WHEN THE WOLF RISES

Linebacker II, The Eleven Day War

COLONEL G. ALAN DUGARD

authorHOUSE®

AuthorHouse™
1663 Liberty Drive
Bloomington, IN 47403
www.authorhouse.com
Phone: 1-800-839-8640

First published by AuthorHouse   12/23/2011

ISBN: 978-1-4685-2537-3 (sc)
ISBN: 978-1-4685-2536-6 (ebk)

Library of Congress Control Number: 2011962197

Printed in the United States of America

Lieutenant Steve Rissi and Crew
"One More Flight"

PROLOGUE

This is a story about the Vietnam War, not about the fire fights that occurred in the jungle, or of the epic battles around the major cities, or even of the hidden enemy in the hamlets that appeared in the night, but rather about men and machines that were unseen, but certainly heard. Their role, though important in the conduct and outcome of the war, was anonymous to most. The B-52 aircraft and the men who fly and work on them were a segment of the war that little is known about and yet their lives were entwined around their mission and the men who made up the crews and the effect of their efforts.

Theodore Roosevelt said that only those who experienced fear could feel the wolf rise in them. The statement really referred to those facing the possibility of serious bodily harm in combat. Many in the military would indicate that they have never felt real "fear", even some of those who have been in combat, however for those who fly fear is always close enough to be called a companion. In most it is the reaction to fear that makes the difference in individuals. Abraham Lincoln said "all men face adversity, but the character of the man is in how they handle it". Anyone who can subdue the wolf can be considered as having subdued adversity, as they have control of their inner being! Those who cannot, must live with their destiny!

Military flying has some inherent dangerous overtones and can definitely cause even the most gifted pilot anxious moments. Peacetime flying in any military aircraft is a great experience, however you are subject to fate and the fact that all aircraft and their parts are subject to some forms of failure from time to time. Also there is the human factor as even good maintenance men have been known to make

1

mistakes as they work long, arduous hours and they have their own personal problems. Take for instance flying a certain aircraft on a day when "fate" plays a role and something major goes awry. Any of the aforementioned factors could cause compromising circumstances and they combine at the wrong time and cause "fate" to play out its hand. Such a situation has happened to many pilots and it has happened on more than one occasion to me. All pilots train for the possibility of something happening to the aircraft while flying. All military and commercial pilots are aware that they must be prepared to handle in-flight emergencies and they spend endless hours in simulators and studying emergency procedures to guard against those events. You should react in a measured pre-planned fashion for any event that endangers you or your aircraft. There are certain emergencies that are categorized as "immediate reaction". These become second nature moves due to the simulator rides and mistakes with these emergencies could very well result in loss of life. Yours included! One such incident happened to me in the best of aircraft, the B-58. It was an ordinary training mission on a beautiful day out of Grissom AFB in Indiana. My crew and I were scheduled for a maximum offload from a tanker almost immediately after takeoff. We were then to fly a high altitude navigation leg and follow with a low level on one of the corridor navigation routes and make a number of simulated bomb runs on targets in North Dakota.

This was a flight in the fastest combat aircraft in the Air Force inventory, capable of flying at mach two and above. Initial climb speed is 525 knots indicated. It was a day mission with a standard departure from Grissom. We quickly leveled off at our requested altitude and started our radio calls to the Tanker, a KC-135 out of our home base. After making radio contact we commenced to provide information to effect the rendezvous. It was a beautiful day and the ride was smooth. Everything was perfect for the refueling. I settled the B-58 behind the tanker, made contact with the boom and as the 58 with its wide wing is very stable, got my assigned off-load without any difficulty. We were now a very heavy aircraft, with 105 thousand pounds of JP-4 fuel in our tanks. We were at the end of the refueling track somewhere in western Minnesota and initiated our climb up to our navigation leg altitude. As we leveled off heading west, I heard the VWS (voice warning system) crank out a call that my "hydraulic system was abnormal"! There are two systems for hydraulics in the B-58, the secondary (which is the main system) and the primary (which is the backup! Now that makes sense doesn't it!). The aircraft is very unique, as it does not have a flight control system that relies on wires. It has a hydraulic ram system and those rams work through an intricate hydraulic method that uses both the hydraulic systems to control the aircraft in flight. Every other piston (ram) on the wing is controlled by one of the systems on a coordinated basis. (I've been told that the designer of this system is in a mental institution. Anytime they have difficulty with the system's intricate makeup they would go to him and he can lucidly solve the problem). If one of the hydraulic systems fail, there is sufficient capability to control the flight surfaces with one system utilizing every other ram. A bit sluggish perhaps, but not a problem.

I peered down to the gages on my two systems, which are both very small and noted that the primary (backup) system was low. I proceeded to turn off the system and the VWS. I knew that today's flight activity was going to have to be curtailed, so started my turn back to Grissom AFB, and called the command post to let them know that I had a problem and was returning to base (RTB). At about the same time the VWS again cranked up and again told me that my hydraulic system was abnormal. I couldn't understand why "she" (it is a sweet feminine voice) would call that out again as the system was off. I turned "her" off again and looked down at the two gages, only to see that the secondary (primary) system was now going down and was in the yellow. That's not good, as without either hydraulic system the airplane doesn't fly! I was in a world of hurt as I had a full load of fuel and both systems were marginal and losing fluid. I informed the Grissom command post of my situation and then called Minneapolis Center and declared a "Mayday". I had to get this bird on the ground immediately! The B-58 has the capability to dump fuel and I initiated that capability, while being cleared to a lower altitude. Center asked me if I could make my home station and I told them I didn't think so. The only possibility for a landing between my present position and Grissom was O'Hare, the commercial airport in Chicago.

That would present a great problem according to the "controller" as they would have to clear all traffic in and out of O'Hare to facilitate my approach and landing. I told the controller I would keep him advised of my situation, but right now I was heading for O'Hare. It was only another 20 minutes to my home base, however I told them that might not be an option. In the meantime my command post was reminding me that I also would not be able to lower my landing gear through normal means and I would not have any brakes on landing. It could mean that I possibly would not have a brake chute, which is latched hydraulically, and as my approach speed would be very "hot" I should consider other options! (The B-58 does not utilize a flap system, and therefore final approach is at minimum 160 knots at the weight I was making the approach). I could "blow" the gear down pneumatically, but would do so at the last moment when taking final.

I told the crew (radar navigator and defensive systems officer) that as long as I had some hydraulics we should be able to land. I left one system off and worked from only one. I would turn both systems on when I had to, but would try to conserve the systems as long as possible. We were cleared to descend at our discretion and all aircraft in our path were notified to stay clear of our routing. I told Center I would let them know if I had to land at O'Hare, however I would try to milk this hummer back to Grissom. My crew stowed everything clear of their capsules in the event we would have to leave this now very tenuous aircraft. The two systems were gradually depleting as I was now alternating their use and there were some indications that I was getting into a full blown need to bail out. I could not engage some of the flight control systems and there was some slop in the control stick. I would have to let Chicago Approach know very quickly one way or the other if we were going to land at O'Hare. I did muster a chuckle or two as I knew what it would mean to that airport if we decided to land there. It would be chaos! I would very much rather go to my airdrome as I knew the territory and there would be no surprises with the approach.

Finally it was decision time and I called Approach Control and told them I felt I could make Grissom There was a pause, I believe of relief, and then a very gracious call of "good luck". I thanked them and continued my descent to a "straight in" final approach to my home station. I would minimize my turns and would insure I would be at the lowest possible gross weight. My stick was now very loose and I stopped the fuel dump. There would be no second chance, no "go-around". This would have to do.

I could see the runway and was now set for my final. I initiated the pneumatic system and hoped the gear would indeed do as the book said it would. The lights on the control panel showed three "green" indicating the landing gear were down. At least that worked. The slop in my stick was now very distracting, and if I missed the approach I told the crew we would climb straight ahead and "punch out". I still showed some indication of hydraulics on the gages so felt we would be OK. The flare was normal and I touched down on the end of the 12,000 foot runway at about 165 knots, lowered the nose and pulled my "brake chute" handle. Surprisingly it too worked as I felt the tug of the large chute. I pulled back on my stick to raise the nose to hopefully get some "aerodynamic braking" and slowly decelerated through 90 knots and the nose came down. The aircraft slowly came to a halt as I pressed on the useless brakes. A group of fire engines surrounded the aircraft and a staff car glided to a stop next to the nose. I opened the canopy, using the normal pneumatic system and noticed my Wing Commander, Colonel Frank Voightman, step out of his car in tennis shorts. He waved at me and called out something indistinguishable. I shook my head and as he came closer I made out that he was telling me that I had ruined a very good tennis match. He gave me a "thumbs up" and got back in his car, drove off presumably to continue the contest.

"Peacetime" flying and the "wolf" didn't really show up as I was too busy in handling a situation that I had been trained to solve. I had handled adversity, but I was not subject to fear as we feel it in a fight. War would be different as it is a fight for life, as I would soon find out!

The Vietnam War had received more than its share of publicity, mostly bad! It had been a war where a news report seems to be almost instantaneous and the action of the day is seen on evening television. There are always scenes of the "jungle war" and the air support that is constantly evident. The "behind the scenes" reports are on a street cafe in Saigon or ground forces at rest at some relief camp. Sometimes there is a random shot of a high altitude B-52 dropping a stream of bombs on an unknown target. What is seldom evident is the story behind the actual war that was being fought by those who fly the B-52. The B-52 crew member is an unusual example of how this war was being fought. His life was an unreported situation of frustration and sacrifice, that only those who are involved in combat could be aware. Those who made up the 52 crews were not on a permanent assignment. They were sent to two bases in support of the war, Anderson AFB, Guam, an island in

5

the Marianas, known more for its role in WWII, and U-Tapao, a Thai controlled base in southern Thailand.

There are three models of the B-52, the "D", "G" and "H "that were used outside of training. The "D" is the oldest of the three and was the only one used in the war until the "G" was deployed in the spring of 1972. Before that time individual crews were sent to make up what was known as the "Arc Light" force and flew only the "D" model, which meant that those in the other models had to "retrain" in the "D" before being deployed. The "G" did not have the capability to carry an external (under wing) bomb load as the "D" did. The "H" has a much more powerful set of engines and did not use water-assisted thrust to increase engine capability on takeoff. It was never contemplated for use in the Vietnam War and remained on "nuclear alert" during the "Bullet Shot" ("G" deployment) involvement in Southeast Asia.

The usual tour of duty was for 179 days. Going beyond that number would result in a permanent change of station and a change of overseas return date. This was something that the Air Force assignment process did not want to happen as it depleted their available pilot resource pool for use in the Vietnam conflict. The Temporary Duty classification given to B-52 crews did not compromise the use of those individuals for other aircraft in the assignment process. The rotation of tours was spread among the bases and the crews until the deployment of the "G" force to Guam and then it became life on the island unless you were a "D" crew and then it became UT or Guam more often then you could stand.

Before the full force of the reason is made for writing this story about one segment of the Vietnam War and its aftermath I must lay the ground work for how I got into this business as there has to be a beginning. It is my story of flight and the nuances of my time associated in the greatest of fraternities that is the one of those who fly and fight. I often reflect on my time as a young officer in the Air Force and how much my career means to me. It molded me into the person I am today. I have met many people in my life who played a part in my development as a person and I must say that the vast majority of those I treasure as friends are those I spent hours with on alert, sharing flying experiences with, learning the art of instruction and command and sharing the grief when one of our compatriots met his/her fate in combat or just trying to complete a mission. It is not only about those who fly the aircraft as it also goes out to those who do the real work. My admiration for the men and women who put in the many hours to make the machines fly is unmatched. You only had to see the great effort that went into putting a bird in the air to recognize the dedication of the many who served.

It has not been a simple, easy life nor has it been one of total chaos. There have been trying times, such as you will find in the trials of the Vietnam War. There were many frustrations mostly they were perpetrated by those who lacked the real concept for mission success and victory in war. There were also those who had no idea of life in the sky and the hazards associated with it. There were also those whose only goal was the next promotion or their own self gratification. Despite all of these I would not trade my life and my experiences in the Air Force for any other type of life style. And maybe most important it has always been a source of irritation to me that there are those who do not condone any type of conflict and go out of their way to make life difficult for the men and women who must do their job or there would not be a free country called America.

B-52D Takeoff for mission to Vietnam

Flight of B-52D's Taxing for Mission to Vietnam

THE STAND DOWN PARTY

A December day on Guam is a lot like any August day on this steamy island, with the only difference being that the temperature is around 88 instead of 96. The humidity doesn't change as it stays in the 90-100% range and the clouds form in the afternoon and just like yesterday, they dump a plentiful supply of water in case you need some. It's the 17th of the month and if Christmas could be in the air, it was going to have to be without the seasonal elements back home such as snow and the warmth of a cheery fire! I've been here less time than most of the other guys who are here on temporary duty (TDY) in support of the effort in Vietnam. This is my first time being deployed to Guam as I just completed a tour in SAC (Strategic Air Command) headquarters, completed my CCTS (combat crew training squadron) checkout in the B-52 and went to Mather AFB in California as the newly assigned squadron commander. I found that my new wing, including the commander and staff, plus my squadron, crews and aircraft had deployed to support the "G" model deployment. I was therefore sent to this sunny island in the Pacific to join the crews that I had never met. Most of the crews on this small dot in the Pacific have spent many months in the "Arc Light" program, (a program designed to convert "G" or "H" model B-52 pilots to fly in the older "D" model aircraft). The individual crews go from their home base to a "D" indoctrination and once checked out in that model of the "buff", they deploy to either Guam or U-Tapao in Thailand for a six month tour, flying the "D" in sorties in support of the Vietnam war.

But this is not "Arc Light" and it is definitely different! This conglomeration of crews thrown together is the result of the deployment of entire squadrons from home in the "G" model. In fact it is the entire "G" force, taken off of the long ago (1956) established "nuclear alert", something that has always been considered "critical" to our national defense and not to be compromised with. They've been sent here with all their maintenance support. It is called "Bullet Shot", but for want of a better term it entails being gone from home for extended periods of time. Although the crew time on each temporary tour is limited to six months, they only allow a short stay back home, usually twenty-eight days, and then it's back to Guam. There is no relief in sight, no sign that this constant round robin of deployment-redeployment is about to end!

It is the first time that the "G" model has been used for the air war in Vietnam, and it is an aircraft that does not have the load carrying capability of the "D", as it does not have the under-wing pylons and can only carry an internal load. It is not the aircraft that matters though as it really is all about the load placed on the individual. The constant "Arc Light" tours in the "D" combined with this undetermined length of tour of duty in the "G" have made the term "temporary duty" a bit misused and very old. I came over in September, to join the squadron. Most of the crews have been here since the start of "Bulletshot" in May. Some may have enjoyed a minor rest period at home since then to help set up a steady rotation of crews. But it had essentially turned into a life of separation and a sordid humdrum of life in the combat arena. However, lately something has changed the atmosphere. In the past few weeks the scenario has been charged with apprehension and the warriors have seen a different approach in an attempt to finish this strange encounter, a war, called by many a conflict. We have seen a dramatic shift in targeting, with missions going to the north of the DMZ (the demilitarized zone). We have also seen a step up in the number of sorties being flown and with both Ds and Gs on the island, it is crowded. President Nixon has cinched up the pressure, both diplomatic and strategic, in an attempt to end this war.

However, today, a Sunday, the B-52 flying crews on the "rock", as some call it, are in a royal American funk. We are not flying! The crews have to be kept busy, don't interrupt their routine and give them time to think! However it has now been disturbed and everyone is experiencing island fever, the "I want to go home" syndrome. No one is really indicating that the crews were going to go anywhere, except maybe on more missions to Vietnam at a still to be determined later date. Another of the former Secretary of Defense, Mr. Robert McNamara's type of stand downs, is in effect, as the powers to be were supposedly making decisions based on Henry Kissenger's work at the Paris peace talks with the North Vietnamese. (McNamara the former Edsel automobile maker just loved giving the enemy time to catch its breath and shore up their defenses). The odds, according to wishful crews, were that a peace accord would be signed and the buffs (B-52's) would redeploy home or as the "Tall Tales" wing newspaper stated "let the beasts head east". (You have to know that guys on an island get a little crazy over a period of time! The tall tail refers to the B-52D and its shark like tail. Thus the "Tall Tales" tag. On the other side of the coin and not to be outdone, when the "G" model was deployed to Guam for the "Bulletshot" operation, the enterprising "G" crew dogs started their own weekly and called it appropriately enough "Short Tails", referring to the stubby "G" tail). What we were unaware of was the fact that the maintenance guys were working to bring the numerous aircraft on the island to a higher state of readiness. The feeling they had was supported by the directive to get the force to a high state of readiness. There was also an obvious move of weapons out of the weapon storage area. They in fact knew that there would be a maximum flight effort kicking off very soon and it wasn't going to the east.

It was another day like all days on the island, some puffy clouds that would eventually grow into some towering cumulus and it would as usual rain before the day was finished, but for the moment it was perfect for almost any outdoor activity! The four "G" squadrons had decided it was a good enough reason to have a party in and around their illegal party hut immediately adjacent to the concretes (three story barracks named for their typhoon proof construction) which housed almost all the "G" crews. It was a very proud party hut as it had a roof of palm fronds, supported by a set of 4x4s, having no sides and was constructed by the crews during their free time. It was big enough to provide shade for the beer and whatever we had for food on a particular occasion. We had been ordered by Col. John Vincent, the base commander to tear the hut down on more than one occasion as the typhoon season was upon us and it would be just so much debris when the heavy force winds hit the island. We had promised to remove it repeatedly and thought about it often, however just never seemed to get around to it. And now today certainly was not the proper time, was it? We all acknowledged that it was a beautiful Sunday afternoon, we were all free, no real duty to restrict us, we were depressed and therefore why not a party? Parties were often and cheap as San Miguel beer went for less than a dime a can and the roast pig was courtesy of the bomb loading crews who seemed to hit at least one wild pig a day on the dirt roads while transporting bombs to the aircraft. This one was given to us last night.

The stand down was certainly a sufficient excuse for the party as it was the first time in four months that the crews had a collective break from the around the clock missions that launched from Anderson Air Force Base. It was the set routine of crew life to be flying a 12-13 hour mission, preparing for one, or recovering from one. Spare time was at a premium and it was spent eating, drinking and for some, indulging in something to occupy their time and looking for some variety in the routine, which seldom included being able to find a member of the opposite sex. What spare time was to be had was usually spent with your own crew, an Aircraft Commander pilot, the co-pilot, the radar (bombardier), navigator, EWO (electronic warfare officer) and gunner. The range of activities fell in the same categories, eating, sleeping, drinking and traveling the 26 miles of paved Guam roads. Of course almost everyone had some form of recreation they had become addicted to, whether it was athletic, reading, painting, or staring at the sunset, but there was always something that occupied every waking minute. A real treat was a trip to the other end of the island to visit the Navy base and it's base exchange or BX, they called them NEXs, (I had planned to take this trip before I left the island), that is if you had access to wheels. It had become a practice with the Arc Light crews to sort of rotate through what we called "Guam bombs", cars that were good for only one thing, transportation around the island. They usually were rusted out hulks, with half stuck windows and a minimum of floor boards and most were true bomb like in their appearance and action as they rumbled and belched smoke where ever they went. A vast majority of these vehicles had long ago lost an exhaust pipe, so there was little impediment to the smoke permeating the interior of the car. Incoming crews would buy a vehicle from a crew rotating-home and then in turn sell it to a new crew when they left.

Yes indeed a stand down Sunday with free beer furnished by the Squadron commanders was indeed what everyone needed as it gave all of us a time to wind down a bit. It would almost take our minds off of the families we have long since deserted in the name of "duty". As the 329th sq. commander I along with the other commanders felt an obligation to make sure that the crew dogs enjoyed their short time off before continuing their endless missions to Vietnam. The squadrons of crews came from a variety of bases in the states. My squadron included the crews from Beale AFB CA., Blytheville AFB, Arkansas and Griffiss AFB in upstate New York. Upon arriving I was told that my Mather AFB squadron from home, the 441st was attached to the 65th BS. And that my "super" squadron would not include those crews. I had about 55 crews in my squadron, not including my 441st (Mather) crews who knowing I was their commander at home tended to feel they were really my crews. Their families at home after all, were under the direct observation of my wife, Rosemary. She had been an instant hit among the wives left behind and she was not new to the long separations they were all enduring. It was also well known, that the squadron commander of the 65th, although an excellent pilot and extremely knowledgeable in the airplane, was not too popular with the deployed crews. Therefore the problems emanating from and about home didn't go anywhere else, but to me, as I was directed by my wife to solve these situations.

At any rate the four "G" squadrons had picked a beautiful day for their party, gentle island winds, no real big clouds (yet) on the horizon and as usual, no women. A few of the crewmembers had wives and/or girlfriends on the Island and for some reason chose to spend their time with them. Everyone was in a good frame of mind despite their time on Guam (We referred to ourselves as the POGS, the prisoners of Guam). Some of the crews were on their second tour with a required break at home and most had been involved in six-month rotations well before "Bulletshot". Prior to last spring, the tall tale "D" had been the only heavy bomber used in Vietnam as part of the "Arc Light" operation, all in support of the war in the southern part of the country. Many of the crewmembers, especially the pilots, had also completed a combat tour in Southeast Asia, of course flying in other aircraft. This had compounded the separation time from their families. But today was special! We would put families on the back burner and enjoy ourselves. No flying! No mission briefing, no target study, just free time, friends and San Miguel beer. There was no dress code so the crews came in a variety of tank tops and shorts and most wore clogs on their feet. Some loud island shirts were seen, but mostly whatever they felt like wearing or could find in their drawer. There were no "green bags" (flight suits) on any of the partygoers.

Living as a crew had to live on Guam brought out both the best and worst in each individual as all six crewmembers shared two bedrooms, each which could accommodate three single beds, connected by a latrine. This latrine was one shower and one commode and always had a very serious traffic problem, from which there would never be any relief! Some of the crews became very inventive and bunked their beds in one bedroom and used the other room as a sort of lounge/entertainment center. They were air conditioned with "swamp coolers", but the island breezes sometimes were needed to get the "stink" out, so doors were often open to the elements. It was not the most unpleasant way of life as others had it much worse. (Ground crews lived in tin roofed huts, where the temperature must have been in the 100's during the day. They relied on whatever air could be encouraged to flow through the raised sides of the structure. There were also a number of "tent cities" that dotted the landscape, though fairly sturdy, they did not provide much in the way of "comfort", and most assuredly would disappear when a typhoon approached the island).

This crowded situation did take some getting used to by all the players in this far off war. It could also impact the crew-rest restrictions placed upon the crews preparing to fly and could become very wearing being around the same people all the time. The squadron commanders had to be very sensitive to personality quirks and conflicts and were constantly on the lookout for possible problems among the crews during their non-flying hours. On the other hand there was a sense of togetherness that was very hard to describe, as each crew became an entity unto itself. Very self sufficient and very oriented to the well being of each other. The real paradox was that if you weren't involved with helping and caring for one another, you could be at each other's throats. Squadron commanders knew that dissenting opinions and ideas on a crew could lead to disastrous results. Constant flying into a combat zone and the tears and loneliness from the constant separation could make for some strange situations and could lead to very tense and sometimes serious circumstances.

So today was very much out of the normal! The composite group was having a great time, swapping stories, talking (always) of going home, drinking beer and wondering how long our party area would last before the Base Commander took matters into his own hands and had a work party raze the area. Of course it wouldn't matter if we were going home! The crew makeup was out the window now as pilots were talking to pilots, obviously trading war stories. Navigators to navigators, talking about the last time they bailed out their pilots from making a terrible mistake. Electronic Warfare Officers (EWO's), sharing whatever sort of humor they seemed to relish in and gunners, as always listening intently and supporting the words of their crew. I was in the middle of a group of aircraft commanders (AC's) and co-pilots when the non-commissioned officer (NCO) on duty found me. "Sir, your wanted at Bomber Ops immediately and you are to bring the other G commanders." (Bomber Operations was our mission planning and briefing area). Well I naturally thought this is it, the maintenance crews had been working feverishly on getting aircraft ready to fly and it was now obvious, we were going home and the wing staff wanted to brief us on the redeployment.

I, along with the other commanders, walked the short distance over to Bomber Ops, attired as we were, which was not very professional, but it was admittedly very comfortable. Upon entering Bomber Ops the cool air actually felt cold after the mid-day heat of the island. It was dark and the four of us had some trouble discerning the group standing at the front of the briefing room. As our eyes grew accustomed to the sudden change we could see this was not the typical gathering for a mission briefing or even an announcement. In addition to the two "D" squadron commanders who were sitting in the front row in their summer uniforms, the assembly included both wing commanders, Colonels Rew and McCarthy, the Division Commander, General Johnson and most of their senior staff. Upon seeing us they didn't seem at all concerned by our lack of a duty uniform and politely asked us to sit down. They were looking intently at the large map on the front of the briefing area and at a glance we saw it was not a map indicating a return to the bases in the CONUS (continental United States). It was an all too familiar map of Vietnam and its environs.

THE BRIEFING

As it was apparent we were the last to arrive, Colonel McCarthy, the permanent party, 43rd bomb wing commander, the "D" wing, walked to the front of the stage. He made some introductory remarks and then, confident that everyone who was supposed to be there was in their seats, he started the briefing. In a loud and clear voice he began with words right out of the WWII Clark Gable films I had loved as a young boy. "Gentlemen, your target for tomorrow is Hanoi!" and pointed to the large letters on the map. I felt myself suck in my breath and was aware that my peers in the room were as dumb struck as I. Herb Jordan was actually slack jaw and Hinch Connor and Al Sweney looked as if they had been struck dumb by a topped off bomb loader. He continued his dialogue to include the number of sorties to be launched, the targets to be hit, the approximate launch times and the many other incidentals associated with any mission. The most dominant statement made during the briefing was that we were going into the "most heavily defended targets in the world". He pointed out the many "SAM Rings" which were going to be unavoidable. These were loaded words for all of us as we had all been associated with targets in the USSR while pulling nuclear alert which were supposedly the toughest. There was also a list of items that were covered which would have an impact on who would fly on the first mission.

A cruncher of sorts was delivered when he outlined the various measures that had to be taken to make the sortie count. Among them was that all returning home R&R crews departing that evening on the redeployment (Freedom) bird would have to remain on the island and be utilized for the mission on Day one, tomorrow, 18 December. My thoughts went immediately to L/Col Steve Rissi and his crew. Steve had had a Nam tour in F-4's and had flown B-58's with me prior to that. I had known Steve for a long period of time and knew he was really in need of his twenty-eight-day R&R back home. He had confided in me that his wife was very anxious to see him come home and he was feeling a pressing need to accommodate her. I had surmised that the constant separation was taking its toll on her. He had a relatively new co-pilot, Bob Thomas, who had joined the crew after it had already deployed to Guam. I had subbed him for Steve's regular co-pilot on an earlier mission in November due to that co-pilot's need to return home to resolve some personal problems. Steve had liked Bob's performance on the mission and asked me if he could be permanently placed on the crew. Lt. Thomas was pleased with the chance to fly on a select crew with an experienced instructor pilot. He was very well qualified and fit into the crew like he really belonged. The fact that he was from the same base, Blytheville, made the decision an easy one to make. I immediately did so and it turned out to be a great move as Steve and Bob hit it off and became the best of friends, something I, as a commander felt was essential as Steve was getting a bit war weary and I wanted to keep him happy.

There could be no exceptions to the crews being held on the island, I was told, as the returning crews from R&R had not as yet had their "over the shoulder" indoctrination sortie prior to being cleared for combat status. There was a requirement for all crews whether new or returning to the combat zone, even the most experienced, to fly their first mission upon return with an instructor crew. This of course meant that the holdover crews were necessary for the sortie count. Don and his crew would fly Day 1 and then go home.

It was at first not clear how the squadron commanders were going to be utilized. The Division commander was a little hesitant to use us for flying duties as he felt we would be needed to prepare and schedule the crews and for other planning and logistic needs. Herb Jordan, Hinch Conner Al Sweny and I were not very happy with this scenario. We were joined by the two "D" squadron commanders in voicing our objections to not being a part of the flying operation. It was also obvious that as pilots we were needed to augment the short-handed crews. General Johnson, Col. Rew, Col. McCarthy and the staff were seemingly moved when we stated that it would not be good for our crews to go into a target area of this magnitude without us participating. We lived with them on a daily basis and I'm sure it would seem odd to them that we were holding pilots on the island while highly qualified pilots were sitting on the ground. We must have been very convincing as the General easily relented and after some consultation with the other senior staff stated we would fly as airborne commanders in command of a wave of aircraft.

With this decision the squadron commanders were divided into two groups. Those who would be the Airborne Commanders and fly the first night and those who would be the crew coordinators for the sortie makeup were to be determined by the wing staff. The second night fliers would also take care of the logistics and would schedule the crew composition for the Day One raids. As a relatively low time B-52 pilot I was selected to be in the second group and would not fly on day one. (I was a high time bomber qualified pilot and had checked out as an instructor pilot in the Buff, but all of my bomber time prior to the B-52 training was in the B-47 and the B-58). I was asked to schedule the crews for flying in the various waves and therefore had a hand in selecting the lead crews for each cell within the waves. The task also involved scheduling buses for the selected crews, insuring flight lunches were ordered, crew equipment, survival gear and protective items were in sufficient number and condition. It would be a process of informing the crews of their status and position and placing them into crew rest. Hinch Conner was one of the two "G" commanders selected to fly the first night and Colonel Tom Rew, my Wing Commander, insisted on flying as an observer with one of my wave leaders the first mission day. I was told that I would be the Airborne commander on Day Two and go as the wave leader. I was pleased with that, but really wanted to go on the first day, as most of my crews would be flying that day, so there was a real sense of disappointment.

I truly believe that all of us were genuinely pleased that we were finally going to go North to such targets as Hanoi and Haiphong and those environs, because we all wanted to turn the heads of those who felt that the B-52 missions were milk runs over the south. We knew that the Buff over Hanoi was going to change the course of the war as we had been very aware of the effect it had down south. Although many of us had flown missions north of the DMZ, and we had seen MIG fighter aircraft menacing our routes over Vinh and other targets, these were short duration flights across the narrow neck of Vietnam. Generally our fighter cover usually scared the MIGs off before they became a real threat. Sporadic missile launches were seen, however they were something we could handle with mutual Electronic Counter Measures (ECM) and simple evasive action. Of course I was really unaware of what was in store for the Buffs on the missions into the heavily defended Hanoi area (and neither were any of the other squadron commanders or at least they didn't profess anything but bravado). Most of us had never taken part in a maximum effort bombing mission before, so our gesturing and talk of "joining in" this undertaking was dumb pride! With this, we were dismissed from the meeting and left to set up the raids for what was being called "Linebacker". The First aircraft were to launch less than 24 hours from now and there was much to be done before we could sleep!

Our first order of business was to stop the party and get crews into crew rest (a twelve hour uninterrupted time away from the obvious debilitating activities they were involved in and as the saying goes, 12 hours from bottle to throttle). The shouts as we approached were half-hearted inquires about going home, however these quickly subsided when we shook our heads. The crews were still very involved in their party mood and a bit incredulous when we told them the party was over and to get into crew rest. We also informed them that all the aircraft commanders were to report to their respective squadron operations that evening for their crew assignments on a series of missions that would change the face of the war and would have an immense impact on our role in the war. This indeed got their attention and succeeded in ending the festive mood that we had worked to engender.

There were to be eighty seven sorties flown from Guam the first day, so not all of the crews would fly on day one, the remainder would go on day two and day three. There had to be a certain process to ensure that crew experience was spread evenly over the first couple of days, therefore there would be great care to get all the crews in a mission oriented mode as they were all going to fly before these missions were finished. I started to feel sorry for the maintenance crews as a launch of two thirds of our force on the island was a formidable task, then upon reflection I knew that this was the type of challenge that they loved. The more difficult the task the better they seemed to like it. They wouldn't let us know that though, as they loved to piss and moan about their difficult life. You can bet they would feel very good about their role as they inhaled their next beer. The crews as well as the maintenance folks were left in the dark about the mission but they knew it was big. We could not discuss the targets for the raid in the picnic area, but they knew it was not a trip home. We had a lot of decisions to make and of course we would fly the re-deploying R&R crews on day one to maximize "crew" utilization. With that mission in the books they, then could be released to go home. We would fly the over the shoulder missions the first night for the just returned crews on low profile sorties to re-qualify them for combat. To sustain each crew's role in the sortie and support mix we would determine all the crews' status for the next three days during the meetings in the squadron.

(It is important to note that crews could not fly two days in a row on missions to Vietnam as the duration of the flights was too lengthy—in excess of 13 hours-to allow the crews to turn-around for a second day flight as it violated "crew rest" requirements).

The Squadron commanders scheduled to fly, Hinch and Al Sweny joined Herb Jordan and I to select the flight and stream leaders for the first day. The selections would be fairly obvious and it would not fall to rank, but to experience in flying combat missions in the B-52 over Vietnam. There were a few of the higher ranking pilots chosen, but there were also a large number of captains who had over one hundred missions and some with two hundred and above. It was not a painful process and when I selected Don Rissi, due to his re-deploy status as the second G wave lead, it was a natural choice as he not only had a large number of B-52 missions, he was also among the leaders in buff combat hours. He also had that F-4 tour under his belt and was most likely one of the most experienced pilots in the wing. (The original grouping would have Don Rissi's crew (S-18) fly as the number three aircraft in a cell, however due to his combat experience in F-4s he was made the lead in the cell). Don was a bit chagrined at having to stay over and was certainly more aware of the risks after the AC's were told where the mission was going. He and his crew had worked hard these past few months and they were ready to get off the island and head for home. I had already announced that the redeploy crews were being held over one day so when he looked at me and said "you're going to make me fly one more mission aren't you"? I nodded and I know I probably smiled and said "one more Don" as he grimly shook his head and unhappily departed.

Despite the large number of crews it was a speedy, but professional proceeding. We were very aware that once the first day's sorties were launched we would have to start preparing for day two. I had no trouble selecting the number one wave lead pilot for the first day. It was L/Col Glenn Robinson (Robbie) and of course his passenger, going as the Airborne Commander, was the Wing Commander, Col. Tom Rew who would fly in the jump seat. (This obviously is not a regular position and it was not ejection seat equipped, so egress from the aircraft, if necessary, involved going down stairs and exiting downward through the holes left by the departed ejection seat of the radar and the navigator). Robbie was my closest confidant on the island and without a doubt the most experienced B-52 pilot in my squadron if not in the "G" model. He had flown two combat tours in Vietnam as an A-1E pilot in the toughest of missions, flying close air support, and did not blink when he was designated as the lead for the mission.

We had become good friends on this coral rock and I had flown with Robbie on more than one occasion and knew how good he was. We would always try to outdo one another in landings, air refueling and anything else that required flying skills. He was one tough and savvy guy and the best of pilots. He was essential to our wave makeup due to the great respect the other crews had for him, however I was very happy with the entire lineup we had come up with as we were able to divide our experience for the first three nights. We knew that after those three missions that the crews could be recycled and we could go on from there for the continuing nights. In addition, our rotating crews could go home and their replacements would fly their sorties on day four and beyond.

Now we had to decide on spare and standby crews. The spare crews would be easy enough as we could use day two or three people, as in most cases we would not utilize an entire crew, but instead a specific crew position for someone who could not fly due to illness, injury or some other unforeseen circumstance. The standby crews would be used to preflight spare aircraft in the event a scheduled Buff (Big ugly fat fella or supply your second "F' word) went belly up during preflight, start engines or taxi phase. The standby crews would have a fully loaded aircraft, preflight it, insure it's ready to fly, and prepare to start engines for the assigned sortie crew to "bag drag" to the ready aircraft, load their personal gear, and launch in their wave and stream position. "Bag drag" procedures were an established mode of operation on Guam. It was a real drill when the flight crew established that an aircraft was non-flyable. "Charlie" (a qualified Director of Operations) would be notified that a crew had a "red X" condition that would preclude flight even under the liberal conditions that prevailed during wartime (it was really an unflyable bird). Of course the on-duty "Charlie" would offer suggestions and lend expertise to the AC in an attempt to resolve the situation, but would then make the decision to "go to the spare". An available maintenance or "Charlie" vehicle would pull up to the disabled aircraft and the crew would exit with all their gear and mission sortie and target data, throw everything in the truck and go to the spare aircraft. In the meantime the standby crew would start engines and wait for the sortie crew. Upon arrival the crews would exchange positions and the aircraft would launch in its assigned role.

On occasion the decision to go to a spare was made on the hammerhead, just prior to launch. In this case the spare crew would taxi the aircraft to reach the scheduled crew. It may have looked like an uncoordinated mess, but it was in reality one of the really coordinated procedures that was utilized during Arc Light, Bulletshot, and Linebacker. The question always came up as to why we just didn't launch the standby crew? It was very simple as it was obvious that they did not mission plan the sortie, were not familiar with their role, route or the targets, and it made no sense to try and prepare them for the many sorties that were to be flown.

All of the crews were notified of their roles for day one and beyond. Those involved in flying tomorrow were now in crew rest, the rest would have some time to get ready for their assigned roles. Now it would be the beginning of a long night of activity for the non-flying, first night squadron commanders and the wing and division staff. I personally was of the opinion as evening dragged on, that it would have been much more pleasant to fly than to be involved in all the mission preparation (little did I know what tomorrow would bring). There were busses to schedule, flight lunches to order (we really didn't ask what kind the crews preferred, but ordered two for each crew position as it was going to be a very long 14-17 hour flight), and finally there would be a check on the personal equipment needed. All crewmembers wore a survival vest, carried a weapon (38 or 45 revolver) of choice and because we had never launched this many aircraft in one day, we were not sure if we had the sufficient numbers to provide everyone with the required equipment. After a visit to the personal equipment building I was not only amazed at the number available, but also the condition and quality of the gear. There is no substitute for the professional personnel who take great pride in what they do and what they provide the crews. It was an established fact that the support personnel that were responsible for the aircraft and the crews on Guam and at U-Tapao (the other operational B-52 base in Southeast Asia) were the most dedicated and hard working individuals in the Strategic Air Command (SAC). Curt Lemay who had long since relinquished his position as the CINCSAC, had initiated the command and had instilled in his staff and ultimate successors, the necessity for the professionalism that had become its hallmark. He would have been proud of these men and women who were tireless in, and proud of their efforts.

ANGELS FROM HEAVEN

Sleep deprivation for the crews and staff was not a problem on Guam! We were so used to not spending time in the sack that it was very much out of the ordinary to be in a reclining position for any extended period of time. The life of a flying squadron commander on Guam (and I'm sure any combat outfit involved in a daily war) was something a civilian or a state side staff "weenie" would never understand. The wing morning "standup" briefing (we actually sat down) was held at 0500 hours. Most of us would go to the Officers open mess to eat breakfast right after standup and then go into the business of tending to the daily and nightly launch schedule and ministering to crew needs. There were always hiccups in the schedule and the lives of the crews. There were the drinking problems, hangovers, crew rest violations, the Guam crud which resulted in a status called DNIF (duty not including flying), injuries, fights, personal problems, both at home and on the island and finally the occasional individual you would just like to strangle.

There was a lot of flying too, as it was nothing for the crews to fly beyond the SAC restriction of 130 hours a month and as a squadron commander I felt I had to get my share of missions, so pushed that envelope most months. The squadron operations room was never without a line of crewmembers wanting to discuss some facet, both good and bad of his life. The business of launching aircraft sometimes took a back seat to the many interruptions from my crews. I would run every day around noon on a set route from squadron ops. As much as I was into staying fit, it was really an attempt for some solitude, even if it was for a relatively short period of time. I would actually have crew personnel intercept me, some running and some actually driving their "Guam Bombs", or riding a bike alongside of me, always with the plaintive plea "Sir, have you got a minute"? My winded reply was "see me at the squadron", however most would go right into a dialogue that would make the most sensitive listener cry. And all were about their personal emergencies!

Running every day was an escape, but it was also interesting due to the drastic weather changes on the island. It was always hot and humid, that was a given. But starting out in sunshine and a gentle breeze could end up in pouring rain and a gale was not uncommon. Every day as I would finish my run I would pour out the water from my shoes and set them outside, hopefully to dry. The water in the shoes could be rain water, however it was mostly sweat, sometimes diluted by the rain. I could not have been the squadron commander I wanted to be without those daily runs. When I flew the time and the route of the run would change as I would land, debrief, change into running clothes and start my run. Time of day or night didn't make any difference as many others were actively involved in their pursuits. Everything was open and operating. We were on a twenty-four hour schedule.

All of the "D and G" crews and those closely associated with them were on TDY orders. Their only relief valves were through the TDY staff. This was despite the fact that there was a large permanent Division and Wing structure on the island. The "permanent party", were for the most part on accompanied tours, meaning with family, and had very little relationship with the temporary duty personnel. They, in fact, had regular duty hours, and a social life that did not involve us. It was something we had no knowledge of. Some were involved in our mission, however, unless you had a friend from a former assignment they would have virtually no contact with the TDY personnel. There was a huge wall between the two groups and very little fraternization! Small incidents often became a rallying cry for the permanent party and they often displayed great resentment for the crews. This was very apparent at the officers club when a wayward pilot, navigator or EWO would have a little (or maybe a lot) too much to drink, and go off on a vocal confrontation with a permanent party. It was also common for one of the crew dogs to "ogle" one of the wives just a bit too long or voice an enterprising plea, inquiring into their availability. Despite apologies and reprimands these incidents seemed to pile up and were seldom solved without a lot of lofty threats. Of course, sometimes the rigors of combat flying and the separation from the family would get to a level where control is totally lost and the snowballing effect would pull in some of the most placid of individuals.

One such incident had happened in the club one night in early November and it started rather innocently. Most of the troops ate dinner at the club, as there really weren't many other options on the island. If you found somewhere else to go, you still had a major problem, and that was the matter of finding transportation, which was very scarce, despite the number of Guam bombs. Where ever you ate, the after dinner normal routine was to retreat to one of the bars in the club and have a drink or two or more. This was as much to avoid having to go back to one's room as it was craving a drink. And if you weren't flying the next day, who was to deny you the privilege of staying out late? This particular night was no different than any other and it did not involve a permanent party. It was in fact too late for most of them. But something very insignificant incited one of the crews and it seemed to hit every other crewmember the same way.

The wing commander had recently banned the playing and singing of our favorite songs at the club, "Yellow River", "I Want to go Home" and "Tie a Yellow Ribbon Round the Old Oak Tree". This was due to complaints from some straight-laced permanent party folks that said the troops got too vocal and volatile when one of these was played. The refusal this night by the ever-present Filipino band to play these songs irritated a crew or crews and they made an issue out of it. The club officer emphatically backed up the band-leader, and the fray was on! I was having a brew with L/Col Herb Jordan, the "G" squadron commander out of Fairchild, that I had been with that evening for dinner, when one of the sober co-pilots indicated there was trouble in the air and it had spread to the pool side bar. It was a bit tender in the main bar too, so I told Herb to stay there and I would go outside.

I did so, and found a huge crowd on the perimeter of the pool and a group packed inside this very small bar where Pizza was the bill of fare. This didn't bother me as much as the very visible pile of tables and chairs in the middle of the lounge. It was the stated intention of the group that they were going to set the place on fire! Jumping inside, I found that the instigators were not your usual malcontents, but among the more respected of crew dogs. They were very angry and vocal in their frustration over their plight in life. It was a result of too many days away from home, too many flying hours, too many days and nights in cramped quarters and now no music that they desired to be played. The fact that they also had too much to drink certainly played a role. Seeing me, they sort of retreated to give me some room. I indicated I really wanted to order a pizza and have a beer and needed a chair and a clean table. It sort of calmed the immediate situation, however no one seemed willing to decrease the pile of chairs or to produce a table. I grabbed a chair and set a table close to the pile and sat down.

There was a real undercurrent of dissension and my presence, though momentarily a distraction was not going to rectify the overall climate in this bar. In a very professional manner I was trying to reason with the ringleaders that any action would have long term ramifications on their careers, however they were not concerned with that sort of rationale and really not in a very receptive mood for anything. As I was talking to them I heard a murmur from those closest to the windows, and looking out I saw two gorgeous women looking inside. Now this was not an every-day occurrence, nor was it even an occasional happening as I had been on the island for four months and had never seen even one unattached lady roaming around the club in the wee hours of the morning. A bit in awe of the sight I sensed a possible solution to the problem at hand. I hurried out the door and invited them into the bar. Needless to say, they hesitated, as it looked like a lion's den inside with nothing but sex starved, horny guys leering at them. As I escorted them inside I signaled that the ladies needed a chair. The chairs were quickly put back on the floor and another table appeared.

We sat down and of course a crowd formed on all sides. They indicated that they were Air France stewardesses, who had arrived at the civilian airport downtown earlier that evening. Bored, they had asked a cab driver where there was a good place to go? Knowing a good fare was at hand, he took them to the O Club at Anderson, telling them there were a lot of things going on at the base and definitely there were a bunch of men. It was about as far as he could drive on the island!

They spoke very broken English and so I made an attempt to remember my four years of college French, sometimes with success, but often we were sort of looking blankly at one another. They were laughing at the attempts to communicate and despite the language problems, the mood of the mob became giddy and attentive. I relinquished my seat after about twenty minutes of drinking in the smell of two beautiful women and noticed that my departure went totally unnoticed. The calmness that prevailed was almost church like.

When I returned to the main bar, Herb asked me "what took so long"? I tried to describe what had taken place, but finally said that two angels appeared and knowing that I was in a world of "hurt", they came to my aid. Herb in that soft southern accent of his looked at me and said, "you really are losing it "! He would never understand and so I just nodded, told him I needed to get some sack time and walked out of the club. I never saw those two angels again and to this day I believe there was some Divine intervention that took place! The club was very definitely the breeding place for most of the problems between the two factions on the island. This incident led to the base commander demanding that the TDY wing commander as well as the permanent party "boss", do something to control the crews. It was then that they decided to detail one of the squadron commanders to monitor the club each evening. That duty of course was rotated on a daily basis and led to the six (four "G" and two "D" commanders) of us being referred to as "the sheriff" It didn't matter whether we were performing this duty or not. Despite the six sheriffs there would be more trouble to come at the club, and I always seemed to be the responsible sheriff and on scene when things happened.

STAFF LIFE

When I wasn't involved in the actual flying and oriented activities, my time was totally involved in crew situations, scheduling and problem solving. Keeping track of fifty-five crews, monitoring their comings and goings was a task that required a constant awareness of the prevailing attitude of the composite crew. At any one time all would be on the flying schedule with only the newly rotated crews not cleared to fly combat, each having six crew members, and most had some situation, either at home or on the island, that needed to be attended to. If not within their crew, then it could be something very personal. Some of the problems extended into very serious situations, impacting on the mental health of the crew-member, such as too much alcohol or involvement with someone on the island that impacted on their home life. Some of the home problems were serious enough that we had to send the individuals back home to solve the situation.

Everything of course was magnified by the crowded conditions. There were over 9000 TDY enlisted personnel on a base that normally would have about a 2700 person total force. They lived in those deplorable tin huts and immensely inadequate tent cities. I had the largest B-52 squadron, however the others were not far behind in number, all being between 45 and 50 crews. Therefore there were roughly 300 crews on the island and there was no room at the inn for 1800 crew-members plus the replacement crews and the staff personnel needed to support the "Bulletshot" operation. The crews occupied the concretes, which were ordinarily used by single enlisted personnel, two to a room. They filled every available structure, necessitating the incoming crews to be in a holding area on a temporary basis, until the departing crews going home on their twenty-eight day break, left the island. They were then assigned the area left vacant by the outgoing crew. As was stated before the crews were only "allowed" to stay on the island 179 days. To go beyond that time frame would constitute them not being assigned on temporary duty. Therefore rotation times were always set to allow some buffer time to insure no one was TDY more than the allotted 179 days.

A very unfortunate situation almost occurred that illustrated the frustration of the SAC crews who were caught up in this TDY scenario. Despite their constant separation from their families and the ongoing TDY-home-TDY routine, that often led to the equivalent of a full Southeast Asia (SEA) tour and then some, these guys were not being given credit for a SEA tour. Therefore they were very liable for an assignment to Vietnam to serve a full tour in addition to their already considerable time away from home. It was a situation that the USAF personnel guys refused to budge from. One day Capt Jack Hanfland came storming into my office, stating that he had just been notified by his home base, Griffiss, in Rome, New York that he had received orders for a SEA tour. This would necessitate his return home so that he could out-process for his new assignment. Jack was in the middle of his third TDY tour, and to say the least, he was not happy. Having spent three plus years working rated officer assignments at SAC headquarters I felt I knew enough of the system to cry foul. I called some of my contemporaries at the Military Personnel Center at Randolph AFB in San Antonio, Texas and stated the case for Capt. Hanfland.

I was stonewalled by these staff jockeys and told that he had to report for his new assignment, as he had not satisfied his remote tour requirement and would have to get involved in the war. My protestations were to no avail. They would not relent from the policy. I was very upset at the inequity of this system. What difference did it make if you were fighting a war from an island in the Pacific or from an air base in Vietnam or Thailand? You were still separated from your family, and you were contributing to our little war. It didn't matter what the designation of the tour was. War is war and separation was separation, period. I decided to write a letter outlining this PCS (permanent change of station) versus TDY assignment problem from a general perspective and the Jack Hanfland situation as a more specific case in point. It was a very vitriolic message, one I feel made the point I wanted to make, but could be considered a bit insubordinate!

My background in SAC personnel had placed me in a position to know that the assignment people at MPC were pushing the envelope and this time I was sure they had gone too far. I knew that what I was sending could have a disastrous effect on my future in the Air Force. Before I mailed the letter I stood in front of the mail slot, wondering if this wouldn't be the end of my USAF career. I sent letters to the Director of Personnel Headquarters Air Force and copies to the SAC Director of Personnel and my own TDY commander. My TDY commander, Colonel Tom Rew, was a very conservative officer and after reading his copy merely rolled his eyes and smiled. I was feeling a bit squeamish after his display.

Two days later while in the squadron my administrative clerk notified me that I had a call from the USAF Director of Personnel. Lt. Colonels's don't usually get calls from three-star Generals, especially in remote locations, so the Ops office became very quiet! Knowing that thunder was about to strike, I said, in a bravado voice, "this is Lieutenant Colonel Dugard". I heard this voice on the other end calmly telling me he had received my letter and that he agreed that there was an injustice in the assignment for Capt. Hanfland and that assignment was now canceled. He also asked me to work with the very individual I had talked to earlier to insure that equitable credit was given for recurring TDY tours especially for those crew members currently participating in the B-52 operations overseas in support of the war in Vietnam. He then indicated a policy change would be sent out to the commands and that there would be a review of all the assignments in the pipeline to insure that similar assignments for TDY rated personnel were scrubbed from the system. Not only was I greatly relieved that my career was intact, but I was also very pleased that the system would finally be oriented to the great sacrifices being made by these crews. Of course, I reveled in the discomfort of my friends at MPC, whom I am told spoke of me in very irreverent terms. They had found new words to describe the SAC guy who had rocked the boat, but who were now very humble and cooperative in our subsequent telephone conversations.

All the base functions necessary for crew morale were open 24 hours a day, 7 days a week, such as snack bars, gym, clubs etc. There were great basketball games being waged at 0200 hours, and there were lines at the outdoor snack bar near bomber ops at any conceivable hour. Crews would get into routines, flying every other day, launching for a 12-14 hour mission at 1300 or 1400 in the afternoon and landing in the wee hours of the morning. Their first order of business after landing could have run the gambit from a beer to breakfast, or an early morning run to a handball game. Some would just go to bed, but all were oriented to the night operation, until scheduling changed their routine.

It was very common to forget what day it was until someone spied the church flag flying, telling all that it was Sunday and time to reflect on other things. Some of us would scurry over to the chapel, hit the first Mass and then get on with the day. That didn't change the operation though as we launched every day, seven days a week. (That is unless that mental midget, Secretary of Defense, McNamara or another of the gray flannel suit crowd had ordered another stand down). As learned as Mr. McNamara and his ilk were supposed to be, and in the face of contrary advice from military and international relations experts, they had placed restrictions on our activity, our pursuit, our targets and even our purpose of destroying the enemy. And then when the mood hit them, they would order a pause in combat operations that did nothing more than allow the north Vietnamese to move into more secure areas and hide their stores. Psychologically it signaled to them our lack of resolve and only emboldened them. MacNamara and his pseudo-strategist contemporaries had obviously never heard of Clauswitz, who stated "you must first destroy the will of the people to fight". Maybe he had the wrong country in mind, as his overt contributions to the peace movement in the states certainly had an effect on the American people and their will to support our efforts.

We wouldn't want to deviate from our daily and nightly order of business as it would spoil the day for those Russian trawler's (that sat in the ocean on the end of our runway). Their antennae bristling, they were counting our departures, noting the westward flight, and then transmitting our numbers to the parties that had a reason for knowing of our coming. They were there day and night, rain or shine, sometimes rolling gently, other times, rocking violently from a stormy sea. We didn't have to look to see if they were there, we knew they were. It was probably a very boring existence for its crew! However things were about to get a bit exciting and they were about to get a wakeup call. They would have a lot to transmit during the 11 day war, known as Linebacker II as B-52 after B-52 was about to roll. Their antennae just might be rocking side to side in a "knockdown" fashion from the jet wash of departing aircraft. Despite our wishes to the contrary we couldn't do anything else about that damn piece of flotsam of unprintable description. The only recourse we had, was to ignore its presence as best we could. However I'm sure there was more than one obscene gesture sent its way during the time it sat on the end of the runway near Guam!

The days usually ended with insuring everything was in a semblance of order in the Ops Office and that the night clerk knew to call me if anything came up. It was a reminder I really didn't have to make, as they never failed to wake me if there was a problem. And they didn't have far to go, as my room, shared with another squadron commander, was only about 30 feet away. Late at night was also a good time to make calls home, as in the wee hours on Guam the phone lines were open and it was get-up time in the states. It was usually at least midnight before I could crash in my bed, always knowing that my clerk would knock on my door at 0430 hours, as he had been told to do, so I wouldn't be late for standup. Obviously the duty day never really ended!

After finishing with personal equipment and the bus schedule I grabbed a quick bite at the Palms snack bar and headed up to my room. A bit of rain had fallen as it often did at night on Guam (It often rained during the day too). I couldn't help but look up to the third floor of the concrete that I lived in and shared with most of my squadron's crews, and reflect on a very similar night barely ten days ago. One of my gunners out of Barksdale, had gotten a late snack at the very place I had just left and was carrying it back to his room. The building had external stairs and around each floor was a walkway that granted access to the rooms. The walkways had handrails about mid body level and a lower bar about 18 inches above the walk. These were heavy medal circular rails. As this sergeant rounded the corner, coming off the stairs and balancing his meal, he slipped on the wet walkway. He was wearing the regular foot fare that most would wear when just hanging loose, a pair of clogs. He fell through the two bars to the ground three stories below and died en route to the hospital. The ground on Guam was unusually hard as it was nothing but coral rock covered with a thin layer of soil. The grass would actually wilt if it didn't rain for two days. I quickly tried to erase the memory as I had spent a great deal of time trying to explain how this freak accident had taken the life of a viable man to his family in a letter I had sent to them. His sister had written me a poignant letter asking how this could possibly happen. It truly was a freak accident and everything that contributed to the accident was mind boggling to say the least. Fate truly is the hunter!

I had some immediate things that I was wrestling with and knew I needed to get some sleep, for tomorrow would soon be upon me, and there was going to be a lot going on. I didn't want to miss a thing!

DAY ONE

Day I-This day was not going to be an ordinary one, as our usual 0500 hr standup was not going to be held for obvious reasons. The jump out of the sack time, though fudged a bit, was still early and this day would be long enough without getting out of bed too soon. The crews would all be in crew rest as the mission brief wasn't until 1100 hrs, however the radar navigator had target study prior to that and therefore the busses would be picking up crews about four hours prior to takeoff and one hour prior to target study. Each bus generally carried only one crew and all their personal gear and equipment. But if the cell configuration would allow it we would get two crews to a bus. Each bus therefore had to be identified by the crew numbers and the AC's names.

1000 hrs and now blue Air Force busses were everywhere, lining up in parking areas adjacent to the crew quarters and bomber ops. It was one of the logistics miracles of the war that crew members and busses somehow matched up with their respective crews and arrived at their assigned aircraft!

The mission briefing had to be held in the base theater as bomber operations was not large enough to accommodate all the eighty seven crews plus spares and staff. The crews were straggling into the theater, still not sure if this was a good day or what, however there was a great deal of excitement, even though somewhat suppressed. Those who had already flown a combat tour in Vietnam, were a little more apprehensive than the others as they had an idea that this was not going to be a turkey shoot. Those guys we were going to visit would more than likely shoot back with more than 100mm weapons! The SAMs would be flying and not for low flying aircraft. The B-52 would present a large target on radar and unbeknown to us, our "G" aircraft were particularly vulnerable. The briefing was very specific, noting targets, possible ingress and egress problems, enemy defenses and the weather in both the target area and enroute. Prevaling high altitude winds were very strong going into the targets and therefore egress from the target areas would be painfully slow. There was a statement used to describe circular pieces of territory immediately adjacent to the target areas "lethal SAM rings". The fact that they extended well into our ingress and egress routes and literally surrounded the targets seemed to get everyone's attention. It was a statement that ordinarily was used in a briefing, however it was generally in reference to a potential problem and was based on a possibility, not known as factual intelligence. These were in fact known SA-2 and SA-3 mobile site areas. The SAM (surface to air missile) has some capabilities that most were aware of. First they are deadly and can accelerate to speeds in excess of Mach-1. Add to that, the gunners have been trained by the Soviets and are considered among the best in the business, and finally, this weapon can be maneuvered to meet the changing flight path of an attacking aircraft. They are not heat seekers!

Colonel McCarthy rose and spoke of "Cell Integrity", stating that all aircraft were to maintain heading and altitude on the bomb runs. There would be no evasive action taken. This did not set well with the crews as they were very adept at taking action to avoid SAM firings and to confound the gunners on the ground, who were directing the missiles to a target. There was no explanation for this directive and it would prove to be a tragic mistake.

After the "Intel" briefing on defenses there were few questions as everyone seemed to be duly impressed and now engrossed in their own little world, most of them were now sensing what was in store this night. The fact that the targets were all in the vicinity of Hanoi was expected, however the overlays denoting SAM sites, and the constant emphasis on cell and wave integrity was obviously the cheese that was binding. As the briefing was winding down I was busy making sure we didn't have any last minute fallout among the flying crews, but with only a minor correction we were not in need of the spares that were ready and willing to go. Finally, the much longer than normal briefing was now appropriately near the end with a prayer from the chaplain. I was caught up in remembering the words from an Air Force hymn, "Lord, guard and guide those men who fly". I think it was while the chaplain was concluding his prayer that most of those in this subdued audience realized this wouldn't be a cake-walk!

The briefing concluded, there was a final "good luck" from the 8th AF commander and everyone came to attention as the staff entourage exited the theater, their steps echoing through the very quiet theater. I watched the crews file past as they left the building. Some nervously pulling out a pack of cigarettes in anticipation of getting outdoors and others exchanging brave laughter on the content of the briefing and the role they were to play. Still others saying "see you downtown", referring to the nickname for Hanoi. I briefly exchanged words with Robbie as he was going out the door with Colonel Rew, our wing commander in tow. He wasn't too happy about taking along an extra person as it gave him one more thing to worry about. In spite of this, he seemed resolute and ready to go, as did most of those leaving the theater, but you knew the knots were starting to form and that only the many years of training, kept everything inside. The busses were in an order that allowed those in the same cells, waves and groups, and oriented to their aircraft parking location, to proceed in an orderly fashion to their aircraft. There was no one worried about missing their bus, and everyone seemed unhurried in getting to their wheels, which were waiting to transport them to the flight line.

Anderson AFB, Guam wasn't built to handle the number of aircraft that were crowded on the tarmac anymore than it was to house the number of crews on the station, therefore the north runway was being used as a parking lot for B-52's. The ramp was full, the revetments were full, the refueling pits were full and the north runway was full. At any time there could be 151 BUFFS on any hard, stressed surface on the base. Transient aircraft when arriving at Anderson were told to park on a refueling pit, and were seldom allowed to take up a precious parking space for very long. The airdrome NOTAMs merely stated that transients were not allowed to RON (remain overnight). The daily operation would not indicate these crowded conditions so vividly as there were always assigned "Arc Light" and "Bulletshot" aircraft in the air. Three ship cells would launch every 45 minutes or so 24 hours a day, flying to the west. But today was different! There had been a stand down and all the birds were in their roost. Now to make matters worse, there were so many vehicles going from point A to point B that it would have been easy to get tangled in the traffic or lost on the ramp. In addition to the multitude of busses, there were maintenance trucks of all sizes and mission. OMS for the organizational maintenance squadron had pickups, flat beds, bread trucks and sedans roaming among the many tugs with a full bomb load in tow. And they were complemented by the same array of vehicles from the Aviation Maintenance Squadron (AMS) and the Field Maintenance (FMS) and Munitions Maintenance squadrons(MMS), all of which had a purpose and tasks to perform. At any moment you could hear APU's (auxiliary power units) firing up or shutting down across the ramp. Throw in the busses and you can imagine the potential chaos that existed.

All of the maintenance functions were performed through the maintenance control officer and his immediate staff of officers and NCOs. The aircraft crew functions, to include any aircraft problems, which could lead to a mission abort, were coordinated through "Charlie" tower. This center was a hot bed of activity manned by a group of very highly "B-52 qualified" full colonels, whose full time job for Arc Light and all the related names associated with the B-52 mission to Vietnam, was to provide know-how and wisdom of the aircraft to the crews. They were the decision-makers on whether a bird could fly or not. They initiated the "bag drags", if the aircraft could not go. They were absolutely the authority, and would always seem to come up with the right answers for the flight crews when things got short and tough. The location of the "Charlie Tower" was like being in the cat bird's seat as it was really only a raised one story mobile control situated on the end of and just adjacent to the runway. Most days the Charlie tower was manned by one of these masterminds for the "D" and one for the "G", working a regular shift with his assigned support staff. During Linebacker, one for each type of aircraft would have been enough to send anyone of these wizards to the loony bin, therefore, there was a team of Charlies that would work the launch time frame to assist the crews. This was done to insure everyone had sufficient counsel (and also for the recovery in the event of a returning emergency). The close to two hour time frame required for the Linebacker launching task was elongated by the aircraft pre-flight inspection time, start engines and the "Tango" taxi routines that had to take place to get everyone in position to takeoff in their assigned cell.

I was pretty busy in the squadron after the briefing, but knew full well the start engine times for the first aircraft and would bust out in time to get to the flight line for the beginning of this operation. Herb Jordan and I were going to go out in my truck to witness the action. He was involved in other activities related to the launch, so I made sure I called and reminded him of the time. When he arrived, he mentioned that the "walkways" on the concretes as well as every other available high spot was full of spectators hoping to see the start of a history making event. Getting into my truck, I could not believe the scene. Non-flying crew-members, support people who worked through the night preparing aircraft, staff and even the permanent party, lined every space with a view facing the flight line. The atmosphere was electric and the sparks hadn't even begun to fly! Everyone wanted to witness the largest launch of bomb carrying aircraft since WW II. The only thing missing was a movie making crew, and of course Clark Gable.

The one aspect of a B-52 that many people don't understand is that within that massive frame a crew of six is housed, the pilot and co-pilot being the only ones having a view to the outside. The EWO and the Gunner are situated about ten feet aft of the pilot team (in the D model, the gunner has a station in the tail of the aircraft). The Radar Navigator (bombardier) and Navigator are downstairs, approximately under the feet of the pilots. The rest of the aircraft outside of the bomb bay, is one big fuel tank, therefore the crew portion of the aircraft is limited only to the first 30 feet. Everything aft of the crew could be thought of as where the weight is. Twenty-seven 750 pound bombs in the "G" and the fuel make this monster 525,000 pounds of rolling thunder. The pilots are sitting next to one another, separated by a throttle quadrant. Similar flight instrumentation is in front of both, a myriad of circuit breakers and systems instrumentation are distributed throughout, within the two pilots reach. A gear handle and flap controls are close to both. A trim control knob is on the top of the control columns in front of each pilot and is controlled with the pilot's thumb. The control column is a half a wheel in appearance and it has a direct connection to the flight controls of the aircraft. Pull it aft and you climb, push it forward and you dive, roll it to the right or left and you will turn. And despite its mammoth size the buff, in the air, responds to the slightest touch. It can turn it on when asked and will cut through the sky at almost 600 knots. There is a jump seat aft of the pilots and in the middle of the two seats. An instructor pilot can occupy this seat, but has no ejection capability. This seat was used during Linebacker for some airborne commanders, which was a great mistake. No one needed to fly in this position and many who did were not current in the aircraft and at least one non-current pilot was needlessly killed during the Christmas raids.

We drove through the gate towards the flight line and pulled up to a space adjacent to, but a safe distance from the takeoff end of the runway. I picked a spot next to one of the bread trucks, knowing they would have a radio and we could hear as well as see what was going on. Maintenance and staff vehicles were everywhere, pointing toward the runway. The maintenance chatter was incessant. No matter how small the problem, whether it was engine, system, radar, radio, personal equipment, spilled coffee, or some small quirk (maybe imagined) in the sound of the aircraft, there was someone responding to it. Charlie had initiated the first bag drag on one of the "D" models, and that meant the closest truck in the area of the afflicted aircraft would transport the crew to the first standby aircraft. As they were still minutes away from start engines, it would not be too difficult to manage. The standby crew was told to not start engines, but to bring the checklist to that point for the flight crew. It was a "Roger that" from the standby crew whose day was about to be over. They were more than likely going to fly tomorrow, so they could head back for a leisurely meal and crew rest. Soon a flurry of noise filled the air. Engines, eight on each aircraft, were starting and now the accompanying smoke was rising in the air. It had really begun.

There would be a wave of "D"s going initially, but now the "G"s were starting their engines and movement was seen throughout the ramp. B-52's commanded attention when they moved, and especially today, as they were grossing out at their max weight of 525,000 pounds per aircraft, the D's showing their under wing bomb loads and like the G's were not disclosing the massive load in their bellies. As they moved from all over the Anderson airdrome they appeared massive and indestructible in their movement toward their place in line and their destiny, whatever that might be! There now were voice directions flying over the air from ground control to various aircraft on taxi directions in the ordeal to mate everyone properly in the cell order of the published "frag" (the order of battle). Some of these moves were really around the horn to get Gold 1 ahead of Gold 2 and Gold 3 to follow. The lines for launch were now evident and the ominous looking "D"s in their black war paint, racks of bombs slung under each wing, and ECM antennae jutting from their bellies, were now approaching the hammerhead.

I knew that Col. McCarthy was on one of the wave lead aircraft as an airborne commander flying in that jump seat, but I wasn't sure if this was the wave. The lead's engines came out of the idle stop and he started to move onto the runway, followed closely by 2 and 3. It was about 1450 hrs. All of the takeoffs would be rolling, meaning there was no stopping on the runway to line up, and lead would have his cell buddies at 15 second intervals behind him. They were now all three at different stages of the runway on their roll and three more were taking the active, with a trail of others eagerly waiting their turn. The black smoke from their engines, emphasized by the water assisted takeoff, used all the time and especially necessary when the temperature was a Guam like 90 degree day, by all the B-52's except the "H" model, was now enveloping everything. Only the ever-constant island wind kept it from being a deterring factor to our view. As the first aircraft were rolling the most amazing thing was happening. All around us as we sat watching aircraft going down the runway, the horns of the vehicles lining the runway were blowing in a cacophony that rose in volume as the aircraft lurched by us. Men were standing everywhere in the vicinity, some on the top of their vehicles, loudly cheering and waving their arms in a salute to these mighty beasts and their crews. Being the emotional and patriotic person that I am, a huge lump rose in my throat and a tear started down my cheek as I was caught up in this spontaneous outburst. I thought of a statement that was made by Miguel de Cervantes, "The man who fights for his ideals is the man who is alive". This was the epitome of pride in one's chosen profession.

After the first "D" wave had launched there was a very slight pause in the action and then the first of the "G"s appeared. The "G" was not as menacing looking as the D, as it has a more subtle camouflage, done in a nice pattern. It appeared almost feminine in nature after the black camouflage of the D. It also didn't have bombs under the wings as it only carried an internal load. Neither did it have so many ECM antennae angling from its frame (something we would regret before the 11 days had passed). The first "F" in Buff stands for fat, but the B-52 on this day and every day since has looked to me like the great machine she is. Big, yes, but graceful to the extent that it disguises it's multi-thousand pound capacity, powerful body in a fashion that few aircraft can.

As I mentioned earlier I flew the B-58 as an operational airplane before the B-52, and I will always remember it as the best aircraft I ever flew. It was a beautiful bird with its swept delta wing configuration and coke bottle shaped fuselage it was light years ahead of its time. It was also the most misunderstood and maligned bomber in the SAC inventory. It was capable of Mach 2+ speed (it's only speed limitation was skin temperature) and high altitude flying, but would skim the turf at 600+knots IAS (indicated air speed), and climb at 1.65 mach. It was like a fast lady out for a good time, but if I had to go to war again in a bomber type aircraft, I would take the Buff. It was tough and could take a great deal of punishment and it delivered one hell of a penalty on those who were the object of its mission. Now a "G" came around the corner sloshing water, not yet fired, over the top of the fuselage, an image I will never forget, then the roar of the water going through the engines became apparent as tail number 201 passed by our position about 1000 ft down the runway. For some reason it caught my eye and I can truthfully say, that it is the only tail number I noticed during the entire launch.

One after another the aircraft passed before us, black smoke mixed with the white vapors from the water-assisted takeoffs. The water was being forced through the engines increasing their ability to produce thrust for the individual engines. The "D" and "G" cells mixed their takeoffs to hit their timing boxes near Saigon, before heading north to their targets around Hanoi. Finally they were all gone, there had been a couple more aircraft changes, however, for the most part it was a perfect launch. Now the hard part! For the crews it was the long agonizing trip to the timing boxes near Saigon, for those of us still on Guam, it would be 7-8 hours before they would even get to the target area. So it was a time for waiting and preparation for day two. That would involve me in what I envisioned as a totally satisfying experience. My confidence was only exceeded by my anticipation! I was full of that Miguel de Cervantes' quote. But first I have to make up a final lineup for tomorrow. Events of tonight would later temper my resolve, but not my belief that I am becoming involved in an historic event! In my mind it was a prelude to the end of the war.

The late afternoon dragged on and most of us just did some busy work to keep our minds off of what was going on. The sun finally set and at least a meal interrupted the wait. The club was like a tavern in a ghost town with hardly anyone around. The band silently set up to start their evenings activity, however they needn't have bothered as few were drawn to the music and it was obvious that our favorite songs had little interest tonight. Day 2 crews were not loitering after dinner for a beer, and all seemed anxious to get back to their quarters. Even the staff guys, probably too tired from the previous nights activity, seemed reluctant to hang around. I too had no desire for small talk so I left immediately after my meal, which that evening had little taste. I decided I would much rather be eating a flight lunch.

I had chosen to walk the mile to the club that night just to stretch my legs, so after dinner the walk back was in the dark. It was uncharacteristically quiet, a gentle pacific wind, few clouds, and few individuals, if anyone on the road. Obviously there was no sound of APUs firing up and no sound of engines or airplanes, which normally interrupted the night. My mind wandered back to the pre takeoff briefing and I remembered that the weather over the target area was forecast to have marginal visibility air to ground, with two layers of clouds. There was also a tailwind inbound to the targets, which meant for a faster bomb run, however it also meant a slower exit from the lethal SAM rings. This could greatly affect our chaff coverage which was provided by lower flying aircraft deployed strictly for that purpose, as it would possibly blow out of the target area at about our release point allowing an unencumbered view of the B-52s in their post target turn (PTT).

In all my combat crew years I spent many tours on nuclear alert. Every alert aircraft sortie had designated targets in the event the "Red

Dot "(go to war) message was broadcast. Each crew had studied their assigned targets and they were familiar with every facet of their mission and the potential for their survival. The Navigator/Bombardier drew Radar predictions of the target area and had them memorized on how they would look at different ranges to the target. We knew the terrain, the people, the escape routes in the event of bailout, as well as the post strike base we would go to and the alternates in the event that base no longer existed. We became very aware of the defenses of each target, the potential for MIGS, and the SAM possibilities. It was said over and over that Moscow and its environs was the most heavily defended city in the world. I knew that it was one place where survival would be a crew effort and bombs on the target would be a priority. During the last two days I had learned that Hanoi now had that distinction of being the most highly defended target and the same priority was evident. It was a numbing thought and it stirred me to get back to the squadron.

When I arrived, there was a message for me to go to bomber operations as they wanted someone who had aircraft and crew knowledge to be available in the area if needed. This wasn't a bother as it gave me something to do. Being in a mission oriented spot involved people to commiserate with, and also it gave me access to information that I knew would be coming in at a rapid rate very soon. It was now about first wave ToT (time on target). This also meant that most of the launched force would be over their targets in a rapid sequence, as the compression of the aircraft was essential for mutual counter measures support with the other segments of Linebacker. The B-52s were not alone in this effort, as there was SAM suppression aircraft and MIG Cap (this was a pre-launched group of F-4s loitering at a specific point to intercept enemy fighters if they were to attempt to interface with the buffs) by the fighters, chaff dispensing by the B-66s and even targets being hit by Navy aircraft. Feedback would come after the waves of aircraft had left the boundaries of North Vietnam. The silence while waiting was obvious to everyone in the room. Finally the first pieces of information started to come in. It was very sketchy, but indicated there had been intense SAM activity and many visible lower altitude anti aircraft firings. The 100 "mike-mike" (anti aircraft, so called for its millimeter designation) activity was not a big concern to the B-52 as we operated above its altitude ceiling. The ingress to the target was at 33-35 thousand feet, the 100 mm arced out around 25-28 and maybe even lower,. and was intended for the fighters and the chaff aircraft. As the next hour unfolded it became more and more apparent that the folks around Hanoi were making a fight of it. It was still in the first stages of aircraft exiting enemy territory where they could break radio silence and report results, so now there was a receipt of more substantive information.

BUFF 201

t was about this time that I got a call from Gen. Gerald Johnson's office, asking me to come to the 8th Air Force command center. They had asked for me specifically and not just any squadron commander and that gave me pause to wonder why. I was very apprehensive and when I arrived, General Johnson himself took me aside. General Johnson had been my wing commander in the B-58 program and was known for his ability to dialogue with his subordinates. He was a very well respected officer and pilot. He informed me that Charcoal 1 had been shot down. I was unsure for a second which crew I had put in that position and then it came to me. It was Don Rissi's aircraft position, the lead ship in a wave of aircraft going to the Yen Vien military complex, one of the prime targets of the night! It was confirmed to be tail number 201. Stunned, I asked if they had any word on survivors, and he responded that emergency beepers had been heard in the area by other aircraft. These beepers are tracking devices activated automatically when a chute is opened. It will beep constantly on guard channel to allow search and rescue to find a downed airman. This obviously does not identify what aircraft the chute came out of, only that it signified an opened chute. It could have come from any other downed aircraft in the vicinity of the targets, and in fact another B-52 was down in the vicinity, this however was a "D" model. I also learned later that an F-111, with another buddy of mine, Bob McIlvane, a navigator from the crew of a very close friend from B-58s, Scotty Billington, was also lost in the region.

I really didn't hear all that General Johnson was telling me as I was thinking of the crew that I had to hold over for one more mission. I knew Don was very anxious to get home and I was sure the reasons were very insignificant right now! Gen. Johnson was instructing me to secure the quarters that the crew had lived in, and that I needed to get all the personal effects of the entire crew together as soon as possible. As an aside he asked if I knew if any of the crew had "guests" on the island. I told him I was sure there were none. It was then that he told me that Hinch Conner's aircraft had been hit and had crashed in northern Thailand, but to the best of his knowledge, the entire crew had been picked up. I was in the command post long enough to hear that all the aircraft were out of the enemy's territory and were heading home. Final count for the evening was 3 B-52's down and two of them contained my close friends. What I didn't know at the time was that the "D" that had gone down, was from U-Tapao, the SAC base in Thailand, where 42 B-52D's had launched to join our 87 buffs. We had 756 Airmen, in the sky and all at risk on this raid.

I left the dimly lit command center in a virtual fog, and walked aimlessly until I found myself back in familiar ground, at the concretes. I walked into the administration office adjacent to my room and realized it was well after midnight. I instructed the NCO on duty to seal off L/Col Rissi's rooms. I would take care of other matters in the AM. Maybe I could get my Ops officer, Maj. Woods to take care of the personal effects. That thought quickly was dismissed as he also was flying tomorrow. Before going to bed I decided I would go by debriefing to see if any of the crews had returned. The debriefing area (the gym was being used to accommodate the large number of sorties that were flown) was rather empty when I arrived. In fact they were still setting the area up in the various segments of intelligence, maintenance, operations and a special place with some liquid refreshment to help the crew members to unwind. I hung around long enough to see a couple of the "D" crews walking in the door, looking as crews ordinarily do when returning from a long mission. There was something different though, it wasn't too obvious, but these were guys who looked like they had a secret and they wanted to tell someone about it! I left, knowing that I was pushing my crew rest requirement to the limit, plus I really needed sleep!

As tired as I was I couldn't nod off! I usually had very little difficulty getting my sack hours, but I was aware of what I was going to face this coming day and it was extremely unsettling. I tossed and turned for an interminable amount of time, but finally succumbed to my exhaustion. I don't know how long it was but it seemed very short, when my room door crashed open and as I came straight up in my bed, I was faced by a crew cut figure in a flight suit. It was Robbie. I got an earful about his flight, as according to this battle-tested combat veteran, Colonel Rew was literally at his ear throughout the bomb run asking questions about their position, SAM sightings and other general items. This wasn't done over the inter-phone as the wing commander was well aware of the need for keeping chatter over that medium to a minimum, rather he pulled on the right earflap of Robbie's helmet and yelled into his ear. Finally on the bomb run Colonel Rew yelled to Robbie with some conviction, that he was going downstairs to observe the target on radar. This was a great relief to Robbie as he and the copilot were too busy to take care of the sightings and questions of the commander.

As the lead crew, Robbie (Barksdale crew E-62) had an obligation to manage all the aircraft in his wave. It was a hellacious mission and nothing was going very well for him. Robbie then enumerated to me all the SAMs he sighted on the inbound leg to the target. To make matters worse only the first bomb in his racks had released and the rest were jammed through some malfunction in the system. He now had 26 bombs still in his bomb bay. He indicated that the turn back towards Laos and the ensuing egress from the target area was long and crazy to say the least. He was very upset with the restriction that had been placed on the crews during the bomb run that dictated there were to be no altitude or heading changes inbound to the target, despite the SAM presence. He indicated that this was a stupid directive and that the tactics should be changed for tonight's sorties. He then cautioned me to keep the wing commander on the ground, as he was a distraction in the air. Now I was awake and sitting bolt upright in bed! I asked about Don's aircraft, but he hadn't seen too much. He did indicate that he heard the very ominous sound of multi beepers on guard channel. Then in his typical fashion, my good buddy now decided he had disgorged his criticism, aroused me sufficiently, smiled that engaging smile of his and abruptly left to catch some Z,s.

DAY TWO~IN THE HANDS OF GOD

I was supposed to continue my sleep? Forget it! I was in a state that only those who have faced a known combat mission, will appreciate. I had digested Robbie's tale of woe and along with my gained knowledge from last night, I realized that the B-52 was not invincible and that the enemy could actually shoot. I was more than uneasy. Now it was obvious and I realized as I tumbled in my bed that I had all the earmarks of fear. Sleep was impossible, so I got up, dressed in my flight suit, laced up my boots and walked over to bomber operations. Upon arriving, the top news about the previous night's effort was the recovery of Hinch Conner and his flight crew. They had indeed all been recovered and in fact, they were airlifted by helicopter to U-Tapao, where they were put on a re-deploying tanker and should arrive back on Guam almost any minute. This was indeed great news and I was momentarily uplifted by the thought. Then the doubt began to spread about my survival. Had Hinch been lucky or had he really had a bad day?

I had business to attend to and decided that I would need help to seal the personal belongings of the Charcoal One crew. Woody was also going to fly today's mission, and in fact was number two in my wave, so I decided I would let him get his rest and enlisted some help from the squadron. Don's crew's quarters were a very typical crew domain, except that he and his crew had already packed most everything in anticipation of their return home. Only a few last minute things were lying around and these were insignificant items that if we could identify the owner we placed in the appropriate bag, if not we placed them in a small package to sort out later. All of the gear was removed to a holding area for safe keeping, from where it would be shipped to the crew's homes if they weren't recovered shortly. I knew that wasn't too likely! Finishing that chore, I went to breakfast with Herb Jordan, who was also leading one of the waves tonight and some of the other flyers on the pending sorties. Word had it that some of the returning crews had felt sure that the crew of Charcoal One had gotten out, or at least some of the crew. There were visual accounts of the aircraft when it was hit and in its final moments and beepers were heard immediately after it was hit and before it went down. I was buoyed by this information, but knew at any rate, that successful bailout was no assurance of survival, especially in the vicinity of Hanoi. The best we all could hope for was that they had been taken alive and were now POWs.

Finishing breakfast, Herb and I decided that we would go by Hinch's room, not that he would be back, but we had some time to kill before the mission briefing. Upon arriving we found Hinch sitting on his bed seemingly unscathed and undaunted by his experience. He was still in his flight suit, which could use a good wash and he was gathering some things together. We were interested in hearing of his experience and so after some coaching he related his tale of the previous night.

It seems that his crew, like everyone else had numerous SAM sightings on the inbound leg to the target. They knew that as they approached their release point that other SAMs had been fired. Upon clearing the target area and in the PTT (post-target turn), thunder struck. The SAM had apparently exploded under the left wing and fuselage of their buff. Immediately it was ascertained that they had extensive damage to the aircraft and they were on fire. The crew was OK and they were now functioning in the manner of true professionals. The pilot's engine instruments were rotating wildly, giving them no indication of the health of the engines, however they were still flying and though losing altitude gradually, they had control of the airplane and they were determined to try to keep the aircraft flying and get out of North Vietnam. Finally upon exiting the immediate enemy territory, but still over what we all knew as a very unfriendly Laos, they headed towards Thailand.

They now had no usable instruments as all of their indicators were gyrating wildly. A couple of F-4s saw their fire and closed in. The fighters, though low on fuel, came to their side in a loose formation, and asked if they could be of assistance. They informed the B-52 crew that the fire around the wing was very intense. One of the F-4 s had to break it off due to his fuel state and the other was about to when he noticed that the fire was spreading rapidly down the left wing. Hinch asked that he stay with them and keep them informed of the fire condition and if it spread to other parts of the aircraft. The F-4 agreed to remain as long as his fuel state would allow. Now calls of "Mayday" were being answered with the flying inferno now being maneuvered to a Marine Air station in the northern part of Thailand. The runway was long enough to accommodate them, however it was narrow and they had aircraft parked on both side of the runway.

The F-4 pilot was skeptical of their chances of making that airdrome as the fire was getting worse and the altitude of their Peach 1 aircraft was getting lower with each passing mile. As they exited Laos it became apparent that they weren't going to make the air base. The orange "preparation for bailout" light was on. It was now a matter of how far into Thailand and how close to rescue aircraft they could get. The F-4 pilot was saying they ought to think about the inevitable. The fire was engulfing the entire wing and the Phantom driver, according to Hinch, said "Hey pardners, you better leave the burning building".

The order for bailout was given and the orange light was now replaced by the red light signifying and ordering bailout. It was time to go. And they went! Hinch stated that as he rolled out of the aircraft he saw the left wing fold up over the body of the stricken bird. Once his chute had opened he started looking around to see what he could see. The bailout had taken place at a fairly low altitude so he not only didn't pick up any other chutes but he was now aware that he wouldn't have much time before he was on the ground.

As he floated down he started to pick out the fires of a small village in the darkened area around him. It was obvious to him that he was going to land very close to that village. Close was a good estimate as he landed in the middle of what he felt was the town square. A group of the natives were quickly congregating in his vicinity. As the chute collapsed and he stood up, they were wary about approaching him, but slowly they encircled him. He released his chute from the harness and began to remove his survival vest. The crowd, though seemingly friendly, was very unnerving and Hinch, in an attempt to keep them happy, started handing the various items from his survival vest to the people closest to him. He gave almost everything in the vest away, but was careful to protect his side arm and the knife strapped to his leg. This seemed to keep everyone in a quiet though curious mood and he was now beginning to discern the sounds of an approaching helicopter.

The Marine "helo" had launched from their intended emergency base. It suddenly appeared and now hovered over him. A lanyard with a halter was being lowered and instructions boomed out for him to secure himself in the inviting loop. He did not need any further urging and grabbed the life-saving device. He said the last item he gave to the villagers was the vest itself and then with the crowd watching him, he was silently hauled to safety.

He was transported to the Marine base to find the rest of the crew already there. All of them were then airlifted to U-Tapao, got in a re-deploying 135 and returned to Guam, arriving not too long after the last of the returning aircraft. It was a great story and a harrowing experience that only added to my building concerns about my activity for this day. I jokingly told Hinch he was back in time to fly tonight and he laughed and told me that because of his bailout they were sending him and the entire crew home that day. He was actually preparing his stuff to go home. He said he didn't have much time and had to take a badly overdue shower. I noted a sense of great concern for us coming from Hinch. He had seen the horror of war and we had not. He was hesitant to say much, but wished us luck. We said our strained good-byes and left to take care of business.

As we walked away in silence we noticed the base activity was starting to gird up for yet another maximum effort mission. We hopped into my truck and headed to the squadron to pick up some material that I needed. Once there I thought I would try a phone call home through the command post. It worked. Rosemary answered the phone and started to tell me all that was going on, interrupting her I told her I didn't have much time and she immediately knew that I was flying that night. She told me to be careful and put my Mom and Dad on the phone as they had been visiting her from their home down south. I talked very briefly to them, said "I love you" to Rosemary and darted out of the office. I had to get to the bus which would take us to personal equipment and then to our pre-mission briefing.

The crew was already on the bus when I arrived. A bit of nervous chatter was emanating from the two navigators and the EW jokingly asked if I knew what time first station was. I looked at my watch and noticed I was two minutes late for departure. I apologized for holding everyone up and there was some obvious forced laughter from everyone. The bus first went to personal equipment and we went inside to pick up our chutes and vest. I strapped my chute on and made sure the straps were adjusted properly. I took out the chute status booklet, didn't read it, but knew that the data would be current and placed it back in the miniature pocket. I put on my vest checking the various pieces of survival gear and then placed the bullets for my revolver in my pants pocket. I checked my 38 and put it in the holster, and stuffed it in the leg pocket of my flight suit. I would secure it in my vest on the way to the target area as it was too bulky to wear the entire mission. All of this was being accomplished in silence by all six of the crew. The personal equipment personnel watched each of us like a mother hen, making sure everything was in proper order, stepping behind each of us in a manner of inspection. Satisfied they would then proceed to the next person and continue their perusal of our equipment. We were about to leave and they too wished us luck and a safe return. We waved as we left and it was then that the knots of concern began to grow in intensity. Boarding the bus once more we headed to the theater. It would be a short ride and a very quiet one.

Arriving at the theater we found that many of the crews had already arrived and the bus traffic was very dense. The driver parked on the coral outside the parking lot. We walked back among crowds of flight suit attired crews disgorging from the busses. Many were standing waiting for their friends from other busses to discuss something more than likely not too important. Whole crews stood together and then proceeded to the second day briefing. Some had been there yesterday as spare or taxi crews, most had not. Entering the theater the crew asked where we would be sitting and I directed them to our sortie number and cell color and we took our seats. Each cell position was marked and the crews were arranged in a takeoff order, the first launchers up front and last in the rear. Standby crewmembers sat in the rear along with the taxi crews. The AC sat in the outside seat and next to him sat the co-pilot, then the radar, the navigator, the EW and finally the gunner. The radar and the nav immediately began to discuss the target data from their target intelligence briefing. Our target would be the Kinh No railroad yards north and west of Hanoi by a couple of miles.

As the commanders entered the theater we were called to attention, followed by the ringing of their shoes on the slanted path to the stage. An "at ease" was called out as they climbed the short stairs to the stage. I noticed with a bit of humor Colonel Rew in the entourage and couldn't help but smile to myself as I recalled Robbie's account of his flight yesterday. It did help to relieve my tension. I had an entirely different outlook on the briefing today as I had acquired some wisdom about the perils of war. The briefing followed the same format as yesterday, but today the crews were very restive and it was obvious that everyone was now really aware of the danger and the personal threats of this endeavor. Most knew the crews who did not return and if not, they were aware of the losses. There was no cavalier conversation. It was all business, but unlike yesterday, today there were questions. Most of them concerned the inbound tactics of maintaining altitude and heading. No evasive action would be allowed, period, was the emphatic reply to these queries. Colonel McCarthy, who flew in the jump seat of a D last night, made the statement that he would court martial anyone who attempted evasive maneuvers. It caused a low murmur throughout the theater! (I felt he had spent too much time watching "12 O'Clock High" and was hopeful he would not bring the same results on himself as Gregory Peck did in the movie).

According to higher headquarters (SAC) this tactic was to insure the most effective ECM coverage and was a method to maintain wave and cell integrity. They also briefed that yesterday's losses could not have been prevented by evasive action. This was not too well received by the pilots as they felt minor deviations would confuse the gunners on the ground as well as compound the effect of their adjustments made after the launch of the SAM. The undercurrent of discontent was obvious to the staff and a stern warning was again issued to adhere to the tactics. The weather again was forecast to have cloud cover in the target area and high tail winds inbound. I was very apprehensive and now realized that my demeanor was something I had to be very aware of. Maybe that's when I realized that being a commander was more than just getting into an airplane and being a good pilot. To use a common phrase I had to "suck it up" and demonstrate a leadership quality that I had not had to display before, courage and resolve.

My crews had found refuge in talking to me in times of their great personal stress. I was now living a different kind of stress. Once again I was beginning to understand fear. The briefing was ending with the chaplain's prayer. The staff walked by my position on the end of the aisle, their steps echoing through the silent theater. General Johnson nodded recognition as he passed. I think I know the kind of person he was and I felt that he was taking this war and the crew's involvement very personally. I acknowledged his gesture and waited for the "at ease" that soon followed. Chattering and loud voices ensued. I then joined the crowd leaving the theater much as one would do at the end of a movie. It was bright outside so I reached for my sunglasses and was reminded of my youth. When coming out of the Rex theater in Hawthorne, California, my childhood home, after watching some furious adventure movie, I was caught up with the events of the story. I would go home imitating the action of the hero in the movie, often using my finger as the barrel of a gun as I shot at an imaginary adversary. I always won!

My truck had been driven there earlier by one of the NCOs (non-commissioned officers) who delivered some papers he thought I needed. He had left them and the keys on my seat in the theater and walked back to the squadron, thinking I would pick it up after the mission. I didn't want it to remain there. Feeling I had to dispose of my truck and seeing one of the AC's, Randy Cradduck who had been a spare and was not going to be used, I gave him the keys. He could use it this evening and return it to the squadron parking area and leave the keys with my clerk. He was happy to have wheels, he thanked me in his southern drawl and last seen, some of his crew was piling in the back and they were driving towards the club. He would fly tomorrow, Day 3.

We piled back on the bus. We were a single crew occupying the vehicle as we were some distance away from most of the launching aircraft. Many of the busses had two crews. Twelve guys and all their equipment and lunches made for a very crowded and hot vehicle. Our aircraft was parked close on the base side of the flight line, not over near the revetments or the north runway. It was again rather a silent ride, however there were some exchanges regarding crew procedures and also discussion and confessed distrust of the programmed tactics to the target. Getting their feelings off their chest we plugged through the gate to the parking location, made a right turn and stopped three parking spaces down just off the south taxiway. It would be a long way to go if we had to go to the spare. The number one spare was on the other side of the active and that meant we would more than likely have to go around the end of the runway by way of the east taxiway and that would be a trek.

THE AIRCRAFT

The crew chief met us as we reached the bottom steps of the bus with the aircraft records. We accepted the book (called the 781) and opened it to the carried-over write-ups from the previous flight. It had not flown since well before our stand down so it had most likely cleared most of the small "discrepancy" items as crew chiefs never let time go by without scrubbing their aircraft's delayed discrepancies. As we were going over the current and delayed discrepancies we saw little that would require even a question of the crew chief. We saw that there were no "red crosses" which meant that the problem had to be fixed prior to the flight, but that was expected. We also noted that there were very few red diagonals or red dashes, both of which you could fly with. This proud sergeant had not neglected his bird in its down time. It was clean and ready to fly and I would wager he had worked on it despite the time constraints that these maintenance guys faced on a daily basis. He most likely worked on his aircraft most of the night and into the morning and there is no doubt he had helped some other crew chief with yesterday's launch. He looked refreshed and was pleased by the comment that the aircraft "looked good" and I handed him back his forms for a needed signature.

He remarked then that we hadn't received our bomb load yet, but the load team was on the way. I quickly scanned my watch and had some real doubt that we could make our start engines time. I was a bit miffed that the bombs hadn't been loaded and I did voice my concern to the Munitions Maintenance Squadron bread truck hovering near our aircraft. There is no doubt that the loading crews had their hands full today, but time was short. The "many striped" sergeant indicated a no sweat attitude, so I moved away in an attempt to make the best of it. I didn't want to vent, as I knew these guys had been working non-stop for the last three days. We could get the pre-flight out of the way up to the start engines checklist and hope for the best. Everything went smoothly on the preflight inspection and so we crawled out of the aircraft after the checklist was completed. It was hot and humid and even with the forced cool air into the crew compartment I was drenched with sweat.

It was a good time to observe some reflection time outside the aircraft. The cockpit was very confining today, as it usually was, but today it seemed to be sucking my breath away. I was experiencing "sweaty palm" time as my gloves seemed to be sliding from my fingers. The bomb loading crew arrived and swung into action. I had watched many a bomb loading, often nuke loading for alert sorties, where everything is done by the book and with a chief master sergeant supervising the action. I had also witnessed a lot of loading here on Guam for our Arc Light and Bulletshot sorties. They were usually done with a methodical and sure air and pace that lets you know they know what they are doing. But this was a scene I had never witnessed before. The loading crew was aware of the time and wasted no time in raising the doors away from the fuselage to allow the dolly with 27 bombs to be fit underneath. I didn't see a checklist, nor did I see someone watching to insure it was done properly. The tug driver maneuvered the dolly into position and seemed to have no problem at all with clearing obstacles like engine nacelles and landing gear struts by the most narrow of margins. The dolly was then placed in a position to hang the load. They hydraulically raised the entire load into position and were locking them in place on the rack in the bomb bay before you could blink.

I know the time they say it takes to put a load of 750# bombs in a B-52, just suffice it to say they beat that time by a very wide margin. I had enjoyed the action and the cavalier, but professional work of this shirtless and tanned team. It sort of relaxed me for the moment. As they swung the bomb doors back into their normal position, the crew chief was signing their load sheet and the Radar was checking the bomb release latches for the pins that were inserted to safe them for the present time. Now it was time to get our act together and crawl aboard. I found it hard to breathe in the now narrow crew space. I pushed open the side window of the cockpit and felt the hot air rush through. The thought went through my mind that this could be the very last time I would suck in the humid island air, or for that matter any air not circulated through the aircraft air conditioning system. It was a chilling thought!

I have had situations that tested my inner strength before and had escaped some very dicey emergencies in the B-47 and the B-58. I had felt that constriction of air that goes with a serious situation. I have had in-flight engine explosions in the B-47 with a full fuel load that precluded an immediate attempt to land and necessitated some drastic aircraft maneuvering to prevent a loss of other aircraft systems. I've also had hydraulic failure in a B-58, an aircraft that is unable to fly without it's hydraulic system and have successfully placed it on the runway with mush for a stick. But this was a new experience for me! Previous combat missions to the north had been in cell formation over quick entry and quick exit targets like Vinh which is in the narrow throat that separates the north from the south of Vietnam, or down in south Vietnam where we were essentially out of harms way. This was different. This was a long bomb run and a very long exit and I was feeling the stress that I'm sure those WWII guys felt when they had to go to the difficult targets like Ploesti, Hamburg and Berlin. Man, this was downtown and some of my friends and charges didn't return from there last night. I was most apprehensive, but I didn't want the crew to know that, as it could be contagious. I'm sure everyone has a different method of suppressing the outward indications of fear, as I'm also sure that all handle it a little differently. I was to see many of those different ways in the remaining days of Linebacker. But I pray, and it's not a close your eyes and clasp your hands type of prayer, it's thought out as I do the things I have to do. It may happen while I run or bike, in this case, while we were starting the engines and counting the bomb safety-pins, and it does calm me.

All eight engines were now in the green on aircraft 479, I pushed the quadrant forward and my "Copper" lead aircraft started to move forward. We were sent off with a smart salute from a very proud crew chief. One had to test the brakes carefully as we were very close to our maximum gross weight of 525,000 pounds. I did not want to upset the folks downstairs or slosh the water. We then made a left turn onto the taxiway, followed by another quick left to cross the active at the 6000 foot crossover point, in order to position ourselves ahead of our other cell aircraft. Bob Woods, my acting operations officer was the number two Aircraft Commander and his bird was patiently waiting for us to turn on the parallel which was actually the north runway, so he and Copper Three could fall in behind. This wasn't at all like flying out of Pease AFB in New Hampshire as I had done for so many years. After all the temperature was different by many degrees and although I had had many thrills while flying the B-47, low visibility takeoffs and landings, loss of hydraulics over a very cold Atlantic and having to land at Thule in Greenland, it was nothing compared to this experience.

I had my MITO (minimum interval takeoff) indoctrination at Pease AFB in the B-47, with each aircraft launching at 7.5 second intervals on opposite sides of the runway and it could get hairy. I recalled the limited visibility from the water-assisted takeoffs and the short distance between airplanes. If anyone heard an abort call on their roll they were to immediately pull their engines to idle if they had not achieved S-1 speed, a designation for a go-no go point. This was the speed at which you could abort the takeoff and still stop on the runway. On the MITO's it was like opening a package at Christmas when you got above the residue from the launching aircraft. You had great visibility and could see the tails of all those in front of you. You were really forced to stay on the runway as long as possible in order to have enough airspeed to come through the turbulence that always lingered just above the runway and out of the "ground effect"

It was a good procedure to hold the nose down and exceed takeoff speed and then lift off and pop through the turbulence. A very wise IP (instructor pilot) named George Knott had shown me that method, and I always employed it on any close interval takeoff. I was often dismayed and then amused when I observed aircraft bouncing up and off the runway and then showing the effects of being caught in the wake of preceding aircraft and wings waggling, struggle through the wash and finally gain momentum to climb. It was seldom though, that these pilots would listen to you if you tried to tell them a method to escape that situation. I was a young post Korean War type and most of the pilots in the wing had flown many hours in multi-engine, prop driven aircraft. They were much smarter than any young pilot that trained in jet aircraft, so I tended to keep my advice to myself. However if asked how I handled it I would tell anyone that wanted to listen "how George Knott does it". They would listen, because George was a respected and extremely capable pilot.

SECOND DAY LAUNCH~
THE SIGHTS OF WAR

Everyone was now in the proper launch sequence and we were taxiing down the north runway, heading west and watching in anticipation of the first "D" model starting its roll. Now I was listening intently to the instructions being barked out by ground control and Charlie tower, they were moving these loaded giants like so many toys in a Conga line. Buffs were in a sashay side to side going to the takeoff point, moving left and right down the narrow taxi way and seemingly were in a concert with the flying gods and those "others" who controlled this action. Cell upon cell, forming into wave groups, "D" and "G" aircraft or as we prefer to call them on the "rock" "tall tails and short tails" nose to tail like a bunch of performing lumbering elephants, moving with their deadly loads to perform, where they'd be much more comfortable, in the sky. As John Gillespie Magee Jr. so eloquently put it in his free verse, "High Flight" they will have "slipped the surly bonds of earth". All aircraft are more at home in the air, and the Buff looks relieved when it breaks ground and sucks up its gear and raises it's flaps.

All crew position reports indicated no problems with the aircraft and now the first of the aircraft commanders were bringing their aircraft engine power up to take the active. I could see the same crowded, truck lined runway perimeter, but quickly concentrated on the business at hand, completing the before takeoff checklist and waiting my turn in pulling onto the hammerhead. As the line of aircraft moved relentlessly forward there was time to take stock of the incredible control of resources that was taking place on this overstuffed island base. We pulled onto the hammerhead and as the takeoff time grew closer, we armed the water and brought the power up to start our roll. Releasing the brakes with partial power, turning to the runway heading down the centerline, advancing the power and firing the water, we felt the surge of power and this beautiful big bird of an aircraft was on its way. The kick in the butt was not as impressive as that in the B-58 as that aircraft had four J-79 engines and an afterburner that provided over 16,000 pounds of thrust per engine. When you popped in the AB's it literally jumped down the runway, and with an empty weight of 55,600 lbs, and a total thrust of 64,000 lbs it climbed like a rocket. It was an aircraft that had little lift aspect ratio, however it's delta wings could support twice its gross weight. With the Buff and its massive load you knew you had an object that was moving, and the book said it would fly, so you had faith every time you started down the runway that it would. You knew it would take a little time and a lot of runway, but it would happen. It didn't rotate like an ordinary aircraft either as the horizontal stabilizer was so large that it actually provided lift to the back portion of the aircraft, so the aircraft didn't rise nose first, it lifted itself in the air. In the B-58 the rotation was dramatic and you had the feeling of a rocket launch; in the Buff it was more like a climbing elevator with lots of forward visibility.

Today, on this very warm December day, it broke ground just where the planned takeoff data said it would, gear up, water burn out complete, a slight turn to allow the cell aircraft to pull into a close climb position. This was not a fighter-close or even loose formation as we were not talking about quick reacting, stick controlled airplanes. We are talking about a couple of acres of wing and a half steering wheel that reacted in a turn with some hesitation and a torque like feeling that lets you know you have a large bird and very heavy gross weight in your hands. So, we flew "in sight" to level off and then flew in tandem, with altitude separation. Of course the radar downstairs is giving you closure information on other aircraft ahead of you and the gunner can "see" aircraft on his radar behind you. Pilots tend to do their own thing in a macho fashion, however when the visibility is limited, the radar and gunner and their information is necessary and most welcome. The climb was only interrupted by a turn on course that we were all familiar with. The visibility was unlimited at the level off altitude, the blue of the Pacific was accentuated by some light fluffy clouds below us and seemed to signal calm, serene times. We all knew it was a false indication of what our next few hours would be.

The cell and wave aircraft settled in and the chatter was very sparse, the only comments were spent informing the entire formation of heading changes and level off information. There were occasional questions from one aircraft to another about some system irregularities, especially concerning radar systems. These usually were inquires to anyone who had an answer and the responses could bring about a plethora of solutions from the cell. It appeared that most were caught up in personal thoughts and the general silence reflected this reverie. Breaking that silence would be a routine operation that we would engage in on the way to our confrontation with reality.

It was going to be almost five hours to the timing boxes over Saigon, but first we would take on a small fuel load from one of the "Young Tiger" 135's out of Kadena, the Okinawa counterpart of Guam for the tankers in this action supporting the effort in Vietnam. Inflight refueling was a great challenge in any aircraft and the B-52 was no exception. It was close formation, nose to tail with the tanker hooked up in an aerial dance that is a thing of beauty to watch and a bitch to maintain when you are the receiver and you are in turbulence and heavy. I had occasion one time in the B-58 where I had to refuel right after takeoff and the weather was terrible. The rendezvous was made and I was guided into the pre-contact position without ever seeing the tanker. My radar vectored me to the end of the boom and the boom operator talked me into position and contact was made. The nozzle on the boom was leaking and as it washed across my wind-screen the leaking fuel froze, (I've been told that JP-4 won't freeze. I'm here to tell you it will) making visibility impossible. I tried various positions in the envelope and finally settled in a low-outer spot, where I could make out the boom. I was almost to my offload when turbulence took me up into the middle of the envelope and the boomer and I simultaneously called for a breakaway. I dove to the bottom of the envelope and felt a forced disconnect. I was relieved to be clear of the tanker and to have my off load. Sweat pouring out of my mask, I reached up to close the slipway door and toggled the switch. The red light remained on, signaling that the door wouldn't close. It was approximately twenty minutes later and with the aid of sunlight that I discovered the problem. The tanker's boom nozzle was still in the receptacle! It had broken off at the connection point and I had to fly with it the entire mission. Upon return the command post asked me "if I had something I didn't start out with"? To further remind me of my pilot technique that nozzle remained on a plaque in the instructor section of the wing with my name on it until they needed to place it back on a boom. With every pilot there are different techniques to maintain position and all seem to work well. If you can't refuel you can't fly in a tactical military aircraft. It's as simple as that.

Our tankers initiated a mating call to get together. They were in their orbit and had some gas to pass. We gave them our format speed (the speed at which we would make contact) and the turn range in order that we would fall behind them at approximately 2 miles. Our offload as opposed to the "D"s was relatively small and compared to our peacetime flights was really a snap. The tankers turned right in front of us on track. The cell had gone to an echelon right, with a 500 foot altitude separation between each aircraft. Copper lead closed on its tanker until we arrived at a pre-contact position. Up to this point the rendezvous is totally in the hands of the radar, now it was the boom operator and the pilot. The boomer gives his directions in increments of feet forward and aft and up and down, and references azimuth in right and left of the boom from the receiver's perspective. The tanker also has lights on the belly forward of the boom that are directional in nature and a green light when you are in position. (These lights could not be seen in the B-47 or the B-58 due to the location of the refueling receptacle). The refueling envelope is not large but sufficient. The boom operator will do whatever he can to assist the pilot of the receiver aircraft.

I have experienced some rare comments from these talented men who lie on their stomachs and control your destiny while looking down through a small set of windows. The tougher the circumstances, the better the effort. There are times where extreme turbulence or limited visibility will test the ability of both ends of the boom. The most difficult aircraft I ever refueled was the B-47 and it always seemed the conditions were challenging. Our wing in New Hampshire pulled nuclear alert in Spain and England during my six years in the famous nuclear bomb dropping 509th bomb wing. Our weekly overseas deployment of three aircraft was always late at night so our refuelings were in the dark. Not that it is a greater problem to refuel at night, but these efforts were originally performed with KC-97s, a prop driven aircraft that had very limited airspeed capability and refueling had to take place at their altitude. Our initial altitude after launch was usually around 28,000 ft and the refueling would always take place around 15,000 ft., therefore a descent over the Atlantic was a necessity and it never seemed to fail that the tops of the clouds were always above the tanker's highest altitude. The stars would be bright in the sky, and then we would descend into the murky clouds.

There was more than one circumstance when the boomer really had his work cut out for him due to an erratic and over controlling pilot in the receiver. I heard more than a few "breakaway, breakaway, breakaway" calls on those deployments than in all my air-refueling experiences since those flights. As you got heavier the need for more speed was very obvious, and the KC-97s would accommodate by starting a slow descent to allow your angle of attack to diminish above near stall conditions. It was always a relief to complete the programmed offload, accelerate to climb speed and get back up above the clouds. On the other end of the scale, the B-58 was by far the easiest airplane to refuel. The B-58, as did the B-47, had the refueling receptacle directly in front of the pilot and you could see the boom into the contact position. After contact it was a joy to fly in the refueling position as the delta winged bird had unlimited power. I, as did most of the pilots I knew, placed three engines at a power setting and then took on the gas (JP-4) using one inboard J-79 engine. It could be a little tricky if you popped in an afterburner though, so you had to recognize the normal stop and set your power accordingly. The B-58s large swept wing made it a very stable platform and refueling with a stick is much easier than using a wheel. The B-52 was in between these two extremes, and not too difficult to refuel if the conditions were reasonable and today it was serene and smooth on the refueling track.

The receptacle on the B-52 is aft and above the pilot's position, so you drive under the boom and closer to the tanker and into a spot where the position lights have a real meaning. Copper flight all hooked up without incident and I heard the "contact made" call of three aircraft almost simultaneously. Staring at the "in the green" light can give you a sort of vertigo and therefore I always scanned the tanker from wing tip to wing tip, trying to not notice it's reference to the horizon, but always seeing it if visibility permitted. Turns while refueling were just a matter of flying formation on the tanker so you didn't need to know where the ground was, just parallel your wings with his. The buff was not an airplane that you made large corrections in azimuth when you were right or left of the center line of the tanker. As an instructor, named Ken Lidie used to tell me in the B-47, "just think the correction and it will happen". With your feet firmly planted on the rudder pedals you would press lightly and amazingly you were back on centerline. After a little over eight minutes on the boom and receiving the prescribed offload I asked for a disconnect on my count. "Disconnect, ready, ready, now". The boom was retracted and the tanker accelerated and started a climb, I brought my throttles to idle and started a descent, while the co-pilot closed the slipway door

. With the tanker flight exiting the refueling track and in sight, the navigator sang out a new heading and Copper flight responded with a gentle climbing turn to the east to finally level off on its assigned altitude. We had resumed our cell composure and assumed station keeping and would remain in that configuration to our ingress point in Vietnam. The gunner on the B-52 has gun-laying radar to the rear of the aircraft and can keep track of the other aircraft in the flight. Ordinarily the navigator insures that the pilot is in the proper position aft of the aircraft in front of him. On good visibility days the pilot will just fly in trail of that object in front. There are occasions when a bird in cell would lose its radar and limited visibility precludes sight reference, the gunner could provide a "bonus deal" to keep or bring the afflicted aircraft into and maintain cell tactics. As the lead aircraft in the cell it was incumbent on me to maintain a constant indicated airspeed and to announce all changes in heading and altitudes to the cell and in this case the wave of twenty-one aircraft.

All aircraft in the formation were in the green and heading to the timing box near Saigon. The Philippines came into view as the sun was setting in a fiery ball behind the horizon making the low stratus clouds in front of us glow brilliantly. It would have made a great photo opportunity, but no one seemed to have the time or desire to take a picture (you could always count on at least one personal camera on board, but not tonight) or for that matter to notice the beauty of the sky. Due to the distance and time to Vietnam from Guam, the crew was allowed to take off their helmets for the non-critical phases of flight and wear a headset. The "brain bucket" could really wear on a person on a 14-17 hour flight so this was a sensible war time policy that was absolutely forbidden on our normal "peace time" training missions. We usually slipped the parachute straps off the shoulders too and tried to find some form of comfort in the bucket ejection seat that we sat on while keeping the seat belt and shoulder harness firmly strapped in place. The crew quarters allowed some movement for bladder relief and general stretching. It was somewhat cramped and stooped but you could stand upright on the ladder to the downstairs habitat of the bomb aimer and the navigator. And there was even a bunk of sorts to stretch out right behind the pilot station if the need or desire arose.

THE TIMING BOX

Darkness was now upon us and we were about to hit the coast of Vietnam, the South China Sea dark below us. It was time to get into our chutes, put the headsets away, put on our helmets, fasten our survival vests and prepare for combat. This was the point I would retrieve my handgun from my flight suit and insert it into an inner pocket of my vest. There was a lot of chatter over the air between aircraft cells. Ground radar was assisting us in getting into the timing box so that the wave composition to the target area could be realized. Sequencing and timing was all important and with the U-Tapao sorties and the later departing aircraft from Guam, it was a real circus in the air. There were rotating red beacons and position lights everywhere. I had no idea how many other airplanes were in these boxes, but my head was on a swivel looking for other aircraft and their rotating beacons. One not so startling interference to our radio communications, if you cared to listen was the information being passed concerning our numbers to radio operators up north. They were merely verifying what they had already been told by the friendly trawler almost 2500 miles behind us. We couldn't understand the language, however B-52 came across loud and clear. They knew we were coming as soon as we got our stuff together and they knew we had a message to deliver. Suddenly the time was at hand and we turned out of the holding area. The waiting was over. It was time to go north and downtown.

DOWNTOWN~THE TURN AND HEADWIND

We took up a northerly heading, finally exiting the friendly skies of South Vietnam and crossed into Cambodia. Inter cell communication chatter had subsided and now small talk was a method to cut the heavy atmosphere within the cockpit. Our EWO, who had barely spoken a word, now became very verbose. These guys really come alive when they start picking up the bleep-bleeps of any form of scanning radar indications, and he was getting frequencies on his scope that had him talking. Nothing specifically tracking us yet, but these were not friendly radar indications even though we were now over Thailand, our loyal allies who harbored many bases used to fly into and over Vietnam. All the aircraft still had their rotating beacons on, not that we could see the waves ahead of us, but it allowed the aircraft in our group to keep a visual with our cell, and the wave. It was fast approaching the territory and time where we would have to go dark as the beacon was a homing device for any MIGs in the area and they would love to be able to pick us up on the way to our turn points.

Once the position lights and rotating beacons were turned off it would then be the task of the radar to maintain the cell composition with his radar scope, using "skin paint" measures. It was now too dark for any possible visual contact as there was no moon this December night. We had been briefed that the MIGs would track the B-52s inbound and relay to their ground controllers our heading, altitude and airspeed. This allowed their SAM gunners to set their proximity fuses for our altitudes, precluding their having to maneuver the weapons after launch. As had happened the night before there had been no deviation from heading or altitude inbound to the targets, so this information was readily used to fire their SAMs at incoming targets. We passed over Nakom Phanom in the northern most corner of Thailand. It was a huge rectangle, clearly outlined by bright lights on all four sides, showing up like a friendly island, a refuge in the darkness below. Naked Fanny, as it was called by Bob Hope, was on the border of Vietnam and Laos, two very inhospitable countries. Enemy sappers, who were trying to get inside the fence to demonstrate their disdain for the American Air Force stationed there, often tested them at night. Therefore the lights, which in reality outlined the outer perimeter of the double fenced, mined area that protected the base, were lit to illuminate the critical areas of access around the base. I suddenly was more than a bit apprehensive and hoped I would see it again that night on the return trip.

I seared the image into my head. I was getting very nervous and the EW was now literally going bonkers with the now tracking frequencies of enemy radar and his attempts to negate their attempts to follow our flight as we proceeded north. He didn't indicate, but I had a feeling that some of his "hits" were from bogies in the air, which were following us on our route. It made the hair on the back of my neck stand up, that strange feeling that someone is looking up my tailpipe with other than good intentions. I gave the order to go dark to the entire wave and now all exterior aircraft lights were extinguished. We were in the active war zone where SAMs are a way of life and death for our flying forces, a place inhabited by an enemy whose aim was to keep us at bay and away from his turf.

Our role was to carry out the orders of our President and destroy their capability to wage war, something we should have done five or more years before. Too bad Mr. McNamara couldn't have come along for the ride. His disdain for listening to those who understood the mentality of the enemy and his constant meddling into the tactics of war were the reasons for this conflict still being waged. I think all of the crews would have enjoyed his jolly ideas for winning the struggle in the air over Southeast Asia. What a buffoon! We also were informed that one of our favorite people was anxiously awaiting our arrival in

Hanoi. Joan Baez, the singer and an anti-war compatriot of Jane Fonda was visiting in her role of aiding and abetting the enemy, a role that a few years earlier she would have paid a price similar to Benedict Arnold. Unfortunately our liberal press condoned her involvement in the Hanoi effort. Our mission, if we chose to accept it was to keep her there and we desperately wanted to keep her there. The only possible method for egress during these troubled times for the inhabitants of Hanoi and for this star of the NVA was to fly out of Gia Lam, the main airport and also a fighter base in Hanoi. We knew she would love the holes in the runway that would be placed by one of our aircraft who was fragged to place their stores across the runways to preclude fighters from launching and anyone leaving during this time. This would allow her to stay yet another day with her chosen brothers and sisters. It was a constant "frag" and a welcome task for each and every day we went downtown.

We could see the lights of a city to our right peeking through the low undercast. It was Hanoi. We stayed on a north course heading until we were almost to the Chinese border, and the navigator called for a turn to 181 degrees, the direct initial heading to our target, which we passed on to our flight. The EW was going the full range of voice inflection. He informed us of the tracking and "lock on" of our aircraft, from low modulated tones to near shrikes, not in panic but in sheer determination to beat their radars. As they would hit a frequency he would jam it, break the lock and look for more. He was riding up and down the scale of highs and lows. In our start to turn, the co-pilot informed us he had sighted three SAM firings to the right. They were three pinpoint bright lights in an inverted "V". They appeared harmless, but as we continued the turn it became more and more apparent that they were intended for us. Somebody down below was aware of our intended track. On our inbound heading the three of them were permanent fixtures in the windscreen, a sure indication that we were the target.

No matter how we would move our heads to see if the relative position would change, it would not! They took the appearance of a three cornered V and were the constant in the view ahead that we had been briefed to be wary of. We could see other SAMs in the distance actually exploding and intended for the aircraft ahead of us, but our primary concern was below and headed to our location. It was like three phosphorus beams, fiery and with dangerous tails. Eric Maria Remarque, in his novel "All Quiet on the Western Front" said, "terror can be endured as long as a man simply ducks—but it kills, if a man thinks about it". I was really trying not to think about it, however ducking might not be the solution in this case. The EW now became a man possessed as he rode an accordion ride to jam the SAM radar frequencies on his scope. EWOs have a reputation of being a bit different than other rated officers. The consensus is that somewhere in their training they acquire this "bleep-bleep" mentality from listening to the various types of emissions that are audibly irritating and visibly stimulating or maybe it was just a certain type of individual that was attracted to this role. Whatever the reason they become experts on areas that most people and especially pilots gravitate away from. But tonight I took another look at my rated brother as I saw the lower end of the V slip out of my view and obviously not a factor aimed toward our position anymore. And then ever so slightly the two remaining weapons started arcing to our left, ever so slow, (even though they travel well above the mach), and away from our flight now and out of harm's way for us.

I noticed a glow out of the corner of my eye and then a flash as one of them passed slightly behind us and exploded at least a thousand feet above us. It probably detonated at a preset altitude called in by a MIG or from their knowledge gained of the previous nights mission altitudes. The proximity fuse would override that point if it came in the vicinity of one of our aircraft.

About the time that threat was behind us, the most electrifying situation occurred. There had been a sighting called over the air of a single SAM going to our right. Looking to the right side we saw this huge object about the length of a telephone pole, with the flame in its tail obviously on the wane passing us. It had reached its apogee about 500-1000 feet below our aircraft. It actually leveled off in a track parallel to ours, took up a loose formation and accelerated by us to a position about a half a mile in front of us and then suddenly the flame in the rear extinguished and the missile exploded. It was the most awesome sight one could imagine as it spewed various shades of, red and orange mingled with yellow and blue tinges ahead of it and was totally surrounded by a blue hue. It was eerily beautiful and evoked the now silent but later communication of expletives and "wows" among those who witnessed it. It is an image burned into my brain that will never go away. It has ruined the fourth of July for me, as I will never see anything again to compare with that incredible and deadly display.

Mesmerized by the sight, it was difficult to refocus our attention to the bomb run, but the words of the radar that he had acquired the target brought our eyes to the front and then back and forth in a nervous scan for more sightings. The navigator acknowledged this finding by the radar and now both were busy refining the offsets to insure they had the best return to lock on to for the maximum accuracy and effect for the release of our bombs. The fact of the matter was that we could probably go direct on this target due to the massive radar returns of the target area, however to insure we did not lock on to some rolling stock, known permanent offsets were used for pin point accuracy. It was still a good distance to Hanoi, but it was visible slightly to our right, peeking through the now very thin clouds below. I was surprised that there were still visible lights to be seen as I had assumed that there would be a total blackout of the area by the time we arrived. I was hopeful that some of the light was from fires caused by the expended bombs from the "Ds" in front of us, but I couldn't tell because of the partial obscuration and I ws more concerned about our flight path and target.

Our target was northwest of the city and I was visually trying to pick out the Red River, but couldn't discern it from our altitude on this very dark night. There were sporadic weapons fired at the incoming aircraft, but most seemed to be distinctly off to the right of the track of our cells. What I hadn't considered or anticipated was that our egress line from the target area, and still well within the lethal SAM line, was to our right. That was our breakaway direction! Without knowing it I was seeing the attempts to hit aircraft in the post target turn and in their flight to the Vietnamese-Laotian border. Also with the bomb doors opening there would be a possibility of a return that the "Fan Song" tracking radars on the ground could see. We could only hope not!

The mutual ECM activity of our flight of aircraft had so far been effective. The attempts to burn-through for the gunners below was nearly impossible and it was apparent that most of the SAM detonations were pre-set to a programmed altitude counting on proximity fuse detonation rather than from radar lock on and tracking. This, however, was the tactic of the remote gunners and not those close in to our selected targets. What we found out too late for some, many of the B-52G's had an unmodified set of countermeasure equipment that allowed the good gunners to "see" the aircraft in the turn from the target when the bottom of the aircraft was pointed more to the horizon than the ground. The ECM was no longer an effective deterrent to their lock-on. Most "G"s lost during the eleven days were in the PTT(the post target turn), something that we didn't know on the 19th of December.

I was a very anxious warrior on the inbound leg to the target and I was discovering what being scared was all about. Mark Twain had remarked "Courage is resistance to fear, mastery of fear, not absence of fear". I was hoping in my own mind that my resistance and mastery were as strong as my resolve to overcome my fear. I would hear a number of versions of that feeling over the next few days, but mine was something I won't let diminish over time and I will always relate to those who experience that feeling in aerial combat. When I hear of acts of heroism in this kind of arena, under these conditions I marvel at the courage it takes to react in such a manner. I'm not sure I could perform in a like fashion. But, boy I could pray and indeed I did. I always thought my Mom had a direct line to the Man upstairs. I had survived some hairy situations in the past and so far this experience could be added to her list.

I saw one SAM going through our altitude about 200 yards ahead and to the left. It seemed to go upward forever before detonating. It was after Linebacker II that I ran into Jim Shelton on Guam wending his way back to his home base of Beale in California. He is yet another of my B-58 flying friends from Bunker Hill AFB in Indiana. During our short discussion it came out that he too had flown on the 19th, but he was in an SR-71 on a photo reconnaissance mission to collect bomb damage assessment information at a much higher altitude than I was at. He stated he saw numerous SAMs coming towards his position in an ambitious attempt to get his aircraft. At "Habu's" (the SR-71's nickname) lofty perch and at its mach 3+ speed, it was a totally futile gesture.

While watching outside and listening to my radar I was reminded of another bomb run a couple of months earlier, I was flying as the lead in a three-ship cell on a target south of Saigon. We were being vectored to a release point by a radar site on the ground, as was the case when there often were no direct aiming points. This was in a particularly bland area, with nothing but rice paddies below. It had nothing but the appearance of mud. I remarked to the crew something about wasting three B-52s and their bomb loads on a sea of rice. We reached the end of the countdown from the ground site set somewhere in the highlands to the west and released our bombs on the dank brown scenery below. We lazily started our turn to the right and watched the earth below to see the impact of the 750 pounders.

The first weapon caused a sea of ripples, like dropping a stone into water, followed by a burst of mud into the air. The second and third received a similar reaction, as the fourth bomb hit, the scene below was an array of explosions, that were perpetuated by the remainder of our bomb load. The following aircraft's contributions only exacerbated the condition, until the clouds of smoke rose in splendor as secondary explosions from whatever was stored in that muddy pond, and it most assuredly was not rice, added to its climax. Needless to say, there were a few words directed at me for my comment, and a few more to those poor guys stationed in very hostile territory about what a super job they had done. I'm sure it made their day, as it did mine. Unfortunately there usually are not many opportunities to see the results of your efforts, much less the impact of your bombs. I knew for certain we wouldn't see much of that tonight as we would be too intent on doing our job and getting out of there. I had a feeling it would be very intense in the target area.

In the final stages of a bomb run the pilot's directional indicator (PDI) is the primary heading instrument as it directs the aircraft to the release point. The radar navigator places his crosshairs on the target or the offsets used to identify the location of the target and the PDI is the target indicator for the pilot. At this point the pilot will give control of the aircraft to the radar, who now controls the big bird until the release of the bomb load. Then, the aircraft automatically reverts back to the pilot. This passing of control to the radar usually takes place with about 60 seconds time to go (TTG). It can happen later, depending on his target confidence or lack of it, but never more than 15 TTG, unless of course the target has not been acquired. (If the pilot sees his PDI skewed more than 10 degrees off the aircraft heading he will attempt to center it prior to giving control to the downstairs guys with less than 15 seconds TTG, otherwise you will find the aircraft in one hellacious turn). During this critical final phase of the bomb run the bombing equipment gyros are stabilized. Any large deviation will totally disrupt the bombs on target capability. At this heroic juncture you are a sitting duck for enemy gunners as you are confined to minor heading changes and no deviation in altitude. You can understand then why we were concerned, as it was at this point that we sighted another set of SAMs arcing through the light cloud cover below. The fiery tails signaling their launching. Now we were in the territory of their very best gunners and it was at a time that we would have to count on our Electronic Warfare Officer (EWO) and his ability to utilize his electronic countermeasure equipment (ECM) to break the lock that these weapons had on our aircraft. He would once again have to jam the electronic spectrum that controlled the radar of that gunner below. Hopefully his talent, good equipment and a divine source would ward off this latest threat.

Now was the time that we would all have to face what Teddy Roosevelt called that period of time, that eternity, he experienced when facing an enemy. We would know "what it was like when the wolf rises in the heart". These bright projectiles, again three, had our name on them. Nearing release of our bomb load we had lost sight of them and had no idea of their location or trajectory and the EWO was not talking. After release that eternity was present, as we had to hold our heading long enough for the bombs to clear the aircraft. This was a period of seven to nine seconds. To turn prematurely would "drag" the weapons with us in the turn and ultimately "throw" them away from the target. Finally, the interminable countdown from the release was accomplished and the radar called for our breakaway from the bomb run heading. We broke violently to the right. Reluctantly the big aircraft rolled into the turn, groaning all the way. The adrenaline rush took over as we passed the forty-five degree angle of bank that we would ordinarily use for a breakaway turn and approached sixty degrees and maybe more as the big beast was creaking and clawing for lift as we were losing altitude at a rapid rate.

This was not good pilot technique! I would have to diminish the angle of bank to reclaim my exit altitude, but was overcome with the thought that I needed to get away from the target area. I continued to lose altitude, but was not deterred in my turn outbound. There were a series of shudders during that massive uncoordinated maneuver that I attributed to the accelerated stall condition that the aircraft was being subjected to. However with later information during the trip back to Anderson and conversations with other crews after the flight I became convinced of another reason. Fear is an amazing thing as it can give you a "rush", making for efforts and thinking that comes from somewhere in the body and mind that you can't summon in ordinary times. Everyone has experienced fear at one time or another, however the fear that one feels in combat has to be a few degrees above the ordinary momentary feeling of helpless panic.

Combat fear grows and its intensity solidifies in every part of your body. It plays havoc with your brain and creates a throbbing heartbeat that pulsates within you. Right now it was exploding in my helmet. The turn away from the target area was not an example of great flying ability; it was more a struggle to control a suddenly 20,000 pound lighter aircraft, and I failed to stay up with the "trim", adjusting to the loss of weight before I started the turn. We still weighed a modest 360,000 pounds and I was really thinking more about the pursuit of life than I was of flying at the moment. I would find out later how tragically deadly the PTT really was! Rolling out on the egress heading, we struggled to get back on our altitude and fire walled the engines to regain lost speed and that necessary egress altitude. It was now the long journey into the jet stream of 90 knot head winds to exit the lethal SAM rings and other angry gunners down below.

It was stone quiet inside and outside the bird. The only noise was from the wind stream over the canopy, accelerating engines and the whine from the movement of the trim wheels as I struggled to get the aircraft to the exit altitude. Were we waiting for the other shoe to drop? It was like everyone was holding a collective breath. If there were other weapons being fired I was not aware of them. We didn't see another

SAM during egress, although the EWO later described a fairly rich array of signals as we were outbound from the target, but he too rode out without a sound. There was a sense of anticipation that made you sit tight in your seat. Sweat was pouring from my mask as I continued to muscle the controls of the giant in an attempt to get it coordinated. I so wanted to put it on auto-pilot so I could rest my steel grip on the wheel. I just couldn't get to that point, so continued to battle the turbulence and groans of the climbing aircraft and hung on tightly.

I remembered a silence like this once when I was a student pilot flying a T-6G aircraft. I was solo and doing acrobatics. I evidently caused fuel starvation to the engine in an abrupt nose down action during a "lazy eight" maneuver and the propeller came to a complete stop in front of my eyes. As someone fairly new to flying, I was momentarily terrified, but a serene calm came over me as the noise of the engine had disappeared, along with the sight of a propeller stationary in front of me. The only sound I heard that frosty February morning over the Missouri fields was the wind over the canopy, and I was actually upset when without any emergency action on my part, the propeller began to turn and the engine sprang into life. The moment was gone as the powerful Lycoming engine roared anew. I know that period of silence was very short, but it impressed upon me what the absence of noise really is all about. It was a lasting and humbling experience!

The egress was a painful time for the entire crew. We actually had nothing to say or report. All the chatter was perfunctory and direct. We were going through Lethal SAM rings and were most attentive to anything we could see or hear. The cell was still governed by our radio silence directives and our beacons and lights were still off. The integrity of the cell was unknown at the time, but the gunner was silently picking up aircraft to our rear, however not in a direct line behind us, which would be understandable due to our turn dimensions and loss of altitude. His feeling was that the cell was intact and due to the size of the returns did not feel that there were any hostile aircraft involved. And at that time we did not feel that any MIG would be straying into the missile firing zones for fear of being labeled as a target by the gunners on the ground. I know it sounds strange, but I couldn't help but feel that someone was definitely looking over this aircraft. My Mom must have been sending missives to God on my behalf.

It seemed time stood still as we proceeded to the safe haven of Laos. The wind seemed to be holding us in place, a form of limbo that was very unwelcome. Finally the sweetest words I heard all night were uttered by the navigator, "turn left to 140 degrees, we've just crossed the Vietnam border". It was a rare feeling, very free, very airy, very light, almost unreal. It was like a life sentence had been lifted from my shoulders. It was like winning the toughest contest for the biggest prize, this one being life. The big Buff was no longer a lethargic bird. She seemed to sense the movement out of the head winds and threw itself towards the south away from the dangers that she had faced. Turning in a nice gentle 30-degree bank to the left, I looked back over my shoulder toward where we had been only minutes before.

There seemed to be a lot of 100 millimeter guns in action, their residue lingering in the sky like minute bites of light, then fading away. Their reaction was most probably to the B-66s or the F-4s in their relentless attempts to drop chaff to mask the incoming bombers. It was found out later that the high winds did blow most of the chaff cover away and that it had little effect on the radar associated with the SAM sites. On second thought it was probably a bunch of frustrated gunners whose only weapon was one that couldn't reach our altitude.

The sense of relief while heading to a more friendly area was overwhelming and it was shared throughout the aircraft. We had faced an extremely tense time and had not only survived, but we had accomplished our mission despite convincing odds. We rolled out of our turn on heading when a voice erupted in the night. "Copper lead, this is two do you read"? I quickly responded in a jaunty voice "Roger that two, go ahead this is lead". After a pause I recognized my ops officer's voice. Woody said in a calm and modulated voice, "I thought you had bought it over the target. We saw the SAM detonate at the same spot where we had sighted you at just prior to release. We swore it couldn't have missed you, are you sure you are OK"? Looking carefully at our engine and system instruments once again, there was no indication of any problems, nor had we felt anything after release. I turned on our over-wing lights and looking out right and left on the huge wing surface, could not discern any fragment damage. I then recalled the shutter I felt in the post target turn and realized it must have been the result of a blast effect, not a stalling condition that we experienced during the turn after release. It had been very close, but it had somehow missed! There are times when you know someone is watching over you. Or was it that rapid and steep breakaway turn that brought us away from the SAM's destructive envelope? I'll never know.

"We're OK" I uttered to Woody and then decided to take stock of the rest of the group. I asked for the other aircraft to check in. Everyone responded by cell position. We had a successful mission and conversation between aircraft went from bomb release problems to the sight of the formation flight of the unsuccessful SAMs and the one flying formation on the inbound leg to the target. It was an extraordinary experience, never to be seen again, at least until the next mission. The relaxed, almost jocular atmosphere was in sharp contrast to that of the flight from Guam to Hanoi. Going back was a walk in the park! Now the best of sights appeared, it was no longer the last sign of friendly territory, but it was the first sign that we were through with the stress of the day and were on our way back to the friendly skies of the Pacific. Nakom Phanom, in its bright rectangular plumage appeared off the nose, an uplifting sight to say the least. We were now over Thailand and on our way back to Anderson. It was almost five hours away, but it would only be a short time until we would turn to exit south Vietnam, go "feet wet", and get casual again.

I couldn't help but think about another close friend of mine from B-47 days at Pease. His name was Bob Standerwick. He was an Aircraft Commander in the 509th who had a wife and two daughters. I knew him as a very good pilot, a bit senior in rank to me, tall, thin and blond. He had gone to Air Command and Staff college and then to SAC headquarters and I had gone to Bunker Hill and then to SAC. He worked in the Command Post in the "basement" at the headquarters and when his tour was up he pestered me constantly to get him an assignment to F-4s. His boss was the most popular General officer in the building at the time, General "Dutch" Heyser. And he too was pestering the assignment people to help Bob. Finally, he received a coveted F-4 slot.

There was a farewell party at his house before he departed for his RTU (re-qualify training unit). He went to SEA and became the squadron commander of his unit through attrition. He had taken a mission to hit a target on the Mugia pass, a notorious supply route for the NVA going from North Vietnam to the south. Bob was shot down somewhere very close to where we were now flying. They had a tape of Bob on the attempt to rescue him that General Heyser let me listen to. Bob was surrounded and on a slight rise and was returning fire with a 45 caliber handgun. He was trying to evade and told the rescuers as much and not to make any attempt to come in, when his radio went dead. He has never been heard from since, nor has there been any indication that he is a POW. He is listed as an MIA (missing in action). I uttered a small prayer that by some quirk of fate in this crazy war, that Bob could still be alive. "Faith is the substance of things hoped for" (Hebrews book II, verse I). My faith was very strong, however I was tired of hoping as I'm sure was his family.

THE RETURN TO GUAM~STARRY
HEAVENS AND MORAL LAW

As soon as we hit the south China sea crewmembers were asking for permission to go off interphone, primarily to relieve themselves and just as important, to get comfortable. That really meant that the sleeping time was about to begin. It was time for the crew to return to that casual status and they were now taking off their helmets, unstrapping their shoulder harness and unzipping their survival vests. About the only adjustment I wanted to make was to remove my 38 revolver from inside my vest as it had begun to rub against my ribs. I took it out, checked to make sure the safety was still locked and placed it in my helmet bag, along with the spare ammo I always carried in my flight suit. Even though my head felt a bit numb, I didn't remove my helmet. It wasn't an irritant, nor was the chute straps so I just left them on. At any rate it would have involved too much effort to take them off and then have to put them back on before our descent into Anderson. You have no idea how tiring it is to get into and out of all that equipment at a constant cabin altitude of 8000 feet. I was tired and the adrenaline had worn off, but I was far from being sleepy. I soon discovered that the others on board did not share that feeling. The gunner and EWO were the first to go silent, followed by the radar. All were very deserving of their nap-time. The navigator chatted as he refined his heading back to home plate, but he too, soon faded away. The co-pilot snatched some eye-lid down time too, but his was merely a doze. The darkness outside seemed to envelop the moment.

I had run many 26 mile marathons and the feeling I had now was like finishing a marathon, thinking how good it felt to complete the distance, and upon reflection knowing that you would do it again despite the preparation and pain that you had to endure. The sense of accomplishment was unreal but the gnawing fear of having to do the same thing again and especially now with the vivid knowledge of an enemy dedicated to your destruction, would take a great personal effort to think of flying and suppress the fear of another mission. But for now I was enjoying the silent and beautiful night around me. Fate is the hunter and tonight we dodged his mighty glare. I started to wonder about Joan Baez, the counterpart to "Hanoi Jane" (Fonda) and how she was holding up in the Hanoi environs, her chosen home and the side she chose in this war. She and Jane are traitors and should suffer the consequences for "aiding and abetting" the enemy, however our left leaning friends will paint them as some sort of martyrs, I suppose. I personally felt that it would be most fortunate if one of our "items" found her abode! This thought was not very Christian, however I was not feeling any remorse for my thoughts.

Despite the moonless night the sea below was very visible. It was largely due to numerous fishing boats all across the horizon in front of us. There was a myriad of lights flashing on the water, a practice commonly used by the large fishing fleets that the Vietnamese have. I understand that the light sweeping above the water was used to entice the fish to the surface. There were some boats quite a long way from shore, all seemingly unaware of the turmoil in their land. They soon faded in the distance as we got further out to sea and then it became a time to pick out the stars, a favorite habit of mine. Tonight you could see both the Southern Cross, low on the horizon and the North Star found easy enough by the pointer chair of Cassiopeia. I could see both simultaneously, which is something you can't experience very often. We were close enough to the equator and at a high enough altitude to view both, also the belt of Orion and the arc of Capella were evident in the dark skies above. Sirius, the brightest star in the heavens shone like a beacon. All the stars in the heaven above were bright and inside the cockpit, the red panel and interior lights only accentuated the beauty; it made you wonder how much better can it get?

Immanuel Kant said something about the two things that profoundly impressed him. They were "the starry heavens above (him) and the moral law within" (him). Both certainly applied tonight, even though I didn't feel like a totally moral person, having just been a party to the destruction of a major railroad complex! I did feel great satisfaction though that what we were doing was a positive step toward ending this insanity against an enemy with absolutely no moral sense.

Every once in a while another aircraft would break the silence of the night with a statement about what he had experienced that night; mostly to keep awake, not to really start a conversation. For the most part though the night was very still. The lights of the Philippine Islands passed below. Those people had felt the calamity of war, big time. For the first time I began to think about the effect of my actions during this long night. I had been the bearer of over 20,000 pounds of destruction and had dropped bombs on targets where there were human beings doing their jobs. I knew that this had been a military target and our briefings had told us there was little chance of collateral civilian damage, however there were people who worked in that railroad yard and our actions were such that if they were indeed there they would not have survived. It was a sobering thought, and one I didn't want to linger on!

I casually asked the radar, hoping he was awake, if he had acquired the target OK and he sleepily replied that with all the reflective returns from the parked railroad stock there was no chance that he had missed the target. He must have had similar thoughts as I had, as he said that there was no way anything could have gotten out after our wave of aircraft released on the target area! I knew he was right and went back to other thoughts, allowing him to return to the "land of nod". It was always a bit boring on the return flights, as dead heading was not something we usually enjoyed, but it was sort of nice and as there was no refueling for the "G" going back to Guam, one could really sit back and enjoy the night. You could sense the feeling of relief and the serenity among the returning aircraft crews during their flight back from the stress they had faced this night. We had experienced a night of terror and had witnessed heroic efforts among all the crews. It takes a great deal of courage to face hostile fire and remain within yourself, doing a job you were trained to do and doing it well.

I was beginning to pick up the Anderson Tacan now. We were within 200 miles of the base, so it was time to rouse the natives of this returning bird. "Nav, I've got Anderson at just over 195 miles" I called. That should wake everyone up! "Everyone strap in and get on your helmets", we're about to start down. Before I could call announcing our arrival, approach control sang out, "Copper Lead this is Agana approach control, welcome back"! It was enough to bring tears to my eyes and once again it was a reminder of what could have been. We have felt the wolf and we didn't flinch. At least, not too much!

Control gave us clearance to start an immediate descent from our now 35,000 ft. altitude. "Descent checklist" I asked for and it would be a leisurely descent to our pickup by the final controller and it now gave us the realization that it was business as usual. But we knew better, this was an illusion and just the beginning of our action as we would have to go again and we all knew it. For the present though it was a matter of completing the mundane procedures that we had been ingrained within our training. Checklists had to be read and actions accomplished. With a level off at 2000 ft. we were picked up by the Anderson final controller and lined up on runway 24 L, a slight wind in our face.

The Island was dark, but outlined in lights from the city of Agana, the bay, and the base. The runway lights were a very welcome sight and could be seen on my long final approach. It was a clear windless night. No crosswind crab needed to be cranked in. This would be a real no-brainer. An extended final, but a real chance to pick up the land water contrast and to actually note the surf on the coral reef, shimmering with the plankton filled water. Now as the runway end identifier lights (REIL) rushed up and I started my flare, I was carefully watching my final approach airspeed bleed off. It had been almost fourteen hours since we launched from this base, but I was extremely alert and as I touched down on the downside of the famous (to B-52 drivers) runway swale, (a large dip in the runway) I was happy with the smooth contact of the tires on the pavement. The chute was deployed and we were now rolling to a stop, no problems, minor brake utilization, and we were now directed to pull off at an intermediate taxiway with about 4000 feet of runway left (the second most useless thing to a pilot is runway behind you). Ground personnel were running a check on all of the aircraft as they pulled off the runway to insure all the bombs had indeed left the aircraft.

The "follow me" vehicle led me to a position where I noticed a small group in front of the aircraft. I now picked up an individual waving the familiar parking wands, urging me forward and finally crossed the wands signaling me to stop my forward motion. I waited for the plug-in and with a modicum of static there was a very masculine voice on the other end saying, "It's great to have you safely back sir". I have to admit, I was emotionally moved. It was a situation that froze me for a moment; it was a circumstance that I seldom experience. It truly was more than a bit wonderful to be back on the ground at the place we launched from fourteen hours ago. I almost choked with the response, "Thanks sergeant, we're certainly glad to be here".

"Sir, would you please open your bomb bay doors, we have a brief inspection to accomplish. I know you've had a long flight, and we won't be long". "Take all the time you need" I responded. It was indeed a very short delay and they cleared us to taxi to our assigned parking spot. Again as we finished our turn into our parking spot we were motioned to a stop by a figure in front of the aircraft. We were now finally able to totally feel the relief of being in our safe haven. Again a voice came through the intercom, "Sir, thanks for bringing my aircraft back"! My response was that it was entirely my pleasure. I shut the engines down, unbuckled my harness, and waited for external power, which came altogether too soon. I could have stayed longer, but knew it was time to flee the scene. It's funny how you want to freeze the moment, even though you know you have to move on. I was more than a bit curious and wanted to complete a post flight walk around the aircraft. Despite an extensive search for some battle damage, there was none to be found. Aircraft 479 was totally unscathed, not a mark on it!

REFLECTIONS—THE BEGINNING

1t was strange that a former ROTC guy like me would find himself in this position. I had just experienced a most scary night and I was reflecting on what brought me here. When I started college, I had no choice but to be in the ROTC corps. It was required if you were physically qualified. I was not a "gung-ho" participant, but did not embarrass anyone in my actions, both in the classroom and on the drill field. Once in my junior year I discovered that there were a number of people that took their roles as a cadet very seriously. I was not one of them, however I had made the determination that I would realize a lifetime desire and that was to become an Air Force pilot. It wouldn't do to not perform in a manner that was expected of all the cadets, therefore I did try to at least not arouse the ire of the ROTC staff. The last two years were not mandatory, but I was determined to get a commission and go to pilot training, so I stuck with it. Also they gave a small stipend to those who participated in the last two years and that was attractive to me.

At the end of the junior year all those who are still involved must go to a summer camp. It was three weeks of intense training, much like a "boot camp" and was a method used to determine if you were really capable of being commissioned as a leader in the USAF. It was actually fun, and I really enjoyed the challenge, however one fateful day all of us were lined up for a "flight physical". I was not concerned as I had always been in good health and did not anticipate any problem. All went well until the eye exam. I floated through all of the tests until all of a sudden they thrust this book in front of me and asked what number I saw. Unfortunately in some cases I did not see a number at all and in some I saw the wrong number. I was told that I had failed the "color blind" test as I had missed a total of five of the prescribed numbers and four was the limit. I was not qualified for pilot training! I reacted somewhat like someone who had lost the prime choice for my future, but felt I had other options. Once camp was over, though disappointed, I was going to look to other ways to find adventure.

When school started in the fall I took an additional English class in lieu of the senior year Military Science class, this one in composition and felt this was the way I had to go. After the first day of class when the professor gave us the syllabus, I felt an overload coming over me. This guy was looking for more work than I usually had in all my classes in a semester, not just one. As I left his class, I was in a virtual fog and looking for an escape from this burden. I needed the units for graduation, not necessarily the class. I bumped into one of the NCO's (non-commissioned officers) on the ROTC staff and he asked me why I had dropped ROTC. I told him I failed the flight physical color blind test and he told me there were ways I could pass the test I had failed and qualify for pilot training. He took me to his office and showed me the book that the "color numbers" were in and said I could retest at some time and that I could learn to see all the numbers. He showed me some of the easier red against green and I had no trouble seeing the proper number. He convinced me that I was a worthwhile gamble to continue in ROTC. It was more the units I could get for the class than the desire to pass the physical that I was looking for as I had reached the decision that graduating from college was my primary concern and this was an easier path than that writing class. I "reluctantly" changed classes and was told another physical would be scheduled in the spring at March AFB.

I told my sister, Colleen, who was a nurse, about the situation and she said that there was an eye doctor in her building from whom she could borrow the "Ishihara" test book. I had renewed hope that I could pass that test and fly jets. She produced the book a couple of days later and I set out to train myself to see those numbers I had trouble with before. Try as I might, I continued to not see some of the numbers on certain pages in the book. I was very frustrated by this, but felt there had to be a way. I noticed that the color circle on each page had a unique pattern and that all similar numbers had the same pattern in the lower portion of the circle. I memorized this pattern and could tell any number on any page by looking at the setup in that lower segment. Even the numbers I could clearly see, I could use my own method of "seeing" them without looking at the circle interior. Confident that I was ready I asked to have a physical scheduled. The sergeant took care of matters and set a date for me to go to March and take the test.

I retook my physical and did not miss a number, however I was so excited I had to retake the blood pressure test twice before getting though the physical. Needless to say I was delighted and joyfully shared my news with the ROTC staff upon my return. I ultimately received my commission upon graduation and entered pilot training shortly thereafter. Strange what fate has in store for you! My "color deficiency" never hindered my flying, nor did I feel that it was a problem in my proficiency as an officer. I was truly grateful for my state of life, even though the present situation of placing my life on the line did not enthrall me at all.

BACK TO REALITY

Stopping my momentary day-dreaming I knew it was now time to get on with the day. Preparations were already in motion for today's missions. The night was indicating in a small way that dawn was coming up soon and many of the recovered aircraft would be flying today. Our aircraft was a good candidate for at least "spare duty". It was necessary to get our aircraft discrepancies to the maintenance debriefing. We wended our way to board the waiting blue crew bus for our trip to the base gym for that purpose. We didn't say much on the bus, mostly acknowledging that it was nice to be back and that we were looking forward to a shower and maybe even some breakfast at the "Palms". After a short trip the bus jolted to a stop in front of the gym and we ambled off the bus into debriefing. Each section was clearly marked by crew position and of course some novelty handouts were available to warm our innards, and a young medic was handing out the small bottles filled with "spirits" to those who wanted to relax while filling out the flight logs and debriefing the maintenance folks.

After completing the necessary paper work the crew went to an intelligence area, where we retold all facets of the mission that could have an effect on the upcoming raids. I was very critical of the inbound restrictions and noted the fact that the turn to the bomb run heading was met with SAM's already fired and on our track inbound. The enemy was very aware of our intended course inbound to the targets. This piece of information would turn out to be a common complaint by all the crews. After leaving the table I was a little surprised to note that most of the pilots were hanging around and gathering in a group, comparing notes on their experiences during their flight. I would have thought that they were as worn out as I was and would be looking for something other than conversation. This was nothing new as we did that all the time! It was very common to unwind by talking out our experiences.

I was about to leave when in the middle of the group I noticed Woody motioning for me to come over. He looked directly at me and said in a semi loud, but sincere voice what he had intimated in the air over Laos, "Man, I really thought you bought it". I felt a smile creeping into my face and in a moment of bravado, said "Not a scratch on the bird, so it wasn't too close". He shook his head but didn't say anything and I knew it was plenty close enough. I shuddered inwardly, knowing that my Mom was on the prayer mat again and suddenly felt very tired. I really wasn't in the mood to listen to the bitching about the same heading tracks flown two consecutive nights that was going on, so headed outside without any further comment.

It was a typical island night, very warm, but with a nice ocean breeze. I didn't feel like going to personal equipment, but had no choice as everything had to be turned in. I crawled back on the bus, sat down, looked around and saw that the entire crew felt as I did. There would be no breakfast at the greasy spoon. It would be get rid of the equipment and go back to the crew area and hit the sack. And that's exactly what we did. After a brief stop to drop off our personal gear, hanging up our chutes and turning in our weapons and vest we headed back to the bus. We acknowledged our satisfaction of not using any of the issued gear to each other as we left the sparkling clean facility. It was a very short ride back to the "concretes" and it was made without further conversation. As the bus pulled in to the crew billet parking area I noticed my truck was in its parking spot. My keys would be in the squadron. The sun was now peeking over the horizon and I knew that I had to get some sleep before the pre-takeoff briefing for today's sorties. Day three was about to begin! I crawled up to the second floor, and went directly to my room, avoiding the squadron operation office, even though there was obvious activity in progress. I wanted that bed.

Sleep was fast in coming but after a very short stay in the rack I crawled out and headed to take the shower that I was too tired to take before I went to bed. Wrapped in a towel I heard someone trying the door, it wasn't locked, never was! In stepped one of my Mather squadron (441st) radar navigators. "Sir, do you have a minute"? I was momentarily irritated, but after looking into his face, I knew he had something that needed to be said. "Could you give me a few minutes, I really need this shower"? We agreed to meet in the squadron and I hurried through my shower, using soap that I had avoided in my shower yesterday. In jungle survival school the instructors were very explicit on the need to avoid using anything that emits an odor, such as soap, after-shave, or even tooth paste. The reason is that the perfume smell is very evident to those we might want to avoid in any hostile environment if we had to bailout of our aircraft and were trying to escape and evade.

I dressed in a clean flight suit and walked the very few steps to the squadron office. Once there, I noticed that there was a bit too much commotion to really have a private conversation so I motioned to my navigator friend to follow me. The two of us stepped out the back door which was always open to allow the gentle island breezes to go out the front door, thus insuring that paper was never stacked on any desk. It was cooler that way, but could be messy. We turned the corner to the relative quiet of the second floor walkway and sort of leaned out over the railing, looking toward the familiar fringes of jungle meeting the base perimeter. He immediately began by stating he just couldn't fly tonight with his crew as he had too many responsibilities at home. After all he had three children and a wife to look out for!

I hadn't really anticipated this kind of dialogue, but I guess I should have. I had heard a lot of reasons why this constant separation was damaging marriages, how wives were crumbling under the strain of running a house alone and how children were out of hand and needed a father. But this was different! I relied on Rosemary to keep the wives under constant watch to insure they were as happy as they could be under the conditions, but now there was the anxiety of intensive combat on top of the everyday possibility of something going wrong in an airplane. This was war! The guys on the other side were as dedicated to shooting us down as we were in destroying their capability to wage war. A guy could get killed out there and the odds were sure higher now than they were a week ago. He was scared, sure for his life, but he also had a fear of not being around to see his children grow up. He was expressing that fear to me and I had to have an answer to satiate his concerns. Was he a coward? I didn't think so, but I had to find a way to work around his fear.

"Jon, you know that everyone here has some family back home that they are worried about, and you and I both know that we are not involved in some milk run over the south. You have to think out the consequences of grounding yourself. You not only will severely damage your career, which is inconsequential at this point but you will also have to live with the fact that you will put someone else in harm's way, because your crew will fly and someone will go in your place. If something happens to him you are going to regret it forever. No amount of reasoning on your part will ever diminish your feeling that you should have been on that mission. Do you want that"? I let that sink in for a second and aware of his silence, said, "I'll be at the pre-takeoff briefing and if you decide that you are not going I'll have someone ready to take your spot. It will be your decision".

With that he nodded silently and walked back through the squadron and out the door. I stood there a minute and then followed him through the door. It was business as usual as John Woods and Big Al, the 65th squadron commander were in terse conversation over some aspect of last night's mission. I sat down at my desk only to be asked by the clerk if I had seen tonight's schedule. I had not so he carried it over to me to take a look. There were a few surprises and a couple of guys who had taken this opportunity to see the flight surgeon and go DNIF. Under normal flying situations they would have sucked it up and flown the mission, however this was not normal and a slight head cold was now a good reason to sit this one out. On the other hand there were also a few cases of guys who should have been grounded, avoiding the flight surgeon's office as nothing in the world was going to keep them from flying. Personal commitment and responsibility weighed heavily on everyone and some more than others. We had more than one hero on Guam.

THE RECKONING

Day three was going to be a carbon copy of day's one and two. It was going to be the same tactics, same headings, same targets, same altitudes, but different crews. We were a bit short of Airborne Commanders for today with Hinch's departure, so someone pulled one of our ranking staff guys, Lt. Col. Keith Heggan out of an office to fly the mission. They placed him with Lt. Colonel Jim Nagahiro, one of our more experienced combat pilots, who was flying the identical position in the wave that I had flown the previous night. Keith would occupy the jump seat as he was not current, although knowledgeable in the B-52. Jim was a well qualified IP out of Fairchild AFB in Washington, and had flown Monday night as a substitute AC for Captain Goronowski who was DNIF, one of my Mather crews. Jim was one of Herb's guys and highly capable in the airplane. He didn't need a passenger to give him direction!

It was going to prove to be a tragic blunder. The whole concept of the airborne commander was to allow the squadron commanders to fly, as well they should. It turned into a platform for wing commanders to partake in the "fun" which was very explainable if not pushing the limit as they too flew the jump seat, but to allow non-current staff to fly was an unnecessary risk. It would cease after day three! This was another heavy night for my overseas squadron, the 65th, Captain Panza and Captain Terry Geloneck from Beale, Captain Cradduck, Captain McNabb, Captain Biddulph and Captain Cheshire from Blytheville and Captain Jack Hanfland, and Captain Hulgan from Griffiss were the crews flying. Captain Vlad Mancl and Captain Ken Mizner, from my Mather squadron were also going, the latter in the same wave as Jim Nagahiro.

It was now a set routine, the crews were no longer asking a lot of questions, they were in a zone that required a solid mind set of doing what you were trained to do. Although only one or two had flown a sortie north, the others had been spares or standby or DNIF cover on the first two days so they had heard the briefings and were aware of the drill. On previous days there was a lot of directing going on, not today. The bag study, pre-takeoff briefing, even the chaplains prayer seemed to fall in line with the routes and altitudes. There was still the anticipation in the faces of the crews, still the suppressed fear of what was in store and still the dread of "what if"? I had noticed during the briefing that Jon was sitting with his crew. I had another radar navigator go through target study and was prepared to sub for him if necessary, however as Jon walked by, though obviously in distress, he didn't indicate any problem. He was looking directly at me, nodded, put his head down and walked out with his crew.

I was immensely proud of him as he had overcome his own demons. That was real courage, the kind that is never written down in stories but it is real gut wrenching valor. He knew all about Teddy's "wolf". There had been a number of crew changes for one reason or another and some substitutions, but nothing that affected the wave composition. I mused to myself how I had felt the previous day and knew that every individual going out of that theater was holding back their emotions, and hoping that they would be back in their own room tomorrow.

Once again I was mesmerized by the launch. As a spectator to a mass of aircraft taking off, you have to be impressed, but to watch bird after bird lift off, fully loaded with weapons of destruction and not knowing what the night will bring, is enough to make the toughest squadron commander cry. I never said I was the toughest. Herb Jordan was watching with me. He had also flown on day two and he too understood what was going on in the minds of those flying today. We avoided each other's eyes, and turned in opposite directions toward our truck. I suspect he was also as apprehensive as I was. It now almost seemed like a regular happening. There would be the wait for the aircraft to get to the target area, and now we had experienced the fear and knew the feelings of those on the aircraft as they approach the target areas. It was once again a waiting game. There would be a meal and maybe even a beer, but it wouldn't have much taste and then we would proceed back to bomber operations to await any post strike information we could get.

The island was terribly quiet during this waiting period and even the permanent party, who often asked to fly on a sortie over the south to get their monthly tax deduction, retreated to their homes. I decided to go for a run. I was very predictable, always running between the concretes and by the mess hall, to an area across from the VOQs (visiting officers quarters), which were now occupied by the 0-6s (colonels) who were TDY as Charlies and Deltas (the maintenance equivalent of the Charlie who were well versed in any maintenance problems that might arise during a launch and made the determination for maintenance issues for flight) and other staff positions. As I reached the open field, the thought occurred to me as I ran with ever increasing speed, that if I stepped in a hole I would probably damage an ankle or leg to the extent that I wouldn't be able to fly another sortie for awhile. But being the person I am, I was also aware that it would really have to hurt and besides, who would fly for me?

I did my three loops around the field and returned to my office, a very obvious sweat showing on my shorts. My shoes were saturated with water as they always were and I removed them to watch the flow of water out of the shoes as I placed them on end. Some things never change! I was once again focused on today's sorties and picked up the schedule to look at the cell makeup. It was like the normal schedule with a big "Secret" stamped on the red cover. The second page noted the date, the 20th of December, 1972 and had the outline of a "G" model and noted the duty scheduler, a Captain Rose and the wave coordinators, Herb, Al Sweney and I. It also had a cartoon with two characters, one asking the other why the schedule was classified, the other W.C. Fields looking character responded "to confuse the enemy". The first curiously said, "how do you figure that"? W.C., with his feet on the desk says, "how can they know what we're doing if we don't"? The schedulers were getting in some digs and they could get away with it.

I had to wonder why we continued the same tactics night after night, tactics dictated from a headquarters in the state of Nebraska, far from the obvious center of this war. I hoped General Pete Sianis, the SAC Director of Operations, and his boss General Richard Ellis had better vibes than I did. Knowing who was flying tonight, I put the schedule back in my top drawer. I wanted to shower again and get on a clean flight suit. Herb, Robbie and I cruised into the club for dinner where a few of the previous two days fliers were congregating. We hustled into the dining area after one beer and noted the Philippine band was warming up for the night's music. The room was almost empty but there were a few permanent party officers and their wives enjoying a meal. I couldn't help but wonder if the men felt left out of what was going on, but concluded they really didn't care and was sure the wives were more into the daily bridge game than they were the war. After all they had decided they weren't going to cancel their Christmas Formal. Why let a little war interfere with your holidays?

We finished our meal and left to the strains of "I left my heart in San Francisco" belted out by a pretty good, female singer. I hesitated for a moment to watch her but turned toward the foyer, knowing that I really must go and I didn't want to linger any longer as the first of the 99 sorties flying tonight should be hitting the IP about now. Besides Robbie was on my case, haranguing me in that soft Louisiana accent, for not getting him on the schedule for the next night's missions. The truth of the matter was that I was told to not worry about tomorrow as no decision would be made until the results of tonight's sorties were in. It was sort of nice to lead him on though and tell him we needed him on the ground. But I knew that if we go, he will lead!

We stopped by the squadron just to check on the calls that could have come in but there was nothing significant. As we were leaving and walking along the railing towards the stairs, the clerk called me to tell me I had a call coming in from one of my pilots. I walked back and took the call. He was pretty excited and said he just wanted to tell me that he was at base operations and was told that a "D" model with a newly checked out aircraft commander had lost all four engines on the right side and couldn't get them started. He had been in the air for a short time and was going to try to put it on the ground pretty quick. I walked outside to find that I wasn't the first to find out about this dude's situation. The word was that he was on his first solo mission in the D on Guam. He had completed his training at Castle shortly before deploying. The word among those that knew was that four engine out landings were as rare as a happy pilot on Guam, but even worse no one had ever successfully accomplished a go-around with four out on one side.

There was certainly nothing I could do but watch and wait. It was extremely dark out and you could hear the crash trucks bearing down on their positions waiting for this guy to attempt to land. The very experienced "D" IPs would be in Charlie tower talking to this inexperienced pilot trying to calm him down and to give him all the advice he ever wanted to hear. I had been "on-call" as the IP in B-47s one night at Pease AFB in New Hampshire and was busy in the Standboard office at my desk cleaning up some paper work. The direct line phone rang. It was a call from the command post to come downstairs as there was an emergency in progress. I hurried to the mirrored door and was immediately buzzed in. The duty controller filled me in as quickly as he could. The bird had launched as a JATO (jet assisted takeoff) aircraft, which meant that they had strapped a set of jet assisted bottles on a large rack to the underbelly of the aircraft. Immediately after launch they began to experience a loss of boost pumps on the aft auxiliary tank, and this was followed by a loss of their UHF radio.

This was a classic case of a fuselage fire caused by a bottle on the rack turning and firing into the plane surface. The plane was in great danger of exploding. I knew that whatever I said was going to have a decided influence on the safety of the crew and I didn't want them to panic so I was very cautious in what I said, but I firmly believed we had to act fast in order to save the crew. They had passed through 11,000 feet on the Kennebunk departure, which meant he was now over the Atlantic Ocean. I told the controller to advise the AC to turn back to land and prepare the crew for an immediate bailout. About that time the wing commander, Col. Frankosky walked into the room. I brought him up to speed as fast as I could and told him I felt the situation was grave and recommended a bailout.

There had never been a successful outcome from a fuselage fire in the B-47 and there had been more than a few. He obviously had to make a hard decision and was not ready to make it too quickly. The aircraft had lost their UHF radio and was communicating on HF and was continuing to lose boost pumps and had other degraded equipment. This had been the pattern in such cases in the past. The fire was progressing forward to one of the fuel tanks. Colonel Frankosky kept using that old command post term when a decision was in progress and we passed it on to the crew, "stand by"!

I confronted Frankosky, "Sir, this can be catastrophic, I'm strongly recommending bail out."

"Al, let's not rush into this. Let's hold off a little longer."

I could see that his concern seemed less about the crew and more about how he would have to explain a crew bail out to higher headquarters if the airplane subsequently did not explode.

The time delay in making the decision had allowed the crew to continue to a higher altitude. The aircraft was now above flight level 180 (18,000 ft). Equipment stabilized, enough time had passed that the fire had more than likely gone out and the present altitude didn't allow much oxygen to get to the fire, thus sustaining it. Finally the decision was made to burn off fuel and isolate the affected fuel tanks and land as soon as possible. It took almost three hours to get the fuel down to a safe level for a landing. Once getting to a favorable gross weight, the AC put it on the ground safely. Colonel Frankosky and I met the aircraft when it parked. As soon as the engines were shut down we went to the aft portion of the aircraft. It was badly scorched and there was a hole about the size of a "saucepan" in the undercarriage.

Going into the aft wheel well we could see the boost pumps of the aft aux and aft main tank. The wiring was burned away from the tanks and the fire had stopped burning no more than an eighth of an inch from the tank. That was the crew's margin of survival! Colonel Frankosky shook his head and said how fortunate they were to have made it back. I knew they had a lot of help and it wasn't from this world and I was thankful that the time delay didn't result in the loss of a crew. If I had to do it all over again I would give the same advice, because we were damned lucky that the aircraft didn't explode! At any rate all an IP on the ground can do is pass on his knowledge in the very best and calmest way possible.

But back to the current situation, I'm sure that there was more than enough information being passed on to the young gent in the hot seat on this "D"! It's amazing how the many interested people can appear without any announcement, but all of a sudden there was a crowd waiting to see how this guy would do. They had been burning off and dumping fuel to get to a decent gross weight and we now heard the attempt was going to be made. This young rookie AC was prepared to start his approach. We stayed in the squadron area on the second floor and could see the final approach from our vantagepoint, but not the main portion of the runway. We were getting sporadic phone reports on my portable radio now as I finally turned the "brick" on! We could see his landing lights on a long final, inching toward the runway. As he got lower and lower, you could almost feel the strain of his situation amid this now large and growing group of seasoned pilots next to the railing far from the problem. All were offering their own opinion as to how they would react.

The aircraft dipped below the buildings along the flight line and then we heard the whine of the engines that were left, winding up and we all held our breath. He was going around! You could see in the faces of those around the railing the despair. You won't make it they all felt and said, while spitting out any number and variety of expletives. The heads started to shake and the words of doom were emitting as one, we waited for the splash and the explosion. And remember there are aircraft all along that runway. A crash could be catastrophic!

It didn't come. That rookie had pulled it off, he had made it back into the air, truly amazing! It was almost by will that the aircraft rose above the runway. The position lights blinking as it rose back into view. You could see a lot of pilots stretching out a leg as if they were the one on the rudder pedals trying to keep the nose semi-straight. He managed a cross-wind turn and then pushed himself into a downwind for yet we knew would be another try. We lost sight of him for what seemed like an eternity and then the landing lights gave his turn to final away. He was once again locked on the runway and started his descent. As he slowly lost altitude in this second attempt, there was not a whisper of wind, which was a rarity on an island where the wind is always blowing. Once again the aircraft disappeared below the buildings blocking our view. Collectively we held our breath and waited. We then heard the four good engines come back and the silence was an indication that he made it. A yell went up as we spotted him in a gap in the building with his brake chute out. He was down and was braking to a stop. This rookie had pulled off a feat no other D pilot had ever accomplished before. I hoped that this was an omen how the night would go. The assemblage broke up, giving high praise to the unknown "green" pilot. Now there were other things to think about, but this had been an event for the books.

Bomber operations was as usual the last to know how the air battle was going, but unfortunately they had received word that one buff had gone down, but weren't sure whether it was a D or G. They did know that one aircraft, a lead in the 3rd wave had lost its radar, and was changing its position to give number two the lead. He would attempt to release his load using another aircraft's radar. It would be no small task changing position during the night conditions! Other ominous information was being received through the Eighth Air Force command post and it was obvious that this was not a good night. Another report indicated that two more B-52s had been shot down, but no information on the cell or the type of buff. I picked up the secure line to Eighth and got a duty controller, identified myself and asked for the identity of the fallen birds. There were two "G's" and one "D" known down in the 1st wave.

Post strike reports back from one of the cells had one of the Gs not making it to the target area, and another was hit in the post target turn. The D went down after the release of his weapons while heading directly to the gulf of Tonkin. That was a change in tactics that I wasn't aware of and as it turned out it was a bird out of U-Tapao. He also informed me that it was Charcoal lead, in the "G" group that lost his radar. That was Randy Cradduck and his crew. He was very experienced and had flown over 40 sorties this tour, however he had only been a lead four times. That concerned me a lot! Word also was filtering in that the 2nd wave was now exiting the target area. The time on target had been compressed down to 90 and 120 seconds to make the SAM loading time a bit tougher for the enemy. The compression would bring the waves closer together. It seemed to help wave two, which was comprised of our "Gs" and the "Ds" out of UT, as there were no reports of losses on that wave.

But the SAM loading obviously took place while wave two was doing their job, as now reports were flying that wave three was really getting hit. Not only were there a number of SAMs being reported by exiting aircraft, there were also some reports of aircraft sighted in flames near the center of Hanoi being called in. Now there was more traffic than I could keep up with, as the third wave was beginning to get their post strike reports out. Again one G did not make the target area and the preliminary reports were that it was the aircraft without radar. That would be Randy Cradduck! Randy had recently had his wife on the island as some crewmembers had made the decision to bring their wives to Guam to alleviate the strain of separation of this constant Arc Light-Bulletshot TDY. There were no regulations that prohibited it, and although it was discouraged, it was a common practice for some of the young married crewmembers. The rent was cheap downtown and when not involved in flying duties the crews were free to do what they wanted.

Randy had sent his wife home as there had been some personal difficulty that caused her to leave, however his copilot George Lockhart had also brought his wife over and she was still here. That would present a big problem, but I didn't have time to reflect on it though as I turned to Herb, he quickly informed me that Jim Nagahiro, his aircraft commander from Fairchild who flew as a substitute on day one, got it in the PTT. He was going after the same target that I bombed last night. That gunner on the ground didn't make the same mistake twice! He offset his aiming point for the turn, not the release point. We now knew that we had lost a total of six B-52s. We were all stunned, but I was in absolute shock. Besides Randy in my squadron, Terry Geloneck's aircraft was seen going down in the first wave. He was also hit in the turn after release. I was not aware that some members of Terry's crew had their wives on the island, but as the "emergency data cards" were pulled the next of kin addresses were in Agana. I wasn't in the mood to face the wives of those now listed as missing men, but I knew that someone would be looking for me to do exactly that.

Now that the aircraft were in the return mode I found myself looking for some sort of refuge. I didn't want a drink, but I did want company and searched ops to see if I could spy Herb who had disappeared or even Al Sweney would do. Not seeing either one I started to leave the building when I noticed a crewcut headed guy in a flight suit just hanging around the various phone banks looking directly at me and seeing my recognition, smiled the Robbie smile while shaking his head from side to side. He came towards me and asked if I wanted to get something to eat. The thought was a good one, so I replied "good idea, how about the pool bar at the club"? We jumped into my truck and didn't say much on the way to the club except to acknowledge the bad night. Six buffs down was a disaster to us, even though we later learned these were supposedly acceptable numbers to the powers to be, back in Omaha. It might have been acceptable to them, but I couldn't fathom six big birds down and the loss of 36 crewmembers. I was outraged, at the thought of not changing tactics more significantly on the third day!

We ate a bit, discussing the events of the night and then after feeling the effects of not being in the rack since early yesterday, combined with my bitter feelings toward our stupid tactics, decided to leave. As we were walking out of the front of the club I suddenly wanted to know more about last night. The sun was trying to bounce up out of the Pacific and I knew the first wave should be close to landing. We decided to go talk to the crews to see if we could learn any details about the downed aircraft. We hustled to the flight line, went past base ops, down to the west loop and then up the north runway to where the aircraft would recover. The first movement I saw was a maintenance bread truck moving among the aircraft nestled on the ground. I hailed them down and asked when the first of the aircraft was due in. They informed me that the first aircraft was on final now.

I looked back over my shoulder and could see the landing lights of an aircraft some distance out. The puffy, fair weather cumulus clouds sometimes obscuring them. If there was one aircraft there would be a lot more very shortly. I looked at my 20 December schedule and scanned the crews. Terry had been in the first "G" cell and was the number three aircraft. In the second cell Vlad Mancl should have some information about Terry's aircraft, as he would have been less than three minutes behind as the number two aircraft in that cell. I inquired at Charlie tower about his parking spot and drove to the center taxiway and proceeded to the designated spot. The aircraft were landing less than a minute apart now and the action on the flight line had gone from calm to raucous. The noise of moving aircraft and the whine of their engines was only somewhat muted by the closed cab of our truck. We watched silently as the buffs moved through the weapons check-point and then around the field as they proceeded to their parking spots.

When I was in the B-58 program I had looked down my nose at the B-52. I thought that it was indeed a big ugly fat airplane and of course it was slow and ungainly looking. I was among the elite who flew twice the speed of sound in the sleekest aircraft ever made, the Hustler. Many of my former crewmembers had told me that I too could one day be a buff driver, and I always responded "NO WAY"! Well when General Paul K. Carlton called me into his office at SAC Headquarters where he was sitting in for the CINC SAC, and told me he wanted me to be one of his 15th AF squadron commanders, I was smart enough to say that it was really an honor. I had actually asked for Fairchild AFB in Washington as my base of choice. The fact that I ended up at Mather was because my friend Herb Jordan had many hours in the bird, was already checked out, was resident on the base and had better timing than I did, but Mather was certainly a great consolation prize. I was not happy to be going to this big bird, but I had no choice. I would have to suffer the taunts of those I had so steadfastly told I wouldn't be caught in that ugly bird.

My first two or three flights in the CCTS at Castle were a mystery as I was once again flying an aircraft that took off in a leaping fashion with zero angle of attack and landed in much the same fashion. It was not difficult to pick up the refueling aspect and it was comfortable to fly once you were in the air. The fact that the receptacle was behind your head was a minor distraction at first as I was totally used to seeing the refueling boom into the receptacle on contact and now it was a matter of seeing the boom pass over your head and out of view. The directional lights on the tanker, however now made sense and were very easy to follow. The B-52 also had this cross wind crab knob that allowed you to land looking out the side window in some situations, and flying low-level using the archaic radar in the pilots position was true agony. But then I discovered the real beauty of the airplane. She was a graceful lady, a big lady, but a lady. My remaining flights were made solving her intricacies or maybe it was just a reawakening of the meaning of bomber.

The B-58 was a nimble single pilot, fighter with nowhere to roam in the cockpit, four engines, a stick that maneuvered the aircraft at the slightest touch and two additional crewmembers along for the ride. But hey, they were the best of the best. All B-58 crew members were handpicked for this aircraft. The Navigator/Bombardier had a sophisticated stellar, inertial, guidance system tied into Doppler Radar for accurate ground speed and the ability to update the inertial system with precise Radar fixes. It could, in effect, drop bombs on target through the inertial system alone if Radar was lost. The Defensive Systems Operator (DSO) was a combination EWO and Gunner. His system could not only disperse chaff, but also intercept enemy Radar and send back false Radar positional information that completely confused the enemy. And when he fired his 20 mm Gatling gun, the aircraft literally jumped ahead with each burst.

Each crewmember flew in a separate capsule that could close on initiation in microseconds to protect you during a high speed ejection. The capsule was self-contained and had all the essentials for survival, but it was very constricting and obviously did not allow one to get up for any reason. The B-52 on the other hand was roomy, had eight engines, five additional people to worry about and coordinate with and required a heavy hand to fly by a yoke (half a wheel). There were constant requests to leave a station and move about, sometimes even to sack out in the rack behind the pilot station during long flights. With the past over and the future in front of me I was caught with the strength and character the B-52 displayed and was very pleased to be a part of the contingent that made her fly.

Vlad's aircraft ground to a halt as the crewchief crossed his wands and then motioned to the pilot to cut his engines. The familiar whine of the shutdown was now replaced by the power unit sparking into life as power was now being furnished from outside the aircraft. The hatch on the bottom of the aircraft opened and the crew began to come out into the now very sunny morning. The crew bus pulled up in front and the crew was now regurgitating their equipment from the belly of the bird. The amount of equipment that is carried on any mission is staggering and now the pile seemed adequate enough, so I walked toward the crew as they were lifting the gear to carry it to the bus.

The look on their faces was like reading a scary novel. They were tired, this was not only their second mission, as they had flown on the 18th, but they had been involved in circumstances last night that could affect their psyches forever and most of all they were mad. Crews don't really talk to you as a commander, they talk to each other in a voice loud enough to be heard at five yards with the power unit going at full bore. I waited for Vlad and his copilot to exit and motioned him towards me. He is taller than I am (as are most people), but not too tall. I asked him if he had seen Geloneck get hit and he said he had indeed. He thought maybe by two SAMs in his turn after bomb release. Instantly, he didn't think anyone survived the explosion, however the crew heard multiple beepers after they saw the missiles detonate so were pretty sure some of the crew got out. Vlad repeated, in anger, what his and other crews had been saying;

"Al, this is really dumb to go in on the same heading night after night and without using tactics. What the hell are we doing? Are we training these SAM crews on how to shoot us out of the sky?"

"I agree Vlad, it's a tough situation and we're like sitting ducks up there."

There is no avoiding a SAM in the final stages of the bomb run and especially if you haven't had a chance to maneuver prior to release. I agreed with him as much to mollify his ire as to let him know that all the pilots were upset with the present tactics. (The G squadron commanders had voiced this opinion repeatedly to Colonel Rew and I know he had gone forward with our concern). Vlad had not seen any of the other 52s go in, but once more he heard lots of beepers. Of course the beepers could have been from an aircraft other than a buff. Vlad and his crew departed and Robby and I now decided we would wait for the third wave crews to get in. We didn't have to wait long as a trail of Gs appeared on final and the second wave was already down, so we charged back to Charlie tower, walked in, grabbed a cup of coffee and got the information on the parking for Captain Ken Mizner and Captain Jack Hanfland.

I had flown with Captain Hanfland on the 5th of December and found him to be a very savvy and smooth pilot. He had called in to the command post with a report that he had received some battle damage, however he had no control or instrument problems to speak of. He said that they had experienced a close explosion that had rocked them pretty well at or shortly after release. Jack was not prone to overstating a situation so I was anxious to see his aircraft. We finished our coffee and jumped out of the mobile control look alike, but Charlie tower was a larger air conditioned model, and walked to the truck. We watched as a G landed on the runway immediately to our right and stared long enough to insure his brake chute had deployed. We headed down to the other side of the 6000 foot crossover position and awaited the two aircraft. Ken Mizner's aircraft would be the first one in. He would have been behind Jim Nagahiro's craft, but in front of Randy Cradduck's bird.

So once again we went through the drill of watching the post flight exit of the crew from the aircraft. Ken was the kind of guy you loved to have around because he loved to fly and he was always talking the good fight, so I prepared myself for a thorough and long dialogue. When I saw Ken alight in his sweat stained flight suit, I joined him in his walk around the aircraft. He still had his flight gloves on and his skullcap pushed into a little point on top of his head, and being short and heavy of stature, and gesturing wildly and talking in demonstrative terms about his flight, he looked like a chubby leprechaun. You could see he was having some serious thoughts about what he had been involved in on his night adventure. As I caught up with him and before I could ask him anything, he was recanting in varying levels of speech the various SAMs he had either encountered or seen.

It was a litany of expletives and wild gesticulations. He felt he had been very fortunate to make it safely back, and from his description of the events I had to agree. I asked him about Cradduck's aircraft when he slowed down to take a breath. "Oh sure I saw him and heard him. He was really in difficulty and was at first asking for a gunner assist, using the aft gun radar "bonus deal" to give him a position relative to his cell. He had ended up totally out of the stream to our 3-4 o'clock position. He then asked anyone to go "Christmas tree" (that would involve turning the exterior lights of the aircraft on, Not a good idea), which would have been suicide with all the MIGs around. I asked, "What happened then?'

"We were barely inbound at the time. I didn't see the first SAM, but I saw the flash and turned to see his aircraft in a slight descent. He was on fire and started to bank to the starboard. But as he turned away back towards Laos, he was hit again and it just went up in a ball of fire."

Ken grit his teeth and I could see his eyes getting moist. I said, "Go on Ken."

"Al, I don't think anyone got out! It was one huge fireball. The second SAM seemed to hit him mid ship and with his full bomb load still in his belly, it just seemed to break in half".

I asked him if he heard any beepers and he said he was too busy at the time to notice and there was a lot of chatter in his aircraft from the bomb-nav team and his EW advising of the various uplinks he was encountering. I left Ken still muttering to himself and proceeded to Jack Hanfland's buff. He was already outside and had drawn a crowd of maintenance guys as well as his own crew at the back of his left wing. As I got closer with Robbie in tow, I could see the "swiss cheese" design tattooed on his left flap and wing. There were a number of small holes and a couple you could put your fist through. Jack noticed me and just kept rolling his head from side to side, with his eyes fixed on his wing area.

In a strange silence we walked under the fuselage to the other side. His right wing trailing edge and flaperon had large holes gouged roughly through its structure, giving the impression of impending collapse. There was a collective intake of air as we all gasped at the sight. The weird aspect of this was that there was no apparent damage anywhere else except in the wing areas. We later found out that there was a total of 149 holes in the aircraft, some on the top of the fuselage that we had missed on our brief walk around. The fact that none of the shrapnel penetrated a vital or critical area speaks well of someone's relationship with the Man upstairs. The other point that was made over and over by crews that suffered damage to their aircraft was how tough the B-52 was. Jack had flown over six hours and 3000 miles after the incident and didn't have any indications of a problem, nor did he feel threatened. Even those who were shot down later told tales of the strength of the bird. Some of those whose aircraft were severely damaged were able to get to relative safety before they had to punch out, as was the case with Hinch Connor and his compatriots.

I did take the time to ask Jack the same questions about the two G's that went down in his wave and he told me pretty much the same story as Ken, reiterating the magnitude of the explosion that occurred on Cradduck's bird. The corroborating story made the outlook for the crew's safe egress very doubtful! I wasn't going to prolong the issue or take the time on the ramp to discuss it further, so we jumped in the truck and headed for debriefing. The gym as usual was full of crews telling stories about their night over Hanoi. I would catch a piece of one harrowing tale and then part of another and still another as I tried to gather my wits and digest what happened last night. I was sitting on the edge of a gym bench when I saw Colonel Rew walking towards me and knew immediately, I should have gone to bed. He was a stricken man and as I would later discover he was a most sensitive human being. He wanted to know if I knew where the wives on the island would be at this hour, slightly after nine o'clock in the morning and I said I really wasn't sure and couldn't help him. But I offered maybe the BX or Commissary if they were not at home, pretty obvious guesses

However I really didn't socialize with the married crew personnel, as they spent most of their free time off base and I hadn't left the base since my arrival in September, not even to the Navy exchange on the south end of Guam. Colonel Rew had someone already check the homes and they weren't there, and I'm sure further calls were being made around other base facilities. I wasn't sure how many wives we were talking about, but later learned there were three in the G squadrons that were being sought. I informed the General that Randy's wife had gone home as he seemed to not be counting her. One of the other pilots standing close by heard our conversation and volunteered that many of the wives were in the habit of going to the pool in the morning before it got too hot. With a chaplain in tow, Colonel Rew told me to come along as he mentioned George Lockhart's wife as one we needed to see, but I was not sure if any other members of Randy's crew or any of Terry's crew were included. I had been through this notification process before and wasn't too keen on repeating it.

When stationed at Bunker Hill AFB in Indiana my wife and I were asked to accompany the chaplain to my neighbor's house across the street. A student crew in the B-58 Combat Crew Training Squadron (CCTS) had gone in off the end of the runway. As an Instructor Pilot I had taken this crew through the launch process of preflight and base operations weather briefing and flight plan filing for that flight. All student crews had to be monitored on their solo "B" missions, but I had been relieved when the weather was marginal and the launch was in doubt. The commander of the CCTS (combat crew training squadron) took my place and authorized the launch when the field went above student minimums. The Defensive Systems Operator (DSO) was my neighbor, and his wife, who my wife and I had met at one of our squadron softball games, was a petite lady of French heritage from French Morocco, and spoke English with a distinct accent. My squadron commander at the time asked if I could go over as he and the operations officer were involved with the other two crewmembers.

My wife and I met the chaplain and went to the door. The chaplain was brutal, no tact, just launched into the will of God and all that. Needless to say it was a very tough encounter for my spouse and I. His wife kept asking me if there was a chance that he survived, and I kept assuring her that there was always a chance that he punched out. I knew full well that they, the crew, had not reached a really high altitude before the pilot, Major Galen Dultmeier lost control of his bird, but I felt this was the only hope she would have until we knew for sure there were no survivors. Finally after three to four hours, there really was no more that we could do and after it was pretty well ascertained that the crew had gone down with the aircraft, we left the new widow with a friend of hers and walked across the street to our base house. I was drained at the termination of that experience and retreated to my living room and had a very stiff drink, while my wife retreated to bed.

I wasn't looking forward to a repeat performance today. As we were leaving I waved at Robbie who was now looking to find a way to silently split the scene. He dove out one of the side doors of the gym and I couldn't blame him. We arrived at the pool in sort of a caravan of blue vehicles and our mission was obvious to those who saw us. There were a number of crewmembers there with their wives, as well as another group of officers with wives mingling with some unescorted women on the other side of the pool. Trying not to be too obvious, we asked one of the crew dogs near us if they knew any of the women we were looking for. Yes they did and we were pointed in their direction. I definitely lagged behind as Colonel Rew and the chaplain briskly headed over towards the women. I saw one of my Aircraft Commanders from Mather and stopped to tell him what was going on and in reality it was to escape the events that were transpiring on the other side of the pool.

I glanced over to where the group ended their short journey and saw one young woman in a bathing suit turn as the contingent arrived. She had obviously been in conversation with someone, but now was caught up with the uniformed group in front of her. She immediately knew they were there to see her and the news was not good. Colonel Rew reached out to grab her hand, which now had gone to her face to suppress the gasp that emitted from her throat. This chaplain had a better grasp on the situation than the one I had previously experienced and seemed to calm her almost immediately. One other wife was found and it was George's wife. Though close by I took no part in the dialogue and marveled at her calm demeanor. I finished some conversation with a group that had gathered around me and headed back to my truck. Colonel Rew was in real distress and had taken this chore very personally. He sort of nodded that I was excused and got into his car with the chaplain. The two wives had been surrounded by friends and hustled to cars for their trip to their island quarters. This day had gotten out of hand and I desperately wanted to go back to my room and get some sleep. There was no need for a drink. I was already too numb to care any more!

A CHANGE IN TACTICS

A very short, furtive sleep was interrupted by a knock on the door. It was one of the clerks from the squadron operations office. He said Colonel Rew wanted me to report to bomber ops immediately. I put on the same smelly flight suit I had worn all day yesterday as I hadn't bothered to wash anything in a couple of days. I made a mental note that I would explain to the good commander that I had been too involved to do such mundane things, knowing that he already knew I had been flying and planning since Sunday night and it was now Thursday morning. The sun was especially bright and the humidity had reached its usual 90+ percent. It was in the short walk to the operations building that I noticed a lot of crews sort of wandering around, more than I would have expected on a maximum effort fly day.

Colonel Rew was in front of the building talking to some of the staff when he saw me and abruptly ended his conversation and walked over to intercept my travel. I naturally saluted smartly and tried to position myself upwind of him as both my body and flight suit desperately needed cleansing. He was a very thin man who was actually surprisingly tall, but seemed to disguise it with his habit of bending forward when in an upright position and slouching forward when sitting. With a proper inspection I would have noticed that he had long legs and a short torso, just the opposite of my body makeup. He was a very proper officer, totally dedicated to his country and service. You could only watch him for awhile and know that he was a real professional. "Al, I need you to seal off Captain Cradduck's room and gather his crew's personal effects, I've already sent someone to take care of the other crews rooms".

I was about to ask any number of questions about the downed crews and to also let him know I would have to tend to my pre-launch duties. He stopped me in mid sentence when he informed me that tonight's "G" missions going north of the DMZ had been scrubbed and that we would only be launching a few "G" sorties down south. I must have allowed my mouth to drop open as he said that SAC was reevaluating our tactics. I didn't say it was about time, but it most certainly was. This was now a normal day for the short tailed G, however the Ds from Anderson and those out of U-Tapao would fly some sorties up north, but no target locations were disclosed. I then asked about the crews who had been shot down. He didn't have too much information about yesterday, but did say that some of the crews from the December 18th missions were known to be POWs. Being aware of my friendship with Steve Rissi, he quickly added that he was not among those who were identified

I thanked him and saluted again and walked away admittedly relieved that we were not going north today, partly due to the dull throb from yesterday's losses, but also it would delay my need to fly north at least another day. I had felt "the wolf rise in my heart" and wasn't proud of my reaction. I knew also this would slow down the incessant pleas of "Sir, have you got a minute"? I needed a respite, but now was not the moment. I found one of the ops officers, Major Dale Drummond in the squadron and asked him to go with me to Cradduck's crew quarters. We wended our way along the second floor railing until we found the right room. Unlocking the door, we saw that this was a crew who had worked very hard to allow some privacy for each of the members of the crew. It was relatively easy to find where each of the crew had his own space.

I was very sensitive to personal letters that were lying about, being careful to have separate envelopes to place individual items of correspondence in. I was concerned that there would be items sent home that might reflect on a married couples relationship, but not knowing the relationship of names on the letterhead it was virtually impossible unless we only sent known family member's items to the listed next of kin. I was particularly moved by the personal items, the pictures that belonged to Bobby Kirby, the radar navigator, of his wife and children and his pipe. I had remembered him using the pipe in his more reflective moods, that along with the aromatic tin of tobacco, were some of the things that I had great trouble putting in a box which I then quickly taped shut. I was very careful to mark each envelope with the name of the officer and very careful to not mix things up.

We finished that distasteful chore and put a seal on the two entry doors. It would remain that way until we had some word on the crew or there was a declaration of their status. All indications had been that no one had survived! We would learn much later that the gunner somehow managed to get out and was a POW, the remainder of the crew had perished. In ensuing days I was asked to take calls from George Lockhart's father, a retired full colonel. He was merely looking for some hope that possibly George II had survived. I was very close to the vest, but told him until we knew otherwise, there was always a possibility that he could have escaped the explosion that a number of witnesses had seen. I knew it was unlikely but there were beepers after all! His calls faded as time passed and he heard no word of his son's fate.

The next two days were a mixed bag as there were so few sorties being flown by the Gs that we actually were able to catch up on our paper work and I caught up on my sleep. The command was already asking for medal recommendations. With all the missions that were being flown it would be a monumental task. All the "G" sorties now being flown were down south and once again had revolved into the regular Arc Light type missions. Smiles were returning to the crew's faces, but there was also a sense of anger as everyone was very upset by the first three days tactics and that was the source of considerable questioning and public consternation. All felt that the third day was just the culmination of poor tactical planning. Despite reports that the losses were less than anticipated, everyone knew one or more of the crews that were now listed as MIA (missing in action) and in some cases prisoners of war. Therefore when it was announced that General Meyer and his staff, notably General Pete Sianis, his Director of Operations were going to visit Guam and U-Tapao to talk to the crews, you knew there would be some direct questions on the matter. Everyone had some personal reason for being upset and I was especially in a funk as I had three crews down and they were people I saw and talked to almost every day.

There had been two D losses on the 21st going after a particularly well protected airfield called Bac Mai, with no losses on the flights on the ensuing day's missions. We were preparing to go back and we knew it was not because we were going to give the North Vietnamese time to regroup in Secretary McNamara fashion. We all knew that this was only a pause to review the G's first three days work and that we would have to go back over the Red River that ran through Hanoi. While looking at some of the BDA (bomb damage assessment) photos) at the intelligence shop I learned that one of my closest friends from B-58s was the AC of one of the Ds that had gone down over Hanoi after the release of their bombs on Bac Mai. John Yuill was a smooth operator, a very athletic person, great tennis player, a super pilot, a jolly person to hang around with and the father of half a dozen children. He came to the 305th Bomb Wing a class after I did and when he became combat ready I spent a lot of time with him on alert. He made it seem like an adventure and he never complained.

John and his wife were very active in the wing functions and were regulars at Catholic mass on Sunday. They were well known and liked at Bunker Hill and there was never a bad word to be said about them. I had seen John just prior to the start of the Linebacker action. He was returning from his R&R back home. He was out of Carswell AFB in Fort Worth and was on his way back to U-T. I had happened across him walking by the crew quarters toward base operations and though it was getting dark, I recognized him immediately. His was an unhindered athletic gait that was hard to forget! I hadn't seen John since the 305th had disbanded, but had talked to him on the phone a number of times, always about his assignment, but never failing to digress into other chatter. It was really great to see him and I told him so. He had heard I was now a buff squadron commander and instead of ribbing me about my past protestations about the B-52, he seemed genuinely pleased at my status. Caring people always seem to ask how you are and are happy for your success.

We talked for awhile and he related to me that he had probably the oldest crew in SAC. His co-pilot was a captain and his gunner a Master Sergeant, with the rest of the crew all Lieutenant Colonels. We laughed about that and about my helping him to get his assignment to Carswell on his return from a tour in Vietnam. When I left the "Hustler" program and went to SAC headquarters and was assigned to personnel, I was in a position where I had some say in the assignment as well as the reassignment of rated SAC resources. Therefore, when six months after my leaving Grissom AFB, named for Gus Grissom, the astronaut, and the new name for Bunker Hill, the B-58 program was canceled (due to a serious brain cramp by the non-thinking Director of Plans at the headquarters). I was besieged by phone calls from all my "friends" looking for their new posting. For most this was going to be a Southeast Asia position, known as an unaccompanied tour. Of course all the pilots wanted F-4s or "Thuds" (F-105s). Needless to say there weren't enough of those to go around, however I really tried to accommodate everyone.

Most were happy with their new assignments but there were exceptions. Some, as I found out later were less than pleased to go from the Mach Two Hustler to helicopters. But go they did! Then when their inevitable tour in southeast Asia was winding down I was getting calls at all hours of the day and night from Vietnam and Thailand pleading for either a base of choice or an aircraft out of SAC. I found out later that my office phone and my home phone numbers were on just about every bulletin board in SEA. It was nothing to get a couple of calls at home in the wee hours of the morning every night (due to the time differential between Omaha and Vietnam) asking for help. All of the returning rated officers with a SAC history that were not scarfed up by other commands were given to my office, DPRD, the Career Development office and to DPRO, the Director of officer assignments office by the Military Personnel Center at Randolph, AFB in Texas.

Lt. Colonel Guy Winstead and I used to jockey for position on how returning officers were going to be utilized. It was a virtual dogfight on some occasions and we would have to go to our mutual boss, Colonel Ed Fleming, the Director of Rated Personnel (DPR) to crank out a decision. I think I won more than my share of close decisions, but I did lose a few. The Center had become used to my inquiries about former B-58 troops, so they gave me four distinct groups of records on my monthly trip to Randolph. They had pilots, navigators, and electronic warfare officer piles and one pile with all the returning B-58 guys. I was able to effect a lot of good choices for the 305th and 43rd guys and was very sensitive to those who had to go back on a crew in trying to get them at least their base of choice. John Yuill was one of those. Before B-58s he was a long time B-52 driver. He had left his wife, Rosemary (the same name as my wife) and children in Fort Worth. That's all he wanted when I told him he would have to go back to buffs, and that's what he got, and he was happy about it. As we talked you could tell that John was not a person to whine about any problems or his separation from his family. John was the most upbeat guy I've ever known and that was the way he was that evening on Guam. He was at his normal self joking about going back to the D model B-52 and U-T. Little did I know that in less than a week his crew would be flying three missions over Hanoi in four days, and that on the third he would be shot down.

His misfortune actually came with a change of the first two night's tactics as his cell was to be a direct overflight of the target area, entering from Laos, releasing his weapons on the Bac Mai storage area in Hanoi and exiting by way of the south China sea. John's entire crew bailed out of the aircraft safely and as I later found out John had to wait for one crewmember whose seat didn't fire and was the last to leave. All were to become POWs. I was informed of his capture at the same time that I found out he had been shot down on the 22nd, now, that really made for a bad week, and it wasn't over yet! This period of time was one I will never forget. I had three of my crews downed, eighteen men, four of Don's crew were known to have been captured, all of Geloneck's crew were captured, no word on Randy's bunch, and now my good friend John Yuill was a prisoner. Couple that with the knowledge that Jim Nagahiro and his navigator were listed as POW,s and there was no news on the rest of his crew or Lt. Col. Heggan, the unnecessary airborne commander.

In addition to that there was every indication that the aircraft commander and co-pilot of aircraft 201, the only number of an aircraft that launched on day one that I could visually recall, was not all good. Don Rissi and Bob Thomas were not listed as being recovered by the enemy subsequent to Monday night's raid. They went down over Hanoi and there was no chance they were evading. It was painful to realize that we were really feeling the war, and I seemed to have been the recipient of more of its impact than I wanted to think about! The trick now was to get back to business. How do you disregard the events of the last four days? There was no time to reflect on what had happened, it was history, but somehow we had to convince the powers back in the Omaha Puzzle Palace (Strategic Air Command Headquarters) to do it better! All of the crews were anxiously waiting for the CINCSAC and his staff!

THE SAC STAFF

The SAC staff had first gone to U-Tapao and the word was that they had bestowed medals on some of the D crews that had flown the first three days. We also learned that all the missions out of U-T and the Ds from Guam had not gone "Downtown" (the term used when referring to Hanoi) since day four. They had gone north, but to "selected" targets mostly removed from the lethal SAM areas. It was a matter of how long would we wait, or better yet how long would the guys in charge wait! I now was made aware of the fact that some of the G aircraft had not been modified to allow electronic countermeasures coverage downward while in a turn. In other words when we turned in the PTT our protective ECM was being directed at the horizon. Therefore the combat break maneuver was actually exposing the big bird and was aiding the enemy in their attempt to find a target.

For the time being this was not going to be for crew disclosure, I wonder why? They were now trying to arrange sorties so only modified Gs would be utilized for flights into lethal SAM areas where a post target turn would be used and to change tactics to allow direct overflight for the others, that is 'no turns'. I know every AC was of the mind that when they turned after release it was to assist in their safe exit from harm's way, now we learn that we were committing a real blunder if our aircraft was not modified! I for one felt very secure in my extreme turn during my maneuver on day three! I was afraid to ask if 479 was a modified aircraft. But I would make very sure I knew if the next buff I flew in combat was capable of performing a turn after release.

The CINC and his staff were to arrive on Day six, another light flying day for both the Gs and the Ds. The two wings with their six squadrons were to be in their seats at 0945 hrs for a 1000 briefing or ceremony involving the SAC staff, of course headed by the CINC (commander in chief) of Strategic Air Command (SAC.) The theater was alive with chatter as we awaited the official party. All the crews were there and they were anxious to hear about what actually influenced these "decision makers" to utilize the same tactics for three consecutive nights. Of course they were interested in anything else the SAC commander would have to say about the war, like when it would be over and when we could leave this island! I was looking around and saw Lt. Col. Red Maynard, the D 60th bomb squadron commander leaning against a wall at the back of the theater. I knew he had already flown two missions and one of them was after the first three-day raids. I was curious how day five missions were oriented and where they went so I pushed myself through a host of rancid flight suits and headed towards Red.

As I got a bit closer I noticed he was standing with the other D squadron commander (the 63rd), Lt. Col. Dave Rines. Both of these guys were born in the B-52. They had been long time co-pilots, became ACs, then IPs, flew in Standboard and for all I knew had spent a tour in the CCTS at Castle AFB in Merced. Needless to say they were probably the most qualified B-52 pilots on Guam. Red was a ruddy faced guy who could not hide displeasure of any kind. He was like a tomato when he was angry, not that he got angry often because he was a real can do guy. Dave, on the other hand, was very soft spoken and seldom seemed to get upset about anything.

We exchanged pleasantries and I asked both about how the missions went last night. They sort of shrugged their shoulders in unison and said in essence that they had gone to targets up north, but well south of Hanoi. They experienced sporadic SAM activity, but really nothing of a threatening nature. I liked the way these two guys handled themselves. We were often in wing meetings at the same time and they were both class acts. They were at the forefront in the briefing on the 17th in requesting that the squadron commanders fly with their troops.

Today, Red seemed a bit pensive, so I asked him how things were going? His answer was not surprising, but it was indicative of the kind of person he was. "I just hope someone doesn't say something to get himself court-martialed, because there are lots of pissed off crew dogs". Before I could respond I heard the familiar "wing, attention" barked out and the "thunder clap" of almost 1000 men rising to attention and now upright from their seats. This was followed by the amazing silence that permeates a room where everyone is in a brace. Then the footsteps are heard walking down the theater isle, a whole lot of them this time as the SAC staff was joined by the Division staff and both wing staffs. It was quite a procession and it took a bit of time for them to all get situated on the stage and in the first row of seats in the theater.

Finally the group settled in. At least to the extent that they appeared to all be there, and the CINC strolled toward the center of the stage and looked down at the green mass in front of him and glanced back to a member of his staff who bellowed out "attention to orders". The undercurrent of sound started up as the crews heard that directive, but it quickly subsided as we began to hear names of individuals called out for a medal. The first name called out put me into a state of shock and I couldn't help but look at the now very red faced Red Maynard. They were giving the "Air Force Cross" to Colonel James R. McCarthy, now that's not an insignificant medal! Colonel McCarthy flew as an airborne commander the first day and saw some real action as did everyone on the first three days. He evidently made a big deal of it in an "after action" report and the leaders of our command were convinced that he was a hero. There was a definite low mumbling now rolling through the theater as the description of this wondrous deed was read. This guy wasn't even flying the airplane! He was in the jump seat. Unbelievable! I know he didn't direct any tactics to evade SAMs.

There was real disbelief on the faces of the two squadron commanders next to me and I couldn't help but wonder what Colonel Rew, the other wing commander was thinking. He too had flown as an airborne commander on the first day, but knowing him, he probably just stated the bare facts in his after mission report. The awards given today were meant as a token of recognition for the crews for their efforts the first part of this air war and they should have gone to the most deserving crew dogs, not to a staff guy riding in the jump seat. And as we all too soon found out, medals were not given cheaply. That became very evident later when we went through the process of recommending individuals for a medal, as some of the crew members who really deserved a medal were either turned down or the recommended medals were downgraded by Pacific Air Forces (PACAF), the final authority on medals given in SEA.

After the medal ceremony everyone settled in his seat and the CINC strolled to the podium. He was effusive in his praise of the crews and of their displayed professionalism and valor. He indicated how pleased he was with the results of the first four or five days and that although there had been losses, they were less than anticipated. It was easy for him to say that as he didn't know those who did not come back! He went on ad nausium in extolling the virtues of the tough decisions that the SAC staff had to make and of the history behind the "Linebacker" missions. He wandered into dangerous territory when he explained "the reasoning behind the tactics" utilized the first three days and even had his Director of Operations, Maj. General Pete Sianis stand up and tell about the tough decisions that were made on those sorties. You could hear the undercurrent within the theater as the crews were grumbling among themselves. You could tell that the CINC was aware of the dissident din as he was beginning to get a bit red in the face and then as the noise was becoming really evident, there was an "at ease" from the senior gallery.

I personally thought it came from Col. McCarthy, but I wasn't sure. Silence returned and the CINC made another mistake as he then asked if anyone had any questions. There were a couple of mundane queries about the immediate future of the current effort, the usual possible going home date and then the bombshell hit. A captain in the middle of the theater rose and when recognized asked "I really don't understand why we flew the same route, utilizing the same tactics three days in a row". Or at least words to that effect! Again the din became evident. And the CINC, now totally upset roared out "What is your name captain"? After a slight pause and total silence in the assemblage, a strong voice said, "O'Malley, sir, Captain O'Malley"! We all gulped a bit as Red leaned over to tell me he was one of the D aircraft commanders in his squadron, TDY (temporary duty) from Loring AFB, in Maine.

The guy had guts. He asked the question everyone wanted to ask, but were afraid to bet their career on, and everyone knew what could happen. Every one waited! The CINC pulled himself up into his large frame and spit out some vindictive words that were like pouring gasoline on a fire. He could never adequately answer that question to those in attendance. Though not directed at the questioner, there was no doubt that his position standing amidst this flock of flying fighting men was one of obvious distress. After a few minutes the CINC mercifully stopped. I personally think it was apparent to him he had lost the audience and wanted to get out of Dodge. It was apparent there would be no more questions and at that moment I think everyone wondered whether Captain O'Malley would be around to fly another day. Being in Colonel McCarthy's wing I had my doubts, but I'll tell you I would take O'Malley on my side to fly my wing any day and I knew that Red would do all he could to protect him.

The entourage stood and the theater participants were once again called to attention and the party of senior staff started up the aisle to exit the theater, again in that strange silence permeated only by the hollow sound of footsteps going to the rear of the building. They were gone and the crews and other observers started to file out as the noise of a bunch of men, shuffling their feet and looking for the sunshine, now seemed to envelop the scene. It was loud and there wasn't what you would call kind words that were being spoken. The visit had done nothing to improve the morale of the "Prisoners of Guam". It was Saturday and tonight would demonstrate the frustration of the POGs. (someone actually created a bumper sticker "Free the Prisoners of Guam", not that many had a car on the island).

The G force was for obvious reasons flying South Vietnam missions. There were thirty D sorties, a majority out of U-Tapao, and so most of the crews were on the ground and had some time on their hands. This was a signal to relax and forget the war, maybe a day at the beach or just reading a book would be in order, however that isn't how it works and the frustration in the air was apparent. You have to wonder how your life takes the twists and turns to place you in a spot like this and I couldn't help but think about becoming a pilot in the first place. Probably the most significant incident leading to being a pilot happened while I was still in college and an Air Force ROTC student and an aspiring future pilot. ROTC was a sweet deal and there was no reason to think there would be any kind of problem. It gave me four great years at a super school playing baseball and preparing academically for my future. It was not until a medic unveiled the color blind test book at the summer camp between my junior and senior year at school. The first two or three numbers were a complete mystery to me. I could see most of them, but about five of them were totally disguised in the sea of dots. I was amazed that some of the guys around me could see the numbers that I couldn't find in the melange of color. They told me that missing four was the limit for the "flight physical" and I missed five, so I flunked the test and that disqualified me from going to flight school. That was despite the fact that I passed a "yarn" test without a hitch.

When I failed my color blind test going into my final year of college, it was a blow to me, but I just felt that now that the Korean War was over, I would complete an eighteen month stint in the service and go into teaching. Fate intervened however as it so often does when decisions must be made about a future. I was able to retake the color blind test, passed it, thanks to an investigative sergeant and was allowed to continue in ROTC. This was the beginning of a career. I was commissioned on my graduation day from college as a second lieutenant and was ready to begin the military phase of my life. I think in the back of my mind I never felt I would make the Air Force a career. I was sure I would get out after I had served my prescribed time.

THE CHRISTMAS PARTY

Unlike most pilots I can claim an uninterrupted career in SAC, including my Southeast Asia tour as the 307th SAC wing commander at U Tapao in Thailand. I do believe I knew the command and was very proud to be a part of its professionalism. Many of the pilots had come from other commands and were not of the same opinion, however all would perform at the highest level because they had a great deal of personal pride and they were brave men and I was proud of them.

I had a lot of work that was waiting at my desk so I went to the squadron and started in earnest to get my "sierra" together. Despite a few interruptions I was catching up on my very full in-basket. It was almost too quiet! Mid afternoon I decided that I would try a run and changed into my running gear and took off. I managed to get through my route without finding that hole which would cause the injury, which would ground me until this war was over. I showered and walked out of the latrine to find Herb Jordan and Robbie sitting on my bed. They wanted to go to the club for a drink and dinner, so I put on some real clothes and we headed to the O club to have some meaningful drinking time. I was the sheriff that night and upon arriving at the club, I parked the truck out front and the three of us together, upon seeing the array of people going into the club, remembered this was the night of the Christmas formal for the permanent party personnel. The mess dress uniforms and the ladies in gowns were a dazzling display.

The ladies especially were a real sight to behold, and for a bunch of TDY crewmembers that hadn't been close to any kind of a woman for a long time, it was a particularly incendiary situation. I thought it strange that they hadn't canceled the function due to the obvious events going on at the time, but then the permanent party was often not aware that a war was going on anyway, so there you have it. Two factions at the club, one engaged in life threatening circumstances and the other enjoying a "tough assignment" (nee vacation) on a Pacific island.

When we entered the club the situation was made even more tense as the crews were being asked not to go into the ballroom area unless of course you were wearing a mess dress, one item that none of us thought to bring to Guam to fight a war. Col McCarthey and his permanent party staff would be there and they, along with Colonel Vincent would be the main reason for this slight to the crews. This was the place where we usually ate dinner and listened to the band, but they were quick to tell us that the bar was wide open and you could order and eat dinner there and of course you could drink! I'm not so sure many just didn't indulge in the latter! The bar was naturally very crowded and rowdy and was not a place to have a friendly chat if you wore a mess dress. The fact that there were now very few crews flying made for a very full house.

You almost had to yell to be heard. Some of the permanent party ventured in to order drinks, but found the atmosphere and the comments pretty stifling and didn't pause to talk. This was despite the fact that I and others had some good friends who were partaking in the evening's formal festivities. As the evening wore on the Christmas trees and other ornamentation became an object of attention. They were a reminder of not being home for the holidays and it seemed to hit all the temporary duty troops right in the face. Suddenly those trees were in danger of not making it through the night. Cooler heads intervened!

There were also instances of physical confrontations when some crew individuals paid (too) close attention to the wives of the formally attired officers at the ball. Fortunately no fights broke out, but there were near skirmishes all night. The sure sign of a possible major problem was a green bagged crew dog venturing into the forbidden area and asking a stunningly attired wife to dance. This usually ended in a face to face standoff, broken up by an alert squadron commander or a smart buddy of the interloper. It was a very contentious evening for everyone and the squadron commanders did their utmost to hustle the crews out of the club as quickly as possible, however the night did nothing to enhance the combat climate on Guam or the relationship between the warriors and the vacationers. We would hear about this evening tomorrow morning, Christmas Eve, and at standup on day eight!

True to form, Colonel McCarthy, had relayed the events of the previous night to Colonel Rew and it became the first item in the 0500hrs briefing. Colonel Rew was very diplomatic and actually seemed pleased that we had somehow avoided any real damage to anyone or anything, namely the club and its decorations for the holiday season. He didn't belabor the situation and launched into the fact that a twenty four hour stand down was to be in effect tomorrow Christmas day. There would be no Christmas raids going anywhere during the stand down, however there would be the few raids for the G model down south today! He wished us a merry Christmas and cautioned us to be alert for anything that might have an impact on the day or night before Christmas. A very private man, he would disappear from view until the next pre mission briefing.

As the meeting broke up many of us wondered about the wisdom of a once again stand down. In the past this had been a sign of weakness to the north Vietnamese and as we had learned, it gave them an increased resolve in their attempts to win this war. We all saw the pause as a time for the defenders of the north to reload the SAM sites and to make it even tougher for our subsequent raids over Hanoi. I had personally seen how a tough stand could make an enemy blink. On one of my many trips to Spain to pull alert in the B-47, I had already spent a week on the bubble and had planned to take my R&R week going on the base operations flight to Frankfurt the next morning when I was relieved from the sortie I was on. My roommate was Bob Ready, another aircraft commander and good friend who was taking the trip with me. As we were packing our bags in preparation for the trip the speaker in our room suddenly came alive with the voice of our President, John F. Kennedy. He was talking about some missiles that were seen in Cuba by one of our U-2s and how the Russians were responsible for entering our part of the world and how unacceptable it was.

I looked at Bob who was now unpacking his bag and I said something to the effect that they surely wouldn't cancel our R&R, would they? He laughed and said something in reply that there was no chance that we would be leaving this base for some time unless it was to go drop a load of nukes on the mother land. I decided to hedge my bet though and merely stopped packing my bag, after all they could resolve this matter in the next ten to twelve hours and then we could get off alert and catch the plane, right? The next morning we walked out of our alert quarters to get some breakfast and noticed that the entrance to our building had been sandbagged overnight and there was a call on the loudspeaker that indicated that all crews would report to the briefing room immediately.

Bob smiled smugly, but said nothing as I turned to get my crew from their room. All the crews were in their seats when the Division commander, General George McKee entered the room to the sound of everyone rising to attention. His briefing was short, but not so sweet as he told all that we were in a state of the highest readiness and that everyone would remain on alert. The Defcon (defense condition) was one that restricted crews to the immediate area and that until further notice we would be confined to our quarters on ground alert. Now I had already had a month of being under the gun, so to speak, as I had been in Wichita to the CFIC (Central Flight Instructors Course) for ten days just prior to my departure for Spain. I had stopped home long enough to greet my new born second son, Matthew and then took off one Monday night for Zarragosa. Now this, it seemed like too much for a body to stand!

After the second additional day of alert we were allowed to go beyond the quarters restriction, but still we were not straying far from our aircraft and General McKee was giving us the impression that we were going to launch very soon. It was very tense, to say the least and the R&R had faded from our memory bank totally. Now all we had to do was to look up to see that this was a very serious time and that the powder keg we were sitting on had a very short fuse. By looking up into the clear blue Spanish sky we could see the contrails of the B-52s on airborne alert in constant race track patterns.

They were at a flight position in the "war plan" that was called a PCTAP or positive control turn around point. They would orbit at this point until they were given the order to continue to their assigned targets or until they were relieved, but there would be constant pressure on the Russians to blink or they would be the object of mass destruction. There were so many aircraft in those orbits that they actually created a cloud cover over the city extending as far west as Madrid. It was a very sobering sight and you only had to know that each of those airborne aircraft were loaded, as we were, with nuclear weapons. As the days seemed to blur by, the alert regime became oppressive so much so that the tension was really playing havoc with the crews. However as things seemed to be getting a bit brighter, General McKee, who was a real determined, but fair guy, allowed the long time crews on alert to downgrade their sortie and go into town for a meal or some other form of relaxation. There was to be no drinking as we would be going back on alert in six hours.

Bob and I had arrived in Spain in early September and didn't leave until the second week of November. The entire time with the exception of two six hour afternoons in Zaragoza, was spent on alert in a state of nuclear readiness. Finally, the President had been successful in his standoff with Nikita Kruschev and the Soviet missile carrying ships had turned around. We had only decreased the Defcon a bit so when I returned to Pease, I was greeted with the fact that I was to be on a bus in the early morning hour going to Boston's Logan airport to pull alert.

At Logan, which was only about a twenty minute drive from my in-laws house on a decent traffic day, we were housed in the National Guard armory and our nuclear bomb laden B-47s were parked a very short distance away on one of the seldom used taxiways on the airport. We were allowed to have our families come and visit us for meals and on Thanksgiving I had a great turkey dinner with Rosemary and her parents and a number of other crew's families. That was the last day we pulled alert for this national crisis as on Friday morning we were summoned to the briefing room and told that in the afternoon we would launch out of Logan, make a left turn and proceed directly to Pease AFB with our aircraft. They downloaded fuel to the minimum necessary to make this very short, but exhilarating journey, and they were going to chain and cinch the nukes into the bomb bay.

There would be no chance of an inadvertent release, and certainly we would have to get the aircraft safely on the ground as those nuclear weapons were a political nightmare. It was a fun flight of about 20 minutes, one takeoff and one landing, and an end to our long participation in the Cuban Missile Crisis, a success because we rattled a more powerful saber and let the other side know we meant it. Not like our adventure in Vietnam, where we vacillated day to day with the McNamara war dance that looked more like the dance of the fairies to the North Vietnamese.

THE BEGINNING

1 grew up making model airplanes and once finished they would hang on a cross-section of wires my dad had placed on the ceiling of my garage bedroom. In high school I worked for the father of one of my friends who restored airplanes. He would completely tear down old training BT-13s and PT-19s bi-wing aircraft. These he would convert into crop dusters. I was quite drawn to the older vintage aircraft, but one day was introduced to the T-6 as my boss bought one fully instrumented from a marine in San Diego and flew it into our local airport. It was a beauty to behold and I was in awe of this well shaped and maintained aircraft. I couldn't stop walking around it and looking into its cockpit. Unfortunately it would be resold to a South American country as a trainer. I could not imagine that one day I would be flying the T-6. My dreams did not take me that far! I never flew in an airplane of any type before going to pilot training despite my great affinity for them. When I entered college I enrolled in the ROTC program to insure I could finish school and play baseball, but it was the entrée into the pursuit of my flying dreams. Upon graduation from Loyola University I was commissioned a 2nd Lieutenant in the Air Force and it was truly the beginning.

PRE FLIGHT

Pilot training in the 50s Air Force was much different than it is in the 21st century. When I received my orders to report to pre-flight training I was really excited. My long awaited reporting date of December 27th, 1954 finally came and I arrived on time for the start of my Air Force career. Pre flight at Lackland Air Force Base in Texas was a process meant to thin out the ranks of those who were designated through ROTC to go to pilot training. There was no Air Force Academy those days so ROTC, Officer Training School (OTS) and Aviation Cadets were the feeding trough for all flight positions. The OTS and Cadets went to their own indoctrination prior to flight school. There had been a need to reduce the pipe line of pilots into the active force due to the end of the Korean War. The daily routine was meant to cull out those who could not deal with the physical and mental requirements of being a pilot. It was more than anticipated as the running and obstacle courses were demanding and a bit more than just challenging. There were also exhausting physicals which were another method of finding any reason to disqualify someone from going further in the process. Soon the five weeks passed and many of those who started in early January were told they would have to serve in a capacity other than flying. I was found to be suitable to go to pilot training. Those still physically and mentally qualified were given three base choices for the "primary" phase of pilot training. They were Mariana, a base in Arizona, Marina, a base in Florida and Malden, Missouri. The two warm states sounded good to me, however my roommate in pre-flight was from Saint Louis and said

I should ask for Malden, because everyone would want the Florida or Arizona bases and our chances would be subject to a lottery of sorts. Of course, not thinking, those who did not get their choice of Arizona or Florida would go to Malden anyway. I selected Malden.

Author: Last row, fourth from left.

MALDEN

Malden would be my first introduction to flight as I had never flown before, despite the fact that I had always aspired to be a pilot and as stated before spent copious hours making model airplanes which hung in my garage bedroom. Upon arriving at Malden everyone was given the new class indoctrination to include the assignment of a room and a roommate, flying gear, to include flight suits, jacket, boots and gloves. We were also given a green baseball cap with an eagle emblazoned on the front as we were "Eagle" flight in class 56-H. The counter squadron in our class was "Hawk" flight. They divided the class into two sections so when one flight was flying the other would be attending classes in all areas involving the knowledge necessary to becoming a pilot. If you flew mornings and attended class afternoons the first week, you would switch the next week. We discovered that Eagle flight was divided into ROTC graduates, OTS individuals (also commissioned officers) a few foreign students and Aviation Cadets. There were 35 of us total in the Eagle flight.

Our first day at the flight line we were introduced to our instructors, all of which were civilians and I was placed at a "table" of four ROTC officers (2nd Lieutenants) Charlie Englehart, Roland Ford, Robert Oltjen, myself and one cadet, Thurman Chamblee jr. Our Instructor was Clyde M. Pinkerton, a homespun individual who was without a doubt the most patient man alive. We were quickly informed that as the class thinned out (washed out) we would be going to another instructor as "Pinky" was the assistant flight commander. Our indoctrination aircraft would be the PA-18, a high wing training aircraft used to determine whether an individual had the coordination skills and the mental aptitude to manage an aircraft.

First flights were of a very short duration, maybe 15-20 minutes. Explanations of the use of flight controls, trim and basic flight turns, pattern entry and exit and of course what to do if the engine quit were the subject for these flights. They were exhausting! Each day after our initial flights we would trade our thoughts about what we had experienced. It seemed that the use of trim was our most difficult problem. Back is up and forward is down, sounds easy, however it didn't seem right! Each succeeding flight the time would be extended, until we were flying 30-40 minutes, again very trying and very tiresome, however we all seemed to be doing well. Then one day prior to our solo flights Pinky sort of let it slip that Chamblee was having some difficulty with air sickness. It came down to one more flight! If Thurman got sick he would meet a board which was preliminary to being washed out. Thurman was a raw boned Oklahoma kid and we wanted him to do well. We were anxious about this flight and all four of us met the aircraft when it landed. As Pinky got out we looked at Thurman in the front seat and he gave us a thumbs up. As Pinky walked away we surrounded Thurman and asked him how he did it and he smiled and said "I swallowed it".

We all soloed, making our three landings to the satisfaction of Pinky and all others who witnessed them. (To solo any aircraft was an adventure and it was more than likely my first hint that there was a segment of fear in what I did. It would not compare to later bouts of fear I would experience associated with flight, but it was there!) Our table was the exception though as our flight ranks were now a mere sixteen and yet we hadn't been given a new instructor, despite some tables now at only one or two student pilots. We lived in fear of changing to anyone else, but we were told it was inevitable. Finally the last flight-checks in the PA-18 were set. It was given by our civilian flight commander, Carl Hubenthall, an individual much like Pinky and his good friend. We all managed to pass and now we were graduating to the T-6, the real training workhorse and a powerful, but forgiving aircraft. It was a "tail-dragger", meaning you had to weave as you taxied because the nose hindered your vision forward. All aircraft had a set of emergency procedures and of course, normal checklists to prepare the plane for flight. Knowing these was an essential part of our checkout in any aircraft. Pinky was a former WWII Navy pilot (we were told he was shot down more than once and crash landed a corsair on a beach) and he was a stickler for following the checklist and knowing what to do in the event of an emergency. He also was a firm believer in knowing how to stall, both power on and power off and spin an aircraft. We practiced these constantly, as well as entering and flying the traffic pattern. Acrobatics was something he would insure you knew, but he was more concerned about recovery from stalls and spins and how to pick the right field for an emergency landing. The need to solo was again an object we had to face and one day Pinky said to head toward one of our practice fields over in Dexter. It was a grass field and had a mobile tower, manned by some of the instructors from the "Hawk" flight. He told me to make a full stop landing and taxi to the front of the tower, which I did. All of a sudden he was on the wing with his chute and told me to remain in the pattern and make three full stop landings. Jelly legs cannot describe my fear, but one had to do what one is told to do. I taxied to the end of the field, called initial solo as I was instructed to do, was cleared for takeoff and roared down the field, took off, entered my crosswind leg turned downwind and finally rolled out on base leg and made a nice turn to final and put her on the ground, a little bumpy, but not bad. I proceeded to make the next two landings without incident and taxied back to the tower where I had dropped off Pinky. He strolled to the aircraft and asked why I had stopped. I told him I had made three landings and he said "I only saw two! You need to make one more and finish the job"! I was not about to argue so went out and did one more pattern and landing. Now he crawled back in and we went back to Malden. I'm convinced that he saw all three, but didn't like my first one and that became a "do over".

We all progressed rapidly and as time in aircraft went by the table began to shrink. Pinky told all of us we would not go with him beyond the 40 hour check ride, Roland Ford and Bob Oltjen left the table, followed by a very nervous Charlie Englehart. Thurman and I were allowed to remain, until we finished the check ride. Pinky told me before the ride to just follow what he had taught me and I would be fine. All 40 hour checks were given by military pilots. Most were well thought of, however one, Lt. Van der Sluis was considered very tough. He had recently given a ride to a student in another class and on landing the aircraft, he ground looped. This means that a wing tip was damaged and the landing process was somehow violated by a violent 180 degree turn. The lieutenant from that time on was even more difficult.

On the day of the check I proceeded with some of the others who were also due for their ride that day to the military check shack. We all sat down waiting for the check pilots to come out. One at a time they would emerge from a back room and grab the paperwork from the pile on the desk and call out a name. At least four or five had come out and selected who they would ride with until only one other student and I were left. Van der Sluis entered and called out the name Dugard. I almost wet my pants! Why me? I grabbed my chute and followed him out of the shack to my awaiting fate and aircraft. I did the walk around check as he watched and then crawled into the cockpit. I finished the checklist, started the engine and proceeded to taxi out, making sure as I took the taxiway that I maintained forward visibility at all times. When cleared on the active and for takeoff I gunned the engine, put in full rudder to counteract the torque of the engine and started my takeoff roll. I could hear Pinky saying that this lieutenant liked to give emergency landings right after takeoff, so to be prepared. I no sooner got my gear up, maybe a couple of hundred feet high and he took the power off. Pinky always stressed to go straight ahead, complete the checklist and leave the gear in the well. I did all that and I felt the power come back in and a muted "good" from the back seat. After getting to a safe altitude. He put me through a series of stalls, a three turn spin, a couple of easy acrobatic maneuvers and we headed back to the traffic pattern. I made a good 45 degree entry into the rectangular pattern, turned base, came down final right on my airspeed and started to round out for landing. I felt a lot of pressure on the stick! This guy was not going to ground loop another T-6! The landing was perfect, the rollout uneventful and the taxi back without a problem. I parked, completed my shutdown checklist and got out of the airplane. The lieutenant said he would complete the paper work, that I had passed and then said, "It was a very good ride"! I was on cloud nine as I walked back to our flight shack, told Pinky and a great smile emerged from his face. It turned out I was given "9s" on all phases of flight, which were the highest marks you can get on a check ride. The next day I got my new instructor.

The change was rather smooth as I went from a laconic Pinky to a diminutive, quiet guy right out of the comic books named John

Maxim. He was about 5"2, had a very small head and was as efficient in-flight as Pinky. Mr. Maxim was also a navy pilot, but was more oriented to acrobatics than Pinky and because he saw that I was very adept at recovery from stalls and spins, he made sure I became as adept in acrobatics. One day while going through a series of maneuvers he asked me to do a half roll and reverse, and I proceeded to do one and because there is a great deal of torque in the T-6 reciprocal engine and I am a short legged individual, I couldn't get enough pressure on my rudder pedals to keep the nose on a "point". In other words, the nose wandered! Mr. Maxim made me repeat the maneuver and in disgust said, "I'll demonstrate one for you", and proceeded to do one perfectly. How could he do that, being shorter than me, I wondered? It was always the same in ensuing flights until one day in his demonstration I looked back and noticed he was not in sight, so peeked down below and discovered he had "bottomed" his seat and was almost prone in the cockpit giving him full throw of the rudder pedal. With the secret uncovered, I became very good at the maneuver, much to the delight of little John, and he never knew that I found out his method.

Primary at Malden was full of characters I would never forget. There was my roommate, Bob Duggan, a big guy who rowed for the University of Washington, smart, but had trouble figuring how to enter a traffic pattern, using the 45 degree method we utilized. On a solo flight the day of his 40 hour check ride I led him into the pattern as part of a pre-arranged deal to make sure he entered properly. He was a regular downtown at Blondell's tavern. There was Luciano Bonilumi, an exchange Italian pilot, who was always late to the morning flight formation, due to his nightly trips downtown. Charlie Englehart, who had many stories about his exploits, none of which seemed plausible and then there was Richard Coyle, a gung ho aspiring flyer, who one day on a solo flight, hyperventilated, losing consciousness, stirring anxiety with all who heard his voice. Pinky and I were up on a dual ride and heard Dick as he would go in and out of consciousness. It was truly scary to listen! Finally, instructors on the ground were able to get him to breath normally and talked him down safely. Richard met the board the next day and was one of the washout victims in 56-H.

Life went on as we conquered all phases of the program, passing instrument checks, formation flying and the final check flight which in my case was with Mr. Hubenthal. He was a real gentleman and was pre-disposed to pass me as I had been Pinky's student and I know that was a factor. We went through all the necessary functions of flight, even the emergency engine out on takeoff (again). And with that my career as a Tango 6 pilot ended. It also was the end of the use of the T-6 as a primary training aircraft as 56-H was the last class to use the airplane. T-28s were taking its place.

LAREDO

1 was reassigned to Laredo, Texas to continue my flight training and would be introduced to basic jet training, flying the T-33, after twenty hours in the T-28. I was assigned to "A" flight in the 3640th Pilot Training Squadron along with about 40 other graduates from the three primary bases. "F" Flight was our counterpart, having another forty aspiring pilots, making up those who went to single engine training in 56-H. There were others in our class from the primary bases who chose multi-engine training and they went to Lubbock AFB in Texas to fly and complete basic training in B-25s. All of the instructors were military pilots and I drew a lanky guy named 2nd Lieutenant Doug Anson, whose call sign was "Shotgun". All of the instructors had call signs to identify them when in flight. He didn't talk much, but was a good instructor who let you fly the airplane. I was introduced to the T-28 initially and it was not my favorite airplane. Despite a powerful 800 horsepower engine it seemed to be too cumbersome, heavy and well, it just wasn't the T-6, which I dearly loved. It leaked oil onto the windscreen, it was a horse in the air and it actually seemed under powered! I soloed after two flights and spent a lot of time just cutting holes in the sky as I didn't like the way it spun nor was I a fan of the recovery and acrobatics was a chore. On one occasion I was about 15 minutes from the field and working some simple maneuvers when the engine started spouting oil. I couldn't see forward and called mobile to tell them of my situation. They were unimpressed and told me to bring it home, which I was doing anyway. I made a successful landing, told them I couldn't see forward and should I park there. They said to do what I had to do but bring it back to the parking spot. Doug was not impressed either as he

141

said it happened all the time. I was happy to complete my time in that aircraft. And proceed to the T-33.

The T-33 was a big step mentally as well as flying it. Up to this time the student pilots had ground training to learn procedures and to combat emergencies, but all of a sudden we were being thrust into flight simulators to prepare us for this step into jet flight. It was a big help, but it wasn't a motion trainer, just a stationary one meant to orient us to the systems and the normal procedures, plus fine tuning instrument flying. After a few "flights" in the box we were ready to start flying again. On our first day in the jet program another pilot or two and our instructors stepped out of our shack and started to watch an aircraft entering the overhead to the landing pattern. The T Bird pitched left and as he did so the left tip tank fell from the airplane and struck the vertical stabilizer. The aircraft went into an immediate skid and as the occupants attempted to gain control, losing altitude and after an agonizing few seconds went into a slow spin and crashed just off the base, killing the instructor and the student pilot, who was a West Point graduate. The effect was very profound watching as the instructors were trying their best to urge the pilots to gain control and put it into a forced landing somewhere. When it exploded silence came over everyone. It was not an incident to build confidence in starting to fly the T-33.

But start we did and it was a big step and yet a simple one. There were things about this new aircraft that made flying simpler, as there was no engine torque to work against, however there were nuances that you had to be aware of. You had to remember on taxi out not to cock the nose wheel. That was a real indication of a rookie in jets. In flight, spins were not only not practiced, but you were cautioned against any situation that could lead to one, as the T-bird was prone to go inverted, from which recovery was near to impossible. It was therefore reasonable to start recovery from practice stalls as early as possible. We also now could no longer wear a ball cap. It was a helmet and mask for flight. One afternoon late in the day lieutenant Anson walked in and said lets go, Grab your chute, it's time for you to go solo"! Was he out of his mind? I had barely two hours and change in the bird. He proceeded to take me to an aircraft in front of our flight shack and said to start my pre-flight. I did my walk around and crawled up on the wing to check the plenum chamber, which was right behind the canopy. I pushed it open only to see obvious fuel around the area. This was an automatic no-fly! I called Doug up to show him and he agreed I couldn't fly the aircraft. I was extremely relieved and knew that time for the flying period was running out. However Doug jumped in a maintenance truck and "found" another available airplane. The truck took us to the parking spot and while Doug did the walk-around, I got in to start the engine. Helmet on, mask secure, oxygen flowing, ready to taxi. Don't cock the nose wheel, I remembered. Made my turns out of the parking area, taxied to the end of the runway and waited right next to the mobile tower. I was hard pressed to give my call sign and the fact that I was an initial solo because I was sucking air and trying to stop the shaking in my hands and legs. I finally got the initial solo call out and was cleared for takeoff. Power in and the roll began, gaining airspeed and reaching takeoff speed I pulled the aircraft aloft, climbed straight ahead and gently turned into the practice area. I was careful not to exceed 30 degrees angle of bank as I started to calm down. As the time for the period was coming to a close I knew I would have to enter the overhead pattern, pitch left and make a touch and go landing followed by another touch and go and a full stop. To say my pitch out was loose would be an understatement as I made what could be charitably called a carrier approach to the runway. I lined up on the runway, made a reasonable landing and followed that with a standard rectangular pattern, another touch and go and finally my full stop. It was over! I taxied back to the parking area, shut down and crawled out with my chute. Doug nodded his approval, which was as much emotion as he ever made and told me I was the first in class to solo the T-Bird.

Laredo Training photo in the T-33 First Jet Aircraft

Doug had two other students, Dick Clark and George Fong, both were good pilots and would be the ones I would be flying formation with when we got to that stage. Doug seemed convinced that he would concentrate on the other two and that I would build my time as a solo pilot. One day I took off for the acrobatic area, climbed to a safe altitude and began practicing chandelles and lazy eights, two maneuvers that did not present a high level of difficulty, but did provide some factors of skill to do right. I progressed from rather flat routines and slowly was extending both the high and low portions of the "lazy eight" profile. Suddenly as I reached to top of the eight I felt a shudder and recognized I had stalled the airplane. I fell off on one wing and was now pointed directly to the ground. Speed built up rapidly and as I attempted to recover from my dive I would get severe vibration in the stick. I recognized a high speed buffet, but hesitated to check my airspeed as I was too busy to look at anything but my altimeter as it unwound. Slowly I managed to break the decent and get some semblance of control. I bottomed out finally, having lost a considerable amount of altitude. It was later diagnosed that I had reached the "coffin corner" in the T-Bird. A small area where you go from stall to buffet, based on aircraft angle of attack. My angle of attack was straight down!

I managed to catch my breath, slowed my heart rate and went back to base. I managed the entry call as a solo flight to the tower, did another chicken pitch and planted it on the ground. After exiting the aircraft I found Anson in the simulator building with George. Seeing me he asked how the flight went and I responded to him that I needed more dual time. He gave me that smile and asked what happened. I related the incident to him and he said OK I'll give you more time with me, but seemed to indicate that I had a bad experience, but handled it well. I wasn't convinced, but was happy to return to instructional time.

My Malden roommate, Bob Duggan was also my roommate in Laredo. He had an instructor named Lt. Meinig, who spoke with a distinct accent. He had been a pilot in the German Luftwaft and was a hard guy to get close to. Bob had many stories about their dual flights, all of them seemed to indicate that he was a tough guy to fly with. One day I was designated to fly formation as a solo and Doug was doing an instrument flight with Dick Clark. As was the custom I was then assigned to fly with another instructor's flight and I was given Lt. Meinig as the number three in a flight of four. Bob was not a member of the flight but pulled me aside to tell me that Meinig prided himself in losing his formation through any way he could, so watch out. The takeoff was normal and the join up of three and four on lead was smooth. We were involved in normal close formation flight. You would pick a spot on a lead aircraft and hold that spot no matter what the aircraft you were spotted on would do. After some turns and slight variations in flight Herr (we called him that behind his back) Meinig told the flight to go in trail. Now you picked a position behind the next aircraft, slightly below his tailpipe to keep out of jet wash and held that position. Bob had told me that Meinig would sometimes go into a loop when in this position and would start his climb and make the loop wider than normal, which it made staying in position for the three and four aircraft very difficult. I could see I was slipping away from the number two aircraft and knew that four would be falling behind, so I dropped about 20 degrees of flaps to give some increased lift and was able to stay in position. At the top of the loop I could see that lead now felt he had lost at least the last two aircraft and was going to take his aircraft back to the base. Number two was waffling and falling behind and as I gained airspeed I decided to roll out keeping lead in sight, above, but far behind him. I had no idea where the number four aircraft was, nor was two close by. I kept lead in sight and increased my airspeed to close on him, but stayed above him. As he was positioning himself to enter the overhead pattern I dropped down on his wing, knowing he could not see me. He called his entry, announced a full stop landing and proceeded to pitch and enter downwind. I waited the necessary two seconds to pitch and entered downwind behind him. I'm sure he heard my pitch call, as number three, but he didn't respond in the air. After landing and taxi back to the parking area. I parked next to him, took out my chute and went back to the shack to be debriefed on the flight. Number two and four straggled in after some delay. After we all were in place Herr Meinig proceeded to critique the formation and was very critical of our group, but didn't comment on my work in formation other than to tell the others that they needed to stay together in flight and that I was the only one who managed to complete the flight properly. I told Anson about the flight later and once again I got the slight smile.

Having hit a stage in our training we were about to engage in our night flying. Up to this time all of our activity had been with the sun in the sky. Weather in Laredo was primarily CAVU (Ceiling and visibility unlimited). Students did not fly solo unless the conditions were almost perfect. In any inclement weather situation that was above minimums we would have some kind of ride with an instructor. On many days we would be limited to formation flights in other areas with our instructors and on days where we had low ceilings we might be in the back seat under the "hood", practicing our instrument flying. Night would be no different as we had to have perfect conditions to fly solo. Of course we would lead up to our solo flights with dual work. Many of these flights we would be sent out with an instructor to fly instrument navigation flights. Going to various cities in the state of Texas, using the only means we had at the time. Compass heading and time, and verifying position using radio beacons. We all had flown days, both dual and solo, so night was no different. Flying to a beacon, the signal was always heard as an "A" or an "N" in Morse Code. The "A" was a dit-da and the "N" was a da-dit. When you flew directly over the station you would experience an "Aural Null", just no sound at all and that would indicate station passage. You would then turn to the next check point. Of course if you were solo you were doing "dead reckoning", using your map and ground check points to verify turn points. Obviously you had to pick up proper headings and initiate time between points. I did well in my navigation work with one exception which I will discuss on my cross country mission with Doug.

Having completed my night navigation work with an instructor, I was slated to fly a solo night navigation and landing pattern activity. This would be a class activity as all needed to complete a night navigation leg as well as the solo three landings at night. When we entered the flight shack on the chosen night we were greeted by a totally red lit room. We took seats at our tables and were briefed on the hazards of night flying and especially flying at night in a desert environment. A student in the same class as the student pilot in the pitch out accident had flown his aircraft into the ground on his night solo. The aircraft was at full throttle and functioning normally. It was surmised by the accident board that the pilot was a victim of vertigo and was so disoriented that he lost all sense of his position in flight. After further discussion and instructor briefings we were given aircraft assignments and slot times for takeoff. Departing the shack we were given red goggles to use while traversing the ramp as it was bathed in light. We would want to retain our night vision to complete our walk around. Taxiing out in the middle of a set of T-33s I was reflecting on the night accident and once again the little edge of doubt crept over me and I was resolved to be vigilant to any adverse condition that might occur. Taking the runway I watched the preceding aircraft break ground and climb into the dark sky. I stood on the brakes, called my solo flight, got clearance to go and released brakes, starting my roll. As I hit takeoff speed I pulled the nose off the ground, sucked up my gear and was immediately surrounded by darkness. There was no concept of up or down. The sporadic lights on the ground became stars in the sky and vice versa. There was no moon, no horizon and no idea of the orientation of flight. "Never fly by the seat of your pants" came to mind and I looked to my artificial horizon flight indicator. It showed a steady straight ahead climb. I kept my eyes glued to it until I reached a safe altitude and I peeked over my left shoulder seeking the town I knew should be there. Once I caught sight of the lights I was fine. My reference to balance returned. I had experienced vertigo and I reacted properly. It was a lesson I would never forget. My solo navigation mission went well and returning to the base I made my way into the rectangular pattern that students were told to fly and made my two touch and go's and then my full stop.

Returning to the flight shack I learned that one of the later flyers, Jesse Hocker, a friend of mine had not returned from his navigation leg. Jesse was a friend and like others I was concerned, only to find out that the Navy tower at Corpus Christie Texas had reached the lost pilot and gave him a heading home. This would be fodder for conversation for a long time. I would never tell Jesse about my cross country when in Malden where I took a proper heading from the wrong check point out of Cape Girardeau, Missouri, only to be found by Pinky somewhere in Kentucky and sent in a proper direction home. Completing our night activity signaled the downward trend to the end of our training. It was now a matter of getting our flight proficiency and instrument checks and one last needed item, a cross country flight away from the known landmarks and radio ranges.

CROSS COUNTRY

Doug asked where I would like to go on my weekend cross country and after some thought I responded that I would like to go to Denver. I have roots in Denver and many cousins that I had spent a lot of summers with as I grew up. I was particularly attached to my cousin by marriage, Tom Young. He was married to Charlene, known as Chuck. Tom had been a high school football phenom and I gravitated to him as I grew up. I called and asked Tom if he could pick me up when I arrived at Lowery AFB, and he was more than happy to do so. The trip would start on a Saturday morning with a navigation leg to Biggs AFB in El Paso Texas, and then continue on to Denver. I would be in the front seat for the initial segment and fly an instrument mission on the second leg. The instrument segment would be a preparation ride for my final instrument check, which Doug would administer on the trip back on Sunday. The trip to Denver was uneventful and all went well as part of my checkout. Upon arrival we checked into the BOQ (bachelor officer quarters) changed and then went to the Officers Club, where I told Tom I would meet him. Doug was settling in and I introduced him to Tom, who asked him to come along as he was having a family party with all the cousins that night at his house. Doug was most happy to accept. That evening all of the Phelan and Young cousins came and it was a great party. So good that we decided to spend the night at the Young's home as no one was really fit to drive us back to the base. We were awakened the next morning by two of the boys whose bunk beds we had spent the night in. Doug was not feeling too chipper, but managed to eat breakfast before we returned to the base. We took the boys and Tom to base operations so they could have a view of the flight line and our takeoff when we departed. The weather was unseasonably warm and as we got our weather Doug wanted to check our data for takeoff to make sure we could make a safe departure from the mile high city on a runway that was not too long. He decided the conditions were sufficient for takeoff, so we went to our aircraft. I conducted the preflight of the aircraft while the instructor, who was obviously not feeling well, was sucking 100 percent oxygen in the back seat. I crawled into the front seat, finished the checklist started engines and taxied out to the end of the runway. I made sure I waved at the Youngs, who were standing in front of base ops as I pulled out of the parking spot. I was cleared for takeoff, took the active and brought the engine up to full power, released brakes and started down the runway. It seemed forever for the airspeed indicator to get to takeoff speed and as I pulled the aircraft into the air, I noticed we were very close to the perimeter fence. I sucked up the gear and started a slow climb on our departure route. I called the tower to get clearance to departure control and they asked if we had possibly skimmed the fence. I said no we did seem to be well clear. (Later Tom said it looked like we were going to take the fence out). Doug was non-committal so we continued on our way. We stopped at Love Field in Dallas to refuel and Doug and I switched seats. I was to receive my final instrument check going into Laredo. I made the instrument departure out of Love and picked up a heading to the high fix at the base. I homed in on the radio range and picked up the steady "A". I had started my time from Dallas and had a good heading to the station. As my time became close I was listening for the change to the "N". At the expiration of time I waited and still was hearing the "A" dit-da. Doug made reference to station passage and I still was confused. I made a procedure turn and during the turn heard the "N", so I had passed the station and now had to home in again. This time there was a distinct change in the signal and I started my teardrop penetration to an ILS (Instrument Landing System) approach which went very well and now went around to initiate the required GCA (Ground Control Approach) to minimums and Doug would complete the approach and make a full stop. I was on glide slope and airspeed throughout and Doug took over at minimums and put the bird on the ground. We taxied back to our parking slot and went into the shack. We put our chutes on their racks and Doug said we would talk tomorrow.

The next day was an afternoon fly day for our flight, so after lunch we marched to the flight line and went to our tables. All the "shotgun" flight was scheduled to fly. I noticed I was going dual with another instructor on an instrument ride. Doug pulled me aside and told me I needed a recheck as I flunked the navigation portion of my check. It seemed I had passed over the center of the "Aural Null" last night and went from one "A" to another "A", so my navigation and timing were very good, but I didn't call out passage, nor did I recognize it. It was to be the only check ride I failed in my pilot training months, and I felt my execution of the procedure turn when time ran out was the correct method to find the fix. I was a bit miffed, but said OK. It was an uneventful recheck as all I had to do was home into the designated "fix" at Del Rio Texas and declare station passage, which I did without a problem. Lieutenant Spurgeon (Squeeky) said I did well and we finished the ride, going back to Laredo.

The remaining days were a series of final checks in formation, in-flight performance, including the dreaded "flameout overhead" which I took from a Lieutenant Curry (Doulphin). I was always a bit in awe of that pattern as I wasn't that good at it. My first attempt was a bit ragged, but OK, so Curry demonstrated one for me and as he did I set some ground check points for the start and first and final turns. Airspeed was easy to maintain, but the turn points were the key. After he showed his attempt, I took the aircraft back to the entry altitude, where he once again cut the engine back. I entered exactly where he did and executed my turns on the ground check points. He really liked that approach and used it for my grade. Formation was a snap as I was graded as a solo in a flight of four. One instructor, with his student as lead and three solo students made up the four ship and everything was flown in a smooth fashion by the instructor. As long as we stayed with the flight we were fine and we all managed to fly our positions.

Finally we were about finished and our first aircraft assignments were posted for us to select. I finished high enough to get one of the good aircraft, but I declined to sign up for an additional commitment of two years so had to see what was left. We actually did not get a lot of good (F-100/F-86) aircraft choices. There were a couple of F-94s, but most were T-33 assignment to tow targets and instructor positions. There were a number of B-47 assignments in SAC (Strategic Air Command) as co-pilots and I was fortunate to get one of those. At the time I wasn't too happy about it, but it turned out to be a great choice. I was to report to Walker AFB in Roswell, New Mexico. Graduation came on February 6th. We were informed during that ceremony that we were the first class to go through the entire training regimen without an aircraft accident. They were very pleased with that and of course we were very happy to be alive and well after over two hundred and fifty flight hours.

THE B-47

It turned out that I wasn't the only assignment to Walker AFB from Laredo. Gerry Gable, an acquaintance in A flight and some of the guys in the other flight were also going there so, getting together we found a pretty nice rental house and within days acquired two more roommates for our large four bedroom house. Dante Gullace and Don Herbine were happy to find a place in this desert city. We found out on our reporting date that the entire 509th Bomb Wing was on deployment to England so we were sort of on our own, with no responsibility except to report to the squadron ops building each day. This was followed by breakfast and the pool. It was a good routine, but was interrupted by the announcement that there were two ground school assignments at McConnell AFB in Wichita, Kansas. Gerry and I, sort of volunteered and were chosen to attend. It was a good six week introduction into the B-47 and it was a very good city, lots of night activity and the classes gave us some needed insight to our new duties in the six J-47 jet engine, bomber as a co-pilot.

Upon returning to Roswell we discovered that the wing had returned from their temporary duty (TDY) and that we were all assigned to crews. We began in-flight training with our aircraft commanders and navigators as the three position crew had a great deal to do before we were to be declared "combat ready". My aircraft commander was a old head name Bill Stewart and he was nicknamed "Shakey". Indeed he was! I soon discovered that most of the ACs were prone to drink too much and were far from being good pilots. I took an instructional ride with one of the old heads and found he couldn't hold altitude within 300 feet in the pattern. It was so bad that the instructor told me to fly the pattern for him, which I did with no problem.

After becoming combat ready, all crews were on a rotation in the initial stages of "Alert". You would spend seven days in this initial look at what became a SAC staple into the 80's, but the start of this process was a very loose regime. It was not even close to what alert would become. It was a prelude to our "Reflex tours going to Spain and England, not to mention home alert. The beginning of alert we were given a truck and had to spend time in the BOQ if you were a bachelor or married and lived off-base. The married crew members who lived on base could go home and had to be on telephone alert. Our "Q" quarters were in a circular area, among the base bachelor nurses. It was not the greatest of sacrifices! This of course changed to the new concept of being isolated with your entire crew and confined to a secure area, away from the temptations of the base.

I had a squadron commander, named Robert H. Gaughan, who we called "satchel ass" for obvious reasons. He and I were soon to tangle! I did pick up a reputation as a good co-pilot and was slowly progressing from the ready status crews to lead and was being asked to go to a select crew. Major Gaughan was seemingly happy with me in my copilot role until a series of incidents occurred that didn't do much to make me popular with him. He was very proud of a ground safety award that had been bestowed on the squadron. It seems that to go for a prolonged period of time without an incident was worthy of praise from the highest levels and the 715th Bomb Squadron had that distinction. Copilots were routinely assigned to the pits for the express purpose of monitoring refueling operations and then returning the aircraft to the parking ramp. I was moving an aircraft and while parking the aircraft somehow found a power unit that was left too close to the turn radius of a B-47. The outboard engine ran over the top of the unit and capsized it. This was bad enough, but not too long afterwards another power unit was toppled due to "jet blast" while I was on duty and I was the object of Major Gaughan's rath once again.

But the crowning blow was the final incident. Going to the flight surgeon's office one morning I was traveling in my car and out of one of the cross streets a staff sergeant going to work on his motor scooter came out right in front of me. I couldn't avoid hitting him, fortunately he was not badly hurt, however the sergeant did suffer some cuts and bruises for which he was hospitalized. The safety award was gone forever! After all was said and done and even though I was absolved by the Air Police, the good major, saying I was accident prone had me transferred to the 830th bomb squadron.

I was on a spare crew in the 830th until Major Gaughan was transferred and the new squadron commander, Lt. Colonel Dick Arnold at the urging of the crews in the 715th had me transferred back to the squadron. I was a big hit with Lt. Colonel Arnold and would have gone to a standboard (the elite instructor crews) crew if I had chosen to stay in the Air Force. Slowly I had realized that despite the allure of flying and the wonderful relationships I had established in Roswell and with the squadron and bomb wing my three year commitment was coming to an end, so in late December of 1957 I left Roswell for civilian life. It was a decision that I had a hard time making and regretted once I started back to college to work on a master's degree. It was a very dull, beach-going existence, living at home which was great, but leading a life that was not for me. My opportunity to change it came a few weeks before the next Thanksgiving, when one afternoon I received a call from a former squadron aircraft commander I had become very friendly with at Roswell (Walker AFB). He and I had played a lot of handball and softball together and was the standboard pilot I would have crewed with if I had stayed in the service. It seems he was at March AFB for the Strategic Air Command Bombing Competition, with his crew and the wing staff to include the squadron commander, Lt Colonel Arnold. He asked if I could come out to the base and visit. I said sure as it was only about a one hour drive from my home in Hawthorne. Once there I was overcome with the memories of my time in the Air Force. The good friends, the flying seemed to overwhelm me. It was great to see these solid people again and I told them so. After a night of drinking and renewing friendships I was approached by Colonel Arnold, who told me they were having a limited recall of pilots and that he would be glad to push my name if I wanted to return to the squadron. I jumped at the chance and he told me he would send me the paperwork. I drove home the next day on cloud nine and felt that I would finish the semester at school and then go back in the Air Force at the beginning of the year.

Within a week my mother came to my room and told me there was a guy in uniform at the front door. I went to the door and was greeted by a staff sergeant with a package for me. I thanked him, thinking it was the "paperwork", instead it was orders to report to the 509th Bomb Wing in Portsmouth, New Hampshire, the new home of the 715th. I was to report right after Thanksgiving. It was a total setup by Ken and Arnold to get me back. I think he could have given me the orders that night.

SAC Bombing Competition Crew B-47E, City of Dover, 509th BW Representative 1963; Pilot: Maj. G. Alan Dugard/ Capt. Keith Glenn (CP), Maj. Jus Rose (Radar)

I did have to take a physical and they had set the time and day at March AFB to do it. I proceeded to the base at the assigned time, took and passed the physical. As I left the flight surgeon's office I was crossing the street to go to my car and all of a sudden a car which I was waiting on the curb to pass suddenly slammed on his brakes and stopped in front of me. A large head appeared and a familiar voice bellowed out "Is that you Dugard"? Recognizing the voice as well as the face I replied "it was". Then, the now Lt. Colonel Robert H. Gaughan asked what I was doing there and I told him I had been recalled to active duty. He asked where I was going and I told him "Pease AFB in New Hampshire" and his reply was "that's far enough" and sped off. That of course worked both ways!

I reported to Pease after a drive cross country and was very pleased to rejoin friends and be back in the flying game. I was assigned to the 715th again under Lt. Colonel Arnold and put on a crew with one Americus Vespucious Combs III, affectionately called "Monk". Like many of the other ACs he liked to party and take chances. He was a good pilot and I enjoyed my time with Monk. Later he became an instructor pilot (IP) so he gave me a lot of stick time and assistance and slowly let me get front seat time. I was at a time level in the airplane that I could be considered for checking out as an aircraft commander and ultimately put on a "fast track" to do so. I passed my initial standboard as an AC, taking my ride with an old friend and handball player, Ken Lidie. Upon completion I was given my first crew. My navigator was Captain Jean Pierre Beaudoin, called BO. He was a French-Canadian who spoke with a distinct French accent and was to become a life-long friend. My first co-pilot was Lt. Fred Tillman. We hit it off very well as a crew and spent some great time on Reflex to Spain, choosing off-time spots which we traveled to together Fred was not long for his role as he was an outstanding pilot and once he got the time he was placed in the upgrade position to become an aircraft commander. I picked up a big guy, Don Kelly, who worked hard at his position and became a very good copilot. Because I was still a First Lieutenant I was concerned about having a captain on my crew, however that never became an issue as Bo and I hit it off very well. My time with Bo and Don was truly a wonderful experience and we spent many hours in the air, on alert and on reflex to Spain. During our time together we were chosen to fly with the SAC CEVG (Combat Evaluation Group). They would go "no-notice" to bases in the command, select crews at random and fly a rigorous flight check for all crew members. It would entail two flights, one specifically for the pilots and one for the navigator. It was not combat, but it was a testament of your ability and to fail required a great deal of rechecks and recertification, plus more rides by your own "standboard" crews. We were one of the only merely "ready" crews to be checked as most of the checks were given to our instructor "check ride" (standboard) crews. We did well and our critiques and final briefing were very complimentary. It was not long until I picked up a new co-pilot, Norm Butterfield, who was asked to go on my crew as I was picked to become an instructor pilot in the B-47 and Norm was on track to upgrade to the front seat. I also was promoted to captain. Bo then got an assignment to B-52's and I picked up a gem of a radar in Alex Ow, a wild Hawaiian, who was a super radar-navigator while doing his job in the aircraft. He was, however subject to many crazy actions once he stepped away from his position. It was like he had a short circuit to his brain when he climbed down the ladder. Norm and I had a strong leash on Alex, but he still managed to dazzle us with some of his actions in every day activity. He was addicted to gambling and was terrible at it. He would buy cars when he already had two, with no desire to trade or sell one. He would show up for mission planning in the dead of winter in his short sleeve summer uniform. Fortunately we could remedy most of his actions and we did very well as a crew as long as we were in the air.

As I continued to mature in the role of an instructor pilot I was sent to the Instrument Pilot Instructor School, at Randolph AFB in Texas. I ended up fourth in my class in academics and first in flying and was selected as number one in my class overall and was selected as the distinguished graduate. This was well received by the wing and I was asked to go into the standardization section as a check pilot and to conduct the on base instrument class, which was a yearly requirement for all pilots. I also picked up an outstanding radar-navigator in Jus Rose, probably the funniest man I have ever known and one of the best at his craft in the Air Force. We were a select crew and received spot promotions as such. Jus and I both were promoted to Major, a rank we would have as long as we remained a select crew. This meant we were on a tight rope, but it was not a problem as Jus and Norm were the best. We were the subject of two CEVG rides and maxed them both. Life was good and we had a great wing commander in Colonel Frankosky, until one day we were informed they had decided to phase out the B-47 and the wing would close in a short period of time. What would be our new assignment? Where would we go? Vietnam was just warming up, but there was no urgency to select pilots to go there yet.

509TH BW PHASE OUT

1had a former copilot who went to attaché duty and I thought that would be a good career path, so I applied. After going through the qualifying process, having family pictures taken and passing language tests I was accepted as the air attaché for Israel. I was very pleased and after years of alert duty and being on a combat crew I would have a different kind of life. Maybe family separation would be diminished? In my mind it was a great opportunity and I was looking forward to the change. Then one day I was asked to go see Colonel Frankosky. I went into his office and saluted smartly. I genuinely liked the man and so when he told me he had received a call from the command asking him to talk to me about my future I was a bit uneasy. He informed me that SAC wanted me to go to the B-58 program, probably the most prestigious and best aircraft in the inventory. I was a bit humbled, but I would be back on a combat crew and this was something I wasn't sure I wanted to do. He encouraged me to take the B-58 assignment and said it would be a far better career move than going into the attaché world, where I might find promotions and advancement hard to come by. I was not sure and told him I would have to think about it. When I then got a call from the pentagon asking what I was going to do as they also had received a call from SAC about my assignment. They had told SAC that they would not change the assignment unless I asked to have it cancelled. I was in a quandary and didn't know which way to go until the assignment individual at the pentagon, a chief warrant officer said SAC wanted me pretty bad and it sounded like it was a move I should make. I informed him and Colonel Frankosky I would go to B-58s. he then informed me that I would have George Holt, a standboard radar navigator as my radar in this supersonic aircraft. George was probably the top radar in the 509th Bomb Wing and was on a crew with one of my best friends, Cy Sweet. Things were looking up!

There are occasions where despite the fact that everything seems to be going well you are suddenly jerked into a new reality. In flying the B-47, once in the air missions are usually very routine, as you are filling needed crew requirements. One such flight happened to me when of all things my wing commander, Colonel Frankosky wanted to fly on the mission. The aircraft had a 4th man position, which was below the pilots in the tandem seating aircraft. It was more of a step with a folding back to hold a chute in place and had a seat belt and shoulder harness secured to the walkway. Bailout was performed through the radar navigator hole after he ejected if necessary. The flight was a standard night mission, an in-flight refueling after level off with a maximum off load and then a night navigation leg, followed by a low level navigation leg and simulated bomb releases on a bomb plot, tonight it was to be Watertown in upstate New York. Once the refueling was completed, I climbed to our cruising altitude, which was limited by our heavy gross weight to 28,000 feet. As we prepared for the navigation leg Norm Butterfield had to get out of his chute and to place the sextant in the mount above the co-pilot position to get his first fix for the navigator, Jus Rose. I felt a slight tug on the aircraft and thought it was some wind shear and dismissed it. Moments later it came again and I surveyed the engine instruments, only to be interrupted by a flash to my right and a wrenching noise and yawing action that caused me to disconnect the auto pilot and for Norm to scurry back into his chute and my wing commander to secure his position. The 4 and 5 engines had exploded and both were immediately shut down. I was very close to Cleveland and called center declaring an emergency. I was cleared to descend and go to the nearest base which was Lockbourne AFB in Ohio. Due to our heavy weight I started a fuel dump through our large auxiliary tanks which could be jettisoned if necessary. Lockbourne was clear and had good visibility, but I was too heavy to land. Sensing a need to get on the ground quickly I asked if they had an area where I could jettison the tanks. After some hesitation they said I could drop them on an area parallel to the runway and then added that I had to give them a ten minute warning as they had to abandon the GCA shack.

To this point Colonel Frankosky had been very quiet, but asked if I ever jettisoned those tanks before. I said "No", but the book says it would work. After some assessment of the four remaining engines, I felt we could proceed to dump fuel and get to a safe landing weight if we didn't have any further problems, so abandoned the jettison much to the relief of those on the ground. We reached a safe weight and put the wounded bird on the ground. Not my best landing, but good enough. The number 4 engine had seized and took number 5 with it. (It was later determined that a compressor stall had been the cause.) A few minor pieces of metal were imbedded in the area around the engines, but no major damage to the aircraft as the force had been parallel to the level flight attitude. We were met by the 376th Bomb Wing commander who invited us to a wing Christmas party, flight suits and all. It was a strange ending to an exciting evening.

THE B-58

In order to fly the B-58 pilots had to go through lead in training in the F-102 at Perrin AFB in Texas and even before being accepted you had to go through capsule training at Little Rock AFB, one of the two 58 wings. All B-58s were equipped with crew capsules for emergency ingress at high, read supersonic speeds. I do believe that the capsule training was to check to see if you were claustrophobic in a very close quarter capsule. Going into the capsule "training" was in their words to see if you could maneuver to get emergency gear and survival items form the back of the capsule. Once the capsule was closed around you it was pointed out that you still had the capability to fly the aircraft as the stick was in the capsule. Also you could control the throttles to an extent that would maintain flight in the event control of the aircraft was regained. However if you chose to punch out, you were protected from the blast and you were in a clam shell container that had all items for survival, to include floats in the event you were over water. Moving around in the capsule was not difficult, but it was very restrictive. I was happy when told I passed. I then ran into an individual who was an all American football player from Notre Dame. Huge thighs, thick chest and to my way of thinking, could not possibly turn around in the capsule. I was 5'6 and 145 pounds. He was 5'10 and 210. Jack Lee was his name and a greater friend I never had. He passed! So the test was not about movement, it was about attitude and adaption.

F-102 training was a real experience. The SAC B-58 pilots undergoing this training were all experienced pilots, most with 3000 plus hours. This group of six SAC pilots in the F-102 training class was the subject of quite a bit of scrutiny as our instructors were far less experienced in flying than we were and in most cases we outranked them. They did have one advantage as they had single engine time and they knew the 102. It would be an interesting time and a great learning experience. The F-102 was the same design as the B-58, but instead of four J-79 engines it had one and was a single pilot aircraft as opposed to the three man crew of the B-58, pilot, radar and DSO (defensive systems officer). It did require the B-47 pilot to realize that takoff and landing were going to employ new techniques. The 102 had to be rotated, the B-47 did not. The angle of attack on takeoff and landing were severe by our standards and aero dynamic braking was a new method of slowing down once you touched down on landing. (aero dynamic braking was effected by pulling the nose as high as you could to allow the aircraft body to be into the wind. It was maintained as long as you could keep the nose up). On top of that the instructors were always trying to impress us with their flying ability, over emphasizing things like pitch out on the overhead pattern and evasive techniques during flight. On one of my flights while in the pattern, my instructor was trying to impress me with the pitch out telling me to turn within a small road paralleling the runway. He was not the yelling type but was forceful and sort of ham handed. Once he finished with the demonstration pitch out. I took the aircraft, made the pitch out, rolling forcefully to stay within the road, "grayed out" a bit and rolled out to total silence. Looking to the back seat in my rear view mirror, my instructor was slumped over, totally blacked out. He came to as I was rolling onto base but said nothing. On the ground he cleared me for solo flight. I had one other incident in the lead-in training and it occurred on an early evening solo flight. I was to be the "target" for some intercepts by other 102s. In the course of the evening I had a warning light come on for my missile-launch system. It was not a big deal, but the command post told me to break off activity and return to base. As I had been up for a good period of time I was also aware that my fuel state was getting a bit low, but not dangerous. As I arrived to my high entry to the pattern and started my pitch out I was asked to break off the approach due to other slower traffic, which I did. I reentered, pitched out rolled onto base and final and was told there was another slow mover ahead of me and to go around. My fuel yellow caution light came on as I went across the active. Still with fuel for another couple of approaches I told the tower I had a low fuel state and that I still had a hydraulic emergency according to the book. Traffic was now a bit heavy and I was told I would be behind two aircraft and would have a long downwind for a radar controlled approach. As the downwind stretched out the red fuel warning light came on. The call to the tower was received in a casual tone and he asked me if I wanted to declare an emergency. I notified him I had already declared an emergency due to my hydraulic problem and was now issuing a "mayday" due to my fuel state. That got his attention and he then cleared me for an immediate landing, sending aircraft in the pattern in all directions. I landed safely, cleared the runway and as I taxied into my parking spot, flamed out and coasted the last few feet to be chocked.

Once finished at Perrin and with the 102 I was assigned to Bunker Hill AFB (later to be Grissom AFB after Gus Grissom, killed in a space shuttle accident) in Indiana. George Holt and I picked up a DSO (defensive systems officer) named Bob McCormick and started our time as a non-combat ready crew. The training was very intense and of course started with a ground course in the CCTS and an instructor crew who monitored our every move. The simulator was spectacular. The pilot's box rotated on takeoff and actually rolled into turns. We spent nine missions in the "box" before we were ushered out to the TB-58. The TB missions were flown with an instructor pilot and a DSO, no radar. My IP, Buck Carroll was a great pilot and as calm as my first IP in primary, Pinky. To say the B-58 was a hot airplane would be like saying WWII was a minor conflict. The climb speed was 525 knots. The speed would max out well above Mach 2, (I've seen 2.5 on a very cold day at 55,000 ft). The motto of the B-58 crews was Mach Two/Can Do. After four TB rides and a check in the simulator we flew our B-1 mission. We were monitored by our instructor crew through the pre-flight and start engines and then we were on our own to fly a mission as a crew. This would be George's first ride in the bird, Mac and I had already experienced the thrill of this aircraft. George was his professional best and the B-1 solo launched us into the greatest flying experience possible. CCTS lasted six months and we had to complete eight additional B rides and four more TB rides, plus complete a successful standboard ride in the simulator and a pilot/DSO flight check in the TB and then we were declared combat ready. Back to being a ready crew, how humbling it seemed. We were the FNGs. We didn't stay that way very long as George was really good at his craft and the crew was recognized early on as very good. We did hit a snag and almost didn't stay as a crew, as fate dealt me a bad hand. I experienced a collapsed lung one day while playing golf. Once it was diagnosed I actually begged my squadron commander to not break up the crew. He said if I responded to treatment quickly enough he would keep the crew together. My flight surgeon doctor was my next door neighbor, Angelo Massaro. He broke every speed record, putting me back together and then getting the paper work completed to get a chamber check. I had to travel to Wright-Patterson AFB in Ohio for the chamber ride which I passed less than a month after my lung collapse occurred. I was given my crew back!

Once back on the crew things broke our way and we progressed to being an instructor crew and finally we were asked by the chief of CCTS, Makie Sorrel to be one of the instructor crews checking out new crews. It was an honor and also was unprecedented as we had only been combat ready a year. I loved being an IP in that airplane. It gave you license to fly supersonic more than the average bear as all new pilots had to be checked out in that phase of flight. It was a great challenge as the IP, not only conducted simulator rides, but also had to check out the new pilots in the TB. As an instructor you were in the back seat, which offered very little forward visibility, therefore as the IP you had to almost stand up to execute or monitor a landing as the angle of attack on final precluded the IP from seeing the runway. Plus the B-58 had no flaps so the final approach speeds were hot, like 165+kts. Seeing dirt right or left on flare meant you were not over the runway and a go-around was needed. It truly was an adventure!

After four years in the B-58 I was sent to SAC Headquarters as a personnel assignments officer, but that's another story as I became the head of the Career Development Division, which was a hoot of a job. I also started flying the T-39 and became an IP and Check Pilot in the aircraft. Lots of fun and good flights all over the country. I spent many hours in the T-39 and enjoyed the aircraft. It wasn't a B-58, but neither was any other aircraft in the inventory. Probably one of the highlights of my T-39 flying was a flight I was asked to take on a trip to Orange County Airport, now known as John Wayne Airport. It was a normal request to fly headquarters staff to various places. This flight needed an instructor pilot, which again could have been for a ranking officer who wanted stick time. When I arrived at base ops I started my mission planning and proceeded to file my flight plan and asked where the aircraft was parked and found out it was right in front of the building. I walked out to the airplane with the other staff pilot and waited for my passengers. Takeoff time came and went, but no passengers. After a pretty long delay, a file of cars appeared, the first of which was flying a four star flag. The only four star on the base was the commander of SAC. The cars stopped and out of the following cars stepped a number of high ranking officers, but the first car doors remained closed. We waited and finally the CINCSAC stepped out of the car followed by Senator Barry Goldwater. They approached the aircraft and the CINC stopped in front of me and addressed me by name and introduced the senator to me. I told him it was a pleasure to take him and his staff out west on their journey. After some closing amenities we climbed on board, started engines and took off for a refueling stop at Nellis AFB in Nevada. Once we leveled off I told the other pilot to go back and asked the senator if he would like to get some stick time as he was a rated pilot and a retired one star. I had purposefully started the flight in the right seat which was the instructor position. The senator was delighted and post haste he was in the left seat and getting some time on the stick. (Actually it was a half wheel). As we approached the southwestern part of the country he asked if we could descend to a lower altitude and because it was a beautiful day I asked "center" if I could go VFR (visual flight rules) and they cleared me to do so. We left our flight level and decended to a lower altitude where the senator started showing me areas that he grew up as his father was an early Indian agent and he spent time on the reservations in southern Arizona. It was an enlightening time and one that gave me some insight into the life of the senator. We finally arrived at Nellis and the senator made a very nice landing. Our reception and departure were yet another story and our arrival at Orange county airport was a landing that he told me to make due to the short runway and obstacles on the end of the runway. An unforgettable trip!

One day after I was approaching the end of my tour in Omaha and after I had worked with the assignment people at the Military Personnel Center (MPC) to go in a single engine aircraft to Vietnam as a FAC in the OV-10 (forward air controller) I was asked to brief the commander of 15th Air Force, Lt. General P. K. Carleton on a personnel matter. After the briefing was finished I saluted smartly and was about to leave when the good general said he wasn't finished. He then asked me what my plans were as he somehow knew that my four years were about over. I told him about my proposed next assignment and he said to forget it. He asked me what aircraft in 15th did I want to fly, the KC-135 or the B-52? A bit taken back, I said I was a bomber pilot and he then asked where would I like to be stationed? Knowing that he was very serious, I rattled off a couple of choice bases and he said he would have me do some maintenance training first at Offutt, an established requirement for all squadron commanders. I was now a lieutenant Colonel so it was a good career move (after all I was the career development chief) and so from the headquarters I went to the 55th Strategic Recon Wing as the OMS (Organizational Maintenance Squadron) commander, which was a matter of going to the flight line side of the base instead of the headquarters. It was a short six month stint, but most educational, especially in dealing with enlisted personnel who spent hour after hour making sure the aircraft, all RC-135s, could fly their extremely important intelligence missions. This wing also supported the "Looking Glass" aircraft, which was the 24 hour airborne command post flown 365 days a year. I truly enjoyed my time in the 55th and despite being asked to stay by the wing commander, I told him I would rather stay in the flying business. Finally my orders to go to Mather AFB in California were cut and I was on my way to being the 441st bomb squadron commander. First I had to go to another CCTS, this time to check out in the Buff.

THE B-52

The first phase in any aircraft is the checkout time and formal training for the B-52, as it was for any major combat aircraft, was very intense. Having flown other combat aircraft did prepare me for the formal portion of training, such as ground course indoctrination and checklist procedures, but flying the 52 after the B-58 was like driving a tank through the air. It was heavy and cumbersome on the ground, no rotation on takeoff, but light as a feather behind a tanker. It was a different, but not difficult aircraft to land and it was a splendid hands-on airplane. It was the last combat aircraft I would ever fly and experience wise it would compare favorably to the B-47and B-58. Finishing CCTS at Castle AFB I went back to Offutt AFB to pick up my family and head to Mather. A place I would deposit my family, only to find out my squadron was on Guam and I would join them in less than a week. It would be the beginning of my first combat tour in the Vietnam War, but not my last tour and it would be the introduction to the discovery of the meaning that Teddy Roosevelt meant when he talked of his attitude and definition of fear!

Maintenance and support activities became one the most pressing concern to B-52s. The B-52s flew from base to hit targets in North Vietnam during the operations.

Munitions specialists worked 12 hours a day, 7 days a week, to support the flying mission.

General John C. Meyer, SAC commander, talks to air crews at Andersen, following Linebacker bombing of North Vietnam.

Shark-finned B-52Ds line up for takeoff from Andersen AFB, for strikes over Hanoi and Haiphong.

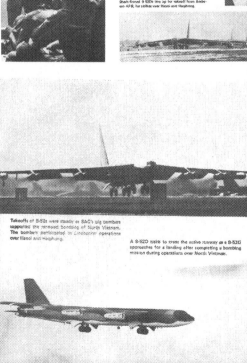

Takeoffs of B-52s were steady as SAC's big bombers supported the renewed bombing of North Vietnam. The bombers participated in Linebacker operations over Hanoi and Haiphong.

A B-52D taxis to cross the active runway as a B-52G approaches for a landing after completing a bombing mission during operations over North Vietnam.

Author and B-52D, Guam

A "G" CHRISTMAS EVE

1t was really a hot, muggy day and it didn't seem like much of anything would happen to make this anything but just another hot, muggy day on this island. I thought briefly about borrowing one of the Guam bombs and going off base, still something I hadn't done since my arrival, but dismissed the thought when I spied a number of the crews already in the bag (not to be confused with bed) at nine in the morning. This could be a tough day and all the squadron commanders had promised to keep the crews in check during this, the seventh day, when only a few of the crews would be flying and throughout the "standown" (no flying day) set for tomorrow. There would be a need to prepare for launches that would require crews and serious planning soon. It was best I hung around and protected my crews! From what,—maybe just themselves!

I drove over to the class VI store and bought a new supply of San Miguel for the crew lounge, which was really only a small room with a refrigerator that was used to store beer. The crews were on an honor code to throw their fifteen cents in the kitty for each beer they took. That was a whopping mean profit of seven cents per can, of course if someone forgot to pay there was a loss to the beer fund. We did OK though, as it was rare when we came up short in that fund. The Class VI store's storage for the beer was in a large ship type cargo container, so you would pay for your beer and then go to the storage to collect your allotted cases, carrying them to your truck for the trip back to the squadron. The only real problem was that the container was not air-conditioned and as the sun beat down the interior was like a furnace. Collecting ten cases of beer was like being in the middle of a sauna.

Just as I finished putting all ten cases in the back of the squadron truck, I was now bathed in sweat and looking like I had just stepped out of a shower, Robbie skipped toward me and asked if I needed any help. I think I said something not so kind and of course he thought it was funny and laughed. He indicated he was going to catch a ride into town and wanted to know if I wanted to join him. I told him I had better stick around the crews, as I wasn't sure leaving the base was a good idea after the close call last night. He chuckled and said that a lot of the crews were by the pool at the club and were already whooping it up, which only solidified my decision to remain on the base. I hustled back to the squadron and unloaded the beer with the help of a couple of crews sitting outside sunning themselves.

I got back in my squadron truck and drove to the club just to check up on things. Arriving there, I walked around to the back of the club by the pizza joint and came upon a number of guys sitting around the pool. Far from what I expected, it was a very serene gathering and didn't even consist of the real rabble rousers that are usually the instigators of any potential problem. I casually strolled through the area, not wanting anyone to think I was checking up on them. I said hello and chatted with a couple of my pilots, Captain Johnny Mook, who had flown on day one, looking terrible, but refusing to see the flight surgeon as he did not want to have his crew go on this mission without him. Upon landing we insisted he go to the base hospital. He was summarily grounded and was now trying to rid himself of the island crud. I asked him when the flight surgeon might take him off DNIF and he said they were very vague and was given no date, however he hoped by the end of the standown. His partner in dialogue was Captain Ted Panza, who had also flown on day one and the two of them were reflecting on their sorties and with my intrusion asked me about my experience on day two. I thought to myself at the time that it would have been totally embarrassing if the squadron commanders had taken the easy road and not flown during this critical series of missions.

We would have lost the respect of the crews and would have missed an event, that having done it, I wouldn't trade the experience, not that I relished the thought of going back as I did not. It was small talk among pilots sharing their moments of this war. It also was sort of like finishing a big race that you didn't want to run, finishing it and then being very pleased with your performance and then wanting to talk to someone who had also run. You shared the race and in this period of time in this war you belonged to the same group having shared a similar experience. A lot of bravado, and a smidgen of pride! Engaged in our war stories we started to laugh when we saw one of the other squadron pilots who had flown a frag with me on an earlier mission before Linebacker. It was a three ship and I was lead and this gent was number three. Captain Mook was in the two slot.

Our target was Vinh, a seaport town which is just above the DMZ and in the narrowest portion of Vietnam. Our track to the target area was similar to the Linebacker missions, as we came up through Cambodia and turned east to our target, just above the parallel (a sort of demilitarized zone ignored by both sides) separating north and south. It was a day sortie and the visibility was good. There had been previous missions flown to Vinh, however I think we were the first "G" cell going there. There had been some "Surface to Air Missle" (SA-2) activity in the area, but no hits. We were, however prepared for the possibility. We were also warned to be aware of the MIG activity that had been going on there and to be on the watch for them. There would be fighter coverage from Red Crown, most likely F-4s from one of the bases down south. It was a very short trip through the neck, maybe eight or nine minutes, so a real quick, bomb run. We had no sooner gotten wings level and barely inside of North Vietnam, heading toward the target on our bomb run when number three started yelling "MIG".

It wouldn't have been too bad, but Captain Rynereson had a high falsetto voice to begin with and it was even higher with each call, and there were plenty of calls. The fighters covering us of course now became involved and they were asking for the location of the MIGs. We were now placing our heads on a swivel to see if we could see anything and our very nervous gunners were on interphone telling us they were picking up traffic at our six o' clock. This could have been "friendly fighters", and naturally to add to the communications traffic, the bomb droppers were trying to get our attention so they could do their job, after all we were on a bomb run. It was utter chaos and in the midst of all this there were fighters crossing through our formation which couldn't be identified as friend or foe, but friendly or not, they did seem to keep their distance while we opened our bomb bay doors and prepared to drop our stores. There was not a confirmed sighting of a bogie by anyone other than Captain Rynereson in number three, and the fighter escort aircraft were hungry for action, but to no avail. I did see a fighter passing on our left, some distance away and I was hardly able to distinguish the type, let alone friend or foe. Finally as we went "feet wet" over the South China Sea, we were able to quiet this noisy guy, who since the incident was called the "choir boy".

I'm still not sure there wasn't a MIG, and he will swear to you that he had a visual and that enemy was after him. The word did get out about the infamous Vinh raid and the good captain was still trying to convince his contemporaries that he had been under attack. After recalling the incident Mook and Panza were ready to rag on the poor guy for probably the upteenth time, something pilots loved to do. They are unmerciful when they have an observed or hearsay item of interest to needle someone on. I left the two of them trying to get the "choir boy's" attention and ducked into the coolness of the club. Entering through the ballroom I noted with some satisfaction the Christmas trees, brightly decorated and covered with fake snow, standing elegantly on both side of the bandstand. There were very few people in the club and those that were there were mostly there to grab something to eat. The bar was empty, which I considered a good omen and so I just continued out the front door and proceeded to my truck.

I picked up a crew that had just hit the road in front of the club and asked them what they were going to do on this lovely day before Christmas. They weren't too sure, but thought they would catch a bus down to Tarague beach. Now that was a good idea! I told them I would take them down and hurried to see if I could catch Herb Jordan. Stopping long enough to change into some swimming gear and finding Herb slouched in the corner of his room writing a letter home, I asked him if he felt like going to Tarague with me. He said he had too much to do and so I went to my truck to find not one, but two crews waiting for me. There was plenty of room in the back so we took off for an afternoon in the sun. The road to Tarague was an interesting one as it was cut through the jungle and although paved, it was narrow and winding. It provided some great views of the Pacific once you could see that great ocean through the jungle foliage.

The cliffs above the beach were the same ones that the Japanese, not willing to surrender when the island was taken by American forces in WW II, jumped off en masse to a sure death 200-300 feet below.

We wended our way down the cliffs by the now straight shot road and turned into a parking area. The beach is beautiful, the sand white and the sun was at its zenith on this day before Christmas. There are no waves at the beach as there is a coral reef about a hundred yards more or less out from the water's edge. You can see the waves breaking over the reef, but you can walk out for a good distance without the water rising above your chest and it's warm and comfortable. Beyond that reef not too far away is the Marianna trench, supposedly the deepest point in any ocean. In fact Guam would be like the summit of Mount Everest if the bottom of the trench were at sea level. I had grabbed two six packs of beer when I left and told the two crews to help themselves as I spread my towel on the white sand. By the time I settled down the beer was history, which was what I had intended. It was a singularly great day at the beach. I hadn't planned to stay more than an hour at the most, however it was hard to leave the serenity and beauty of this place. After two and a half hours I picked myself up, and told the guys I had to go. All but two of them elected to stay at the beach. I loaded up and headed back to the (I hoped for calm) base.

Arriving at the squadron I was once again struck with the lack of activity. I wondered where everyone had gone, surely they were not lounging in their rooms on Christmas Eve, but finally decided they all went to town. Was that wishful thinking? I yearned for home as did all of my weary crews, but at least we were in warm beds and were eating hot meals. You know some guys fighting this war were slogging through the jungle wondering where the next land mine was or who could be lurking in the next shadowy grove. Also some of my best friends were living in the Hanoi Hilton and their Christmas was going to be a lot more difficult than mine or the crews grousing around the island feeling sorry for themselves because they were locked up on Guam and not home with their families.

On the other hand there were people like Jane Fonda, the Benedict Arnold of the twentieth century, Joan Baez and their media friends who spend their time undermining the effort to the point where those fighting this war on the good guy's side were made out to be the villains. That of course includes all of us here on Guam. It's one thing to oppose the war, it's yet another to aid and abet the enemy. I hope Joan's time in Hanoi is long and grueling. She belongs there with her friends and not back in the states! She is experiencing what war is really all about, destroying the enemy's capacity and will to wage war. Her actions and those like her are actually causing this war to be prolonged and it's causing precious loss of life.

It was also causing people at home, egged on by the war protestors to malign those who were fighting. When in the 58 business, my crew and I went from place to place presenting a briefing on the mission of the Strategic Air Command and specifically the B-58. We were well received by most, however we made a presentation at Ball State University to the ROTC detachment and when finished had to be escorted out of the theater due to protestors. It was humiliating and an experience that has remained with me.

I decided to take a shower and get the salt off my body. The beach had been a real treat and the water had been like an enveloping cloud, washing away the island stink and the worry of flying yet another mission up north. I knew it was coming and I wasn't looking forward to the experience. I would be the first to admit that my mission to Hanoi had duly made an impression on me and it had destroyed any bravado that I may have had at the onset of this extreme exercise. I had already lost more crews than all the other squadrons combined and that was on my mind. Was it in the cards to have me join those at the Hilton, or even worse? It was indeed something to think about as my turn was next. I finished showering, lingering there only long enough to cleanse my body. On reflection my soul was OK too!

I dressed casually, of course, as there was no other way to dress on Guam and was now ready for a quiet night, dinner with my usual friends at the usual place, the officer's club. However I couldn't find anyone, despite going to the respective rooms and the downstairs crew lounge. I suspected that Robbie was having dinner at the Navy base and that Herb had found somewhere special and maybe met some of the crew dogs to spend the eve of Christmas with. I gave up and walked down a flight of stairs, walked across the coral parking lot and got into the truck. There was a group of guys just hanging around and drinking some red wine out of the bottle, and we exchanged pleasantries and joked about the difference between here and their home base, Griffis AFB, in upstate New York on Christmas Eve.

They were ragging on one of the lieutenants, Figallo, for some reason, but he was enjoying the banter so it must have been about something that he was not ashamed of. They seemed reasonably happy so I wasn't too concerned! I started the engine of the blue Air Force truck, pulled out of the gravel parking lot and drove to the club. I was caught up in the fact that I was clean from my recent shower, not in a flight bag, among my contemporaries, and doing what I was trained to do, but languishing in the reality that I still missed my family and that I was about to spend yet one more Christmas away from my wife and children. It hurt! As I pulled up in front of the club it was obvious that I was not going to see a great number of the permanent party, as the parking lot was empty.

With the exception of the few crews possessing "Guam bombs", those stationed here had the motorized vehicles that would be parked in front of the club. It was the only real fine dining facility (eating in most O clubs is not like eating at the Ritz, however when you have no other choice but a mess hall or a snack bar, the club can be termed as "fine") on the base. I proceeded to the entrance of the club and opened the door. The sudden blast of air conditioning combined with the sudden dim interior seemed to subdue and envelop me. I took the left turn toward the bar, bypassing for the moment even looking into the dining room.

As I entered the bar there were a decent number of crew members having a drink, however there wasn't one staff person around. I wondered aloud where they all were as I noticed Captain Bob Crouch, with his crew at a table. Bob and his navigator were big guys! They were constantly at the gym, working out with weights and their bodies had responded to the time spent. Bob, obviously hearing my inquiry which was really not directed to anyone, looked at me and said he hadn't seen any of the squadron commanders or operation officers all day. I found a chair and sat down at the table. Bob and his crew were stationed at Barksdale AFB in Shreveport, Louisiana, so at least the weather was similar. We all acknowledged that the bar was a better place to be than the outdoors as it was a very warm December evening.

I again spied Captain Mook, one of my ACs from Beale AFB, who I had seen earlier that day. He had been to the flight surgeon again after I had talked to him and was told he could not return to flight status. He was in a state called DNIF (duty not including flying), and from his downcast look and his pallid appearance, seemed to be ready for an extended stay on the ground. Seeing the group he stopped to ask if we had seen any of his crew and I with the others gave him a negative response. He headed off toward the dining room as Major Don Bogue, one of my Mather aircraft commanders sidled up and sat down. Don and his crew were known for the laugh track they play on takeoff that they let spill onto the tower frequency. They also throw a pirates skull and cross bones flag out of the pilot's window on roll out after landing and taxi to their parking slot. He was joined by various other crew members and they seemed to have something on their minds, so I waited for the first of them to sound off.

Don didn't make me wait too long as he said, "Is there any truth to the rumor that we will be going full strength up north after the standown"? He and others had obviously been discussing the fact that the Gs had not gone north since day three and that SAC headquarters wouldn't think of allowing that to continue. Most of the rumors started at the bar and with any sort of help and with a grain of unsound reasoning and a couple of beers, any suggestion became an intelligence secret that needed some verification. I was the verification in this case! I smiled at the now fairly substantial group and said, "How would I know what the plan is for the end of standown"?

Not the least affected by that statement, they launched into all the reasons why I would be privy to such data. I responded "I'm sure that the "frag" (battle plan) for the end of standown (no fly day) is being closely guarded and only those with a great need to know are aware of those plans. And furthermore I firmly believe that no one on this island will be brought into that circle of need to know until SAC has a finalized battle plan, which probably won't happen until tomorrow night"! That made a little sense to them and they sort of ran out of steam for the moment. It made sense to me that whatever "they" had in mind, it would have to include the Gs going north as our squadrons were too valuable a resource to waste on missions down south right now.

It was too late to modify all the unmodified aircraft with the needed ECM, (electronic counter measures) however there were sufficient planes that had been modified that could fly and provide the needed coverage. I wasn't about to share that opinion with these crews as it would only grow into a monster statement, becoming gospel in mere hours! It was a good time to go eat. I picked up the beer I had ordered and struck out to the dining room. Entering, I found some crews, or at least pieces of crews there, but not a large number. It was quiet! I sat down alone, something I don't usually do. I ordered and ate my food with only minor interruptions from passing crew members. I finished, paid my bill and walked back to the bar. Not much doing here either, those I had seen here earlier were gone so I ordered a beer and sat down without any plan for the night. I sucked on my beer, had a few conversations with a new group that had arrived and listened to some tales of woe about being away for the holidays and left. I jumped into my "one each" Air Force issued truck and drove back to the squadron.

The same group of guys I had left were still there now sitting in the dark on the railroad type ties that delineated the parking area. They were still drinking a little wine from the bottle and so I joined them. Not for the wine necessarily, but for the laughter they were involved in. They were having a great time, joking about some of their experiences on the island and elsewhere. It was a rollicking affair and they were still after Figallo, but he was laughing right with them! After a fairly long period of time verbally jousting with one another and in the middle of all the kidding around, another of my aircraft commanders appeared and wanted to know if he could borrow my truck. He added that he had to go by the dispensary to pick up some medicine and had an appointment to see a doctor.

He would have walked the moderate distance normally, but it was obvious that he was in some form of discomfort. I threw him the keys and said to go ahead despite the fact that he was going to have to wait for medication and at night it could take awhile. I told him I wasn't going anywhere except to bed so to take his time. He thanked me and drove away. It was about fifteen minutes after he left that the squadron clerk came running out of the office on the second floor and went directly to my door. Seeing him I yelled up to see what he wanted. He couldn't quite make me out in the darkness below, but recognized my voice and yelled out, "They want you at the club right now as there is some sort of riot in progress". Jumping up and realizing my vehicle was gone I started yelling, "has anyone got a car I can borrow"?

I frantically called it out a couple or three times and a door opened and a set of keys for one of the Guam bombs sailed through the night to my feet and some directions followed about which of the rusted out hulks they went to. I piled into the wreck and started the engine and was immediately engulfed in purple smoke coming through the holes in the flooring of the car. I wrenched it into gear and headed to the club, trailing smoke and sparks provided by a dragging muffler, which was of little use as it had more holes than medal. I screeched into the driveway at the club to see a myriad of rotating beacons on the top of a number of Air Police vehicles. I stopped right behind them, startling a few of the individuals around the vehicles. The smoking Guam bomb seemed happy to stop and willing to rest and as the smoke diminished I ran by the Air Police into the club.

A group of very worried uniformed officers seeing me asked if I was the "sheriff" for the night. "Yes" I replied, not remembering whose day it was, but not wanting to implicate any of my fellow squadron commanders. They didn't need to explain what the problem was, as the playing of the Air Force hymn was explanation enough. I rounded the corner to see a quagmire of crew members standing at attention, or at least trying to as they swayed, like a bunch of off balanced dolls. Where had they all come from or better yet, where had they been? It was incredible as the place was jammed and the tables had been placed end to end in long rows, like in a mess hall or in a boarding house fashion. They must have all come back to the base en masse and come directly to the club.

A group of senior ranking officers was in deep and loud conversation, one or two gesturing wildly toward the tumult that was taking place. The Air Police squadron commander, a usually mild individual, must have been getting an ear full as his face was a high degree of red. The club manager was frantic and seemed to be the one moving his arms in the most gyrating fashion. The base commander was exploding, and I was hearing some very off colored language, effusive in his catalogue of items that this group had already destroyed. It included all the prized Christmas trees, which were now serving as life rafts in the club pool. The wreathes and garlands and other decorations which were pulled down and were now serving as garnish on the tables and the large club plants were teetering on the edge of the visible diving board. Having spent some crew time with Base Commander Colonel John Vincent in his less than glorious days as a captain on a crew and a party animal of the first order, I was able to reason with him and convince him that I could handle the situation. It wasn't exactly a boys will be boys speech but it did quiet him for the moment. He backed away and I proceeded into the fray.

The last bar of the Air Force hymn came to a close and the din rose as the troops slammed down into their seats. Now raising and slamming their spoons on the table in a synchronized symphonic gesture that was to lead to new renditions of spoon music, providing a level of noise that was sure to render all in the area with a ringing that would remain for hours. It was a coordinated pounding of the table by the many participants with their iced tea type weapons and it was loud. I ran to the bandstand and told the leader who was cowering on the stage, to play the Star Spangled Banner. As the notes began, the ensemble again rose to the near vertical and many began to sing. It was a sobering sight, even if I only had a couple of beers and a single slug of wine. Actually the voices rose in a crescendo now and it didn't sound all that bad.

Given the moment I knew that I had to come up with a quick fix for the situation and I knew I couldn't count on my two long ago disappeared French angels to bail me out. The look on the faces of the group before me told me that the voices of the multitude was a statement of the great respect that they held for their country and it's anthem despite their present plight. It's too bad that the many war protesters do not feel the same way about the United States. I have long kept a quote that I cut out of a story about a great American hero in my wallet. General Douglas MacArthur once said, "only those willing to die for their country are fit to live". Ms. Baez, who is now holed up in some remote corner of Hanoi, has only one concern and that is to insure that her cause supporting the North Vietnamese is in the forefront. It's very obvious that her regard for her countrymen fighting against them is one of total disdain. A very vociferous and extremely damaging liberal press shares her discordant attitude. (Maybe she can find the where-with-all to die for her chosen bed-fellows, although that won't change her category in my eyes, but it would make her a hero to all the protesters)! The anthem came to a close and the noise rose in crescendo to the level similar to that of being in the interior of a jet engine test facility.

Many of the noisy participants as they saw me yelled out my name and the fact that the sheriff was in the house and seemed to try to quiet the masses. I turned to the band-leader and told him to play "Yellow River", the most forbidden of songs. He vigorously shook his head from side to side, telling me he had been told to never play that song. I said "play Yellow River or this club will be a memory and you and your band will be out of work". He knew I was in a serious mood, but wasn't sure I was aware of the ban on that tune. My glare must have convinced him that I was most aware of the story and this group was definitely a threat to his well being. It was also obvious that the numbers were greater than he had seen in this room in his tenure as the resident entertainment. All of this was maximized by their inebriated condition. He was also aware that Colonel Vincent and his authoritative group had retreated to an out of sight area so he turned and told the band to start the music, hoping silently I'm sure that they were out of earshot as well.

"Yellow River" started to the enthusiastic cheers of all those who were still able to comprehend the symbolism of the music. As one, the group sat down and started the spoon symphony on the table. Those who were engaged in some further dismantling of the Christmas reminders in the club stopped their destructive activity and joined in. "Their" song was being played and maybe that was all they really wanted. The mayhem didn't stop, but at least the reasoning powers of most seemed to return. I followed the playing of the most famous of "our" songs with a request for "I Want to go Home", another of the forbidden tunes.

Now this raucous group was getting the idea; and joined in and sang loudly and with deep sincerity this plaintive plea to get them out of this war. They had been most involved for such a long period of time and they were tired of the constant stress, not only of waging war but also of being gone. The separations were truly debilitating and some of these guys had been involved in "Arc Light", and Bulletshot TDYs since the late sixties, not to mention their permanent tours in Vietnam and other remote locations. They were blowing off steam period, they were frustrated and more than likely a little bit (read a lot) scared. Hell, they were a lot scared as they knew that a day of standing down was going to be followed by flights to the north.

They loved those songs as they represented their feelings and desire to go home and see their families. As the last notes died down the crowd was a bit more subdued and now I was able to start some reasoned and loud dialogue and most were listening. I promised that the band would play all their requests the rest of the night to include as many renderings of their favorite songs as they wanted, but they had to cease and desist in the systematic dismantling and progressive destruction of the club. It did not get total quiet, but there were now comments like "The sheriff's right," and "let's get back to serious drinking", and I was happy that they seemed to be responding. I now saw out of the corner of my eye the "D" squadron commanders and Herb Jordan standing to the side looking for a way to get involved.

These were real reinforcements! I motioned them to get into the middle of this situation and talk to their guys and they responded and strolled into the fray. What had been a thunderstorm of serious potential was now a minor drizzle with a little sunshine peeking through. The band was playing "Yellow River" again and everyone was beating the spoons harmlessly on the tables. Even the club manager was now smiling. I wasn't about to say that the condition was over and I wasn't about to leave, but the great majority of the participants had returned to drinking their beer and talking quietly in small groups. A few continuing rowdy crew members were being counseled by their bosses and calm was returning to the club on the day before Christmas. Colonel Vincent gave me a "thumbs up" as he left the club, still disturbed but happy that the building at least was in one piece.

The OWC (officer's wives club) would have a lot to say and would be very unhappy with those "TDY hooligans". We would most certainly reimburse them for the loss of all their trees and decorations and they had enough time to reorder for next year and I'm sure they would ultimately forgive us and realize it was an action by a bunch of frustrated and scared, homesick crew members. God willing we would be home by next Christmas! I knew we would all pay the price for this evening, but for the moment I wasn't going to worry about it. Dave, Red, Herb and I had put out most of the fires and decided we would be as well off in the bar, as we would certainly hear any repeat of the action in the dining area. Somebody had to recognize that when a band starts playing sweet ballads and there is not a female to be had, there is going to be a reaction! Common sense would tell anyone to play those tunes that are best described as masculine and don't bring back fond memories, for that will certainly cause near, if not full chaos!

I hadn't been in the mood for a drink before, but now I craved a beer. I walked to the bar and ordered for the four of us and the bartender told me that Colonel Vincent had told him to put my drinks on his tab. This could end up being a long night! The base commander must have accepted the fact that the forbidden songs were appropriate for at least this evening, hopefully we could get the ban lifted permanently after this stand down.

Herb acknowledged what I had suspected. He had gone to the club at the navy base for dinner with a couple of his crews and no one else, and had just returned to the base and stopped at the club to see if I was around. Dave and Red were in their flight bags and had been at bomber ops getting feedback on their missions and were satisfied that all their planes had come off their targets without a problem. They were pleased that they had no losses for the evening and had only come to the club to grab a late bite. But after seeing the assembled masses and the damage they had managed to create, they decided they weren't too hungry after all.

Colonel Rew would certainly chew on us big time at the first opportunity and hopefully by then would have cooked up palatable solutions to mitigate the problem. However, Dave and Red were going to have to hear the wrath of the permanent party commander of the 43rd. Colonel McCarthy as he had been most vociferous about the crews and their conduct in the club and would have more than a little to say. At this moment I wasn't too concerned about his reaction and was only thinking about what could have happened. This was the second major situation that had occurred at the club and it was a direct indication of the fire that was burning in the ranks of these disgruntled crew dogs.

There was no guarantee that the constant rotation to this island would ever stop! All the crews were being told was that the B-52s were here for the duration. Duration! Of what? This war had been going on for over six years at this juncture and if we kept it in the hands of the politicians, it could last at least another six. Our only hope was the gutsy move by President Nixon to allow the "Buffs" to go downtown over the Red River to Hanoi, with the objective of bringing the North Vietnamese to their knees. This was a strategy long overdue and one which had been thwarted by the previous Secretary of Defense and his continuing war waging restrictions and stand downs.

At least now, in our collective fear, we could see some sense in our actions and best of all we had a feeling that we were finally bringing the war to the enemy and it would hurt him big time. The result could be the end of our involvement and get us off this island. It was the "close to the tough" stance President Kennedy took against Russia during the Cuban missile crisis, if not more to the point for the Asian mentality, which only understands strength. The western mind just can't comprehend the patience of the Vietnamese, mainly because our mentality is to get things over with quickly and the Vietnamese leaders are aware of that chink in our armor. They fought the French for years until they wore them out, destroying their will to support a war in the jungles of Southeast Asia.

The Asian doesn't put a timetable on winning a war. If they can't accomplish victory in one generation, they just pass it on to the next and if need be the following one. They do understand power properly demonstrated, something that the United States had failed to show, up to Linebacker II. With this President there seems to be an understanding of how to make the war a bit more catastrophic to the leaders of the North. At any rate I was deep in thought about what the following days were going to bring when into the bar walked Robbie wanting to know what was going on. I hesitated answering for a moment, but finally mumbled something to the effect that the "boys" were having a little party to celebrate the time off. The group at the nearest table, sucking on their beer chuckled loudly. With that the band struck up "I want to go home" and Robbie, knowing the restriction for playing that tune gave me his hard look and said "I missed something, didn't I"? I laughed and launched into the story.

CHRISTMAS, AT LAST

Christmas day in the year of our Lord, 1972. My daughter, Mary, would be a year old tomorrow. It seemed like I had been here that whole year and yet it had been barely three months. I had logged approximately two hundred hours of combat time in that period, much less than the crews would log, however quite enough! Flying was described to me very early as "periods of total boredom, interspersed with moments of stark terror", and well it was. That statement always brings back the memory of a flight I had when I was a member of the 509th Bomb Wing in Portsmouth New Hampshire.

It was my favorite crew as an aircraft commander and they were the best thing that ever happened to a fledgling B-47 AC. Norm Butterfield was my co-pilot. He was a virtual bundle of energy, totally professional and a true friend for life. Jean Pierre Beaudoin (Bo) was my radar, a French Canadian and a bombastic former hockey player, who spoke with a distinct French accent despite the fact that he lived his whole life in New Hampshire. It was a routine flight with an in-flight refueling shortly after takeoff. It was a nominal off-load of fuel and was to be followed by a fairly often flown low level route in the northeast corner of the United States. Entry was in upstate New York and the route then meandered through Vermont and ended in New Hampshire.

Enroute to the entry point we saw a few embryonic Cumulus clouds near the route, however they didn't seem threatening. When we received our clearance to penetrate from the entry point and descend to the low enroute altitudes, center did not issue any advisory about possible weather problems nor did they advise of any low-level hazards. The normal route was approximately an hour and a half long and that would be followed by a race track pattern to get in a few simulated bomb runs on different targets using different release tactics. The first portion of the route was uneventful but as we progressed through Vermont I noticed that despite the daytime flight, it was getting very dark. I called center and asked if there was any report from previous aircraft through the route of any weather problems and they gave me a negative reply, however they did mention the fact that they had reports of moderate turbulence.

Bo was busy keeping us in the corridor and I was working hard maintaining altitude and airspeed. At the same time Norm was actively trying to raise the bomb plot to give them information for the run and to ask them about other PIREPS (Pilot reports), but was not having any success. I was getting very concerned about the conditions and told Bo to keep a watchful eye on his scope for heavy returns that would signify thunderstorms. In the meantime day had turned into night, despite at least three more hours of sunshine. The turbulence was beyond my tolerance level, and I'm pretty much "mission" oriented. I decided to call center and ask directly about other aircraft who had been in the low level route. "Center this is Axel 27, we're running into significant turbulence in the route, have previous aircraft indicated any problems? The reply was negative, however some recent aircraft cited moderate turbulence on exiting the route. "OK crew, I'm not too happy with the conditions, but we can talk to bomb plot and get an update" Norm, have you made contact with the plot?' "No", he answered. "Bo, make sure we stay in the corridor" "No problem" was his reply. There was a steady increase in turbulence and I told the crew that we needed to get out of the route. The tips of my wings were waving at the cockpit in increasing oscillations. I knew that there was a certain amount of flex in these objects, but I felt looking at the very tip of my wing well above my fuselage was not a good sign.

Flashes of lightning further convinced me it was a very good decision to abort the low level. I told Bo to find us an exit route and he gave me a heading to turn to and we were trying to coach this recalcitrant lady to the "minimum enroute altitude" (MEA) as we were in very mountainous terrain. Bo chimed in that he would tell me when to turn and to do it expeditiously as he was taking me through two immense cells. Norm was trying to get center for clearance to climb out of the route and I was sweating bullets trying to keep the B-47 under control. Without clearance to leave the MEA we couldn't climb any higher without declaring an emergency. When Bo yelled to turn I didn't hesitate to get to the new heading. It was pitch black and the wings were waving like those of a sea gull. I rolled out on the new heading, but felt very little relief.

It seemed like an eternity and then all of a sudden I could see a glimmer of light and it was directly ahead of us. Norm was now talking to center and had received a clearance for us to climb. I added power and started to climb out of the route. Bo had put us on the right heading as after climbing through 12,000 feet, we popped into the bright sunlight and blue skies dead ahead. As we turned to head back to Pease, the gigantic thunderstorms that we had been in the middle of were now obvious deterrents to any flight activity to at least the tropopause (45-50 thousand feet). I couldn't help but wonder what could have happened if we had attempted to tough it out! Too many pilots have challenged those odds and became a statistic!

Combat flights from Guam could fall under the same mundane routine with sometime horrific results as an interjection into the flight. Those incidents were few and far apart as the flights to and from South Vietnam and its environs were no more than long, over water jaunts of a sight-seeing variety, but with the same sights day in and day out, lots of water. Then maybe an hour was dedicated to the actual involvement in the target areas, which for the most part were non-hostile at our altitude. Down south, of course, that hour could qualify as a part of one of many uneventful trips and allowed us to get our wits together. Comparing that to the recent flights made no sense as trips north were now far from that. There was the anticipation of what was going to happen in the target area, combine that with the number of planes involved and it would lead to a myriad of problems.

The normal three ship cells were a distant memory during Linebacker. With twenty aircraft stacked behind you there was always a formation problem. Someone inevitably would lose radar and would be asking for a bonus deal while they fixed the problem. This led to some obnoxious conversation at a time when nerves were already frayed. It seemed to everyone that the once monotonous trip to the target area was now too short. The refueling only added to the worry. It was at night and we would put three receivers on one tanker. For twenty-one bombers we had seven tankers. That's a lot of aircraft in the relatively small airspace at night. Also when we entered South Vietnam entire waves were placed in timing boxes before we pushed north. This was to insure the target release times were totally coordinated. Flight discipline was absolutely essential. The miracle each day was that there were no serious incidents during refueling or in the timing boxes. The enormous amount of aircraft was over whelming. Once out of the target area, I for one, felt like I would like to fly forever. I didn't want to land. The night would envelop me and I was euphoric, the master of the world. What a great feeling! Now if only I could get rid of all the bozos behind me.

I reflected on my family that morning as I joined a large number of crew members at Mass on another Christmas without my wife Rosemary and my five "Ms", Martin, Matthew, Monique, Marc and Mary. There were a lot of fervent prayers that morning for strength and being able to conquer the inner demons that kept conjuring up the worst war scenarios. I took solace in the fact that my Mom had a direct line to the Man upstairs as I knew she told Him to take care of me and He was the only explanation for some of the near misses I had experienced, to include Day two. If "Fate was the Hunter" I wasn't in his sights yet and I asked God that morning to listen intently to my Mom.

I did have thoughts and prayers for Steve Rissi and the others who we had not received any word about being POWs, and in my heart I was apprehensive about their fate in this troubled time. I had been invited to have dinner with some of my friends that I had been stationed with at SAC headquarters, Lt. Colonel Ted Buehler and his wife Kit. They were now part of the permanent contingent on this mountain above the Marianna trench. Major John DeJong, another former SAC personnel weenie, and his wife would join us, so it wouldn't be too bad of a day! I would avoid being overly critical of the permanent party and their commander and besides Kit had great sympathy for the crew members and their long separation from their families. Of course war was another problem that wasn't being addressed too well by the folks stationed here. They were just too far removed and it was more like someone else's problem. They had their trips to take to Hong Kong, Singapore and other exotic places and this stuff going on right now was interfering with their vacation plans.

This attitude didn't go unnoticed by the crews and that was probably the crux of the hostility that existed. The crews also could not see the extraordinary effort that the PCS (permanent change of station) officers and enlisted were making as they melted into the fray and weren't wearing a patch that identified their status. Ted and John were certainly among those who were very involved as they had to track all the personnel on the island to include the temporary toads (crews and support personnel, officer and enlisted). It wasn't all sun and pool time for anyone stationed here! Ted had been a close friend of my next door neighbor at Bunker Hill A.F.B., home of the B-58 Hustler. Phil Sicola and his wife Marge were two of the greatest people I have ever known and the reason for my assignment to the Personnel Division at SAC headquarters. They were large people (not obese, just big), both in physical appearance and in their dealings with others. Their hearts were enormous!

That was an assignment that gave me more background and experience in dealing with people and situations than I could have ever gained in a combat wing. It certainly prepared me for command! Phil was in the non-rated assignment directorate and knew every conceivable personnel regulation ever devised. When I arrived in the personnel business, I sought his counsel, and as I matured in my position I would still go to him constantly for direction, opinion, and yes, for ways to circumvent the system, a practice he was a master at! Marge was, well, she was Marge. She was a compassionate, sensible, lovely woman who had a great attachment to my (then) four young children. She didn't understand the operational side of the base, but that didn't stop her from mothering anyone she felt needed a sympathetic shoulder. She was so good to Rosemary during the tough times of my being on alert and learning to fly the B-58. She loved the sun and spent time in the back yard, slick with lotion, directing Phil in his planting of gladiolas (or gladigoolies as Phil called them) among other things, in their sparse base housing garden.

Phil and Marge introduced Rosemary and I to the Buehlers, and our relationship grew at Offutt. Ted was the director of enlisted assignments at SAC, a tough task, but one he was very capable of. On Guam he was the Director of Personnel and John was his deputy and right hand man. Ted was a bit nervous at times, however an extremely competent officer, who unfortunately was never rewarded for his talent with a promotion to full colonel.

I arrived at Ted and Kit's base house thinking about all the other Christmas holidays I have been away from my family. I had been lucky in many ways as in the B-47 days at Pease. I had avoided the Christmas deployments until one year when it was just my turn. I was to depart for Spain on a "Reflex" tour, leaving a couple of days before the holy day and was to be gone for three weeks. I would have with me two other crews who had also avoided the dreaded separation on the holidays. One of them was John Taylor, the former Aircraft Commander of my co-pilot, Norm Butterfield. John was not a very ambitious AC and had sort of gotten into the routine of just doing what was expected of him and little else. He was an OK pilot and had a bit of a temper, but nothing extraordinary. The other AC was Tom Manning, a very loose individual, but a worrier. He was the type of pilot you wonder about as he could obviously fly, but what would he do in a tough situation?

The day before our departure I received a call from Ted Guidera, a Navigator in the 100th Bomb Wing, our sister wing at Pease. He was the brother-in-law of the Division Commander at Torrejon, our destination near Madrid, General (three finger) Jack Ryan. He wanted to know if I could bring some items over to Torrejon. He and his wife were going over for the holidays and in addition to some of their personal belongings, they had an array of Christmas gifts for the General and his family. I said sure and asked him to meet me at the aircraft about three hours prior to our 2230 departure time so we could load it into the bomb bay. There was a lot of room for additional gear, as they would fasten a platform into the bomb bay that was roughly its length and width. This allowed them to deploy a lot of necessary equipment to the forward location to support the operation, however there was always plenty of room left for crew bags and golf clubs and when deploying home, for electronic items, such as Telefunken stereos and camel saddles.

Ted met me at the aircraft with a couple of large foot lockers and some smaller bags. He explained that they were spending an extended amount of time over in Spain and this would accommodate their needs. I instructed him to make sure someone met us to pick up the items, as I didn't want to have to lug them around through debriefing after our arrival. He assured me that someone would be there.

After the pre-takeoff crew briefing and getting our weather, we proceeded to the airplane and started engines. I was to be the lead aircraft and John was two, with Tom in the number three slot. The takeoff, and departure were routine, with an enroute climb to our initial cruising altitude. The departure was a direct on course routing on our easterly heading as there was no need to fly the Kennebunk departure route which we flew for normal training missions. Leveling off, we were almost immediately in a preparation mode for our inflight refueling. Norm was busy making the call to establish contact with our tanker. Tonight it was a KC-135, which was a stroke of good fortune as the weather was really going to be a factor and the 135 could handle the faster format speeds, not to mention the higher altitude which could keep us out of some serious lower altitude weather. After level-off we were in a loose entrail formation, 500ft altitude separation and one mile between aircraft.

This was a normal procedure for long enroute flying. We would go echelon right (a process where the three aircraft would be in fingertip formation, with separation both vertically and horizontally) just prior to our descent to the refueling altitude. Radio contact was established with the tanker, format speeds were determined, turn radius of the tanker, which was in orbit in the refueling area, and positive rendezvous identification of the intended tanker was established. We went into echelon, started the countdown for the tanker turn range, and started our descent. We briefly saw the tanker during his turn, but then lost him in some clouds. It would be up to Bo to bring us into the contact position using the returns broadcast by the tanker. At three miles we called for an airspeed reduction for the bomber formation and again at two and one mile. Throttles were almost in idle when we closed to less than a half mile according to our radar returns and still no visual. At about 200 yards I could see his lower rotating beacon and called visual and opened my refueling slipway door.

I was to take on 30,000 pounds of JP-4 and knew it would be a bit testy as there was a bit of turbulence and the visibility was not the best, however I had experienced much worse conditions. I edged into position and waited for the boom operator to plug me. The telescoping boom reached out to my nose receptacle, wavered a bit and the boomer gently pushed the nozzle into the hole and as I heard the latches lock on the boom, signifying contact, my green "contact made" light illuminated and I called out "receiver contact". Norm informed me we were getting our fuel and I grimly worked to stay in the "green". Despite some gyrations I managed to hang on until the tanker co-pilot announced, "lead, you have your gas".

"Thank you" was not usually exchanged and it was commonly acknowledged by a simple "roger that", followed by a call to the boomer, "disconnect on my count of three, one, two, three". At this point both the boom operator and the pilot of the receiver push their disconnect buttons and acknowledge the break in contact. The receiver pulls his throttles to idle and descends clear of the tanker and in the case of three receivers on one tanker, turns slightly to the left and flies formation on the tanker, insuring a safe separation. I pulled over to the side, closed my slipway door and waited while John Taylor pulled into position to get his offload.

It was obvious from the start that John was going to have some problems, as he was not getting stabilized as he should have. After two or three aborted attempts to get into position, the boomer started to talk to him as good ones will when they know the receiver is having some difficulty. "OK pardner, forward three and down two", referring to the corrections John had to make to get into a contact position. The boomers all have a different style and some will reach out and drag you into the green. Others are a bit more "book" oriented and will not make contact unless you are in position, totally in the "green". This boomer was going to do whatever it took to make the contact, outside of a dangerous act.

He reached out and reeled John in and the "contact made" call was made. There was a lot of movement on the boom and a constant dialogue was emanating from the boomer. A lot of references to forward and back and up and down, always followed by "pardner", it was an attempt by this boomer to relax John. You could feel the tension and with each disconnect came a calm reassuring set of directions to get back in position. With about 5000 pounds left, the B-47 in John's now very tight grip, started into a roller coaster motion and suddenly lurched up into the tanker. The cry of "breakaway, breakaway, breakaway" filled the air and the lights of the two aircraft seemed to merge. I cried out some expletive, sensing the midair explosion that would surely follow, when as quickly as they came together the lights separated, as the tanker accelerated and climbed and the bomber decelerated and dove.

There was a long pause while everyone got their respective heart out of their throat and then this silence was followed by words I will never forget from the boom operator. "Nice breakaway (long pause) pardner"! I think the collective exhale of everyone involved was heard all the way to Spain. I knew that John was black with sweat and was not about to attempt another contact. We had already determined he had sufficient fuel to get to our destination, and after that close call, was not ready to do anything but get out of the way. Everything settled down and Tom pulled into the pre-contact position of the now very quiet tanker. Despite a couple of disconnects, Tom got his offload without any major problems.

I cleared the Tanker to climb after Tom was settled on John's right wing. He was clear of the now lightweight 135, and then I gave the call to the other two bombers to accelerate to a safe climb speed and then initiated the climb back to our enroute altitude. We suddenly jumped out of the hazy refueling altitude into the star filled and clear skies above. The calm above the clouds was very refreshing and most welcome.

The trips to Spain and England on these "Reflex" tours were very interesting. For in heading east as we were at the hour we always flew, we would go from the end of the refueling track, climb to our level off and suddenly see the horizon start to lighten up, announcing that another magnificent sunrise was about to take place. It also signaled we were over the mid Atlantic, a thought that even during the warmer months had you thinking of the cold water down below and as the sun got above the horizon, the sighting of icebergs was a common occurrence. Even at our normal above 30,000 ft they looked large and ominous. I was very attentive to unusual sounds when over this ocean and was not the least bit afraid to utter a silent prayer, asking for a safe journey the rest of the way. The cold Atlantic was not my idea of the place to practice my open water survival knowledge!

I relished being the lead aircraft on deployment, as I didn't have to worry about my position on an aircraft in front of me. The sun rose directly in front of the aircraft and it was blinding. I would take my map and fold it to fit behind the windscreen panel to block the sun, all the while knowing that two and three could not afford that luxury as they had to keep an eye on the aircraft in front of them. Pilots like to see objects around them despite the radar's requirement to maintain "station keeping" on the other aircraft in the cell. Even with the constant coordinating of any slight turn or change in airspeed, there was always a tendency to drift in and out and back and forth when in this loose formation. Fortunately the trip over always seemed to go very quickly and especially so in the winter as the jet stream was always gushing at about 125 knots and it was a direct tailwind.

The landfall today came suddenly and the plains of Portugal and Spain sped by underneath us. An air traffic controller, picking up our three-ship formation, called in halting English, asking us to identify ourselves, which I proceeded to do. He gave a new heading and announced that we were approved for an enroute descent to Torrejon AB. The brown terrain below seemed barren this time of year and despite the excellent visibility, the familiar pall of smoke was hanging over Madrid. The base was about 10 miles outside of the city and now appeared on the nose of the aircraft. A final controller from the base picked us up and was giving me instructions for the GCA (ground controlled approach) to the runway. Gear down, flaps milked down, and after a no sweat final, a very good landing (in my opinion, and of course any landing you can walk away from is a good one). I deployed the drag chute to slow this monster down, gently tested the brakes and rolled slowly to the turnoff short of the end of the runway. Ground control gave us instructions to our parking area and I pushed the six engines up to move smartly to the appointed spot.

As I was turning into the area I noticed the Air Force blue sedan with the three star flag waving, waiting for me to turn into my parking location. As the wands of the sergeant giving directions into the parking spot crossed, I crunched on the brakes and came to a halt. The blue sedan pulled into the perimeter around my aircraft and a couple of "high powered" guys in blue suits jumped out to await the bomb door opening. When cleared, Bo opened the doors and the two gofers below scurried out of sight under the aircraft. I completed the appropriate checklists, and scurried down the ladder to the cool wind below. I noticed some very industrious crew chiefs already unfastening the lines that held our bomb bay cargo in place, and were passing items to the guys below. Bud had marked his bags and packages very well and as I watched, an assortment of items was being stacked to one side. I glanced at the sedan off to the side to see if the General was actually in the car and he was not! A group was now carting one large stack of bags to the car and without any other exchange but, "thanks Captain", they were a memory. Our crew bags were placed into the standard Air Force bus and we were on our way to maintenance debriefing.

It was not until the following Sunday while in the club, thinking about dinner that the Guidera luggage was even thought of again. While standing talking to one of the other ACs, I felt someone grab the base of my neck and then squeeze very hard. This was obviously an old friend who was giving me this neck brace. I was about to pull the "old elbow into the groin" response when I noted the wide-eyed stare of the guy I had been talking to. I held fast and as the pressure was released I turned to find a rather tall gent with three stars on his shoulder smiling down on me. He stuck out his hand, grabbed my shoulder and said "Captain, I want to thank you for bringing my sister's stuff over with you". Now, I noticed Bud and the General's beautiful sister standing there. I muttered something to the effect that it was no trouble at all. He then told me my crew and I would be his guest at the New Years eve party next week. After he walked away I looked at those now hanging around in the wake of the Generals departure and sputtered out, "Wow, I almost hit the general". Christmas in Spain would have been a disaster!

Christmas in Guam, despite the humid and remote conditions was very nice this year of our Lord, 1972. Kit prepared an excellent turkey dinner and if you let your mind go into reverse, one could forget that a war was going on and that tomorrow was going to be another big day in the lives of a lot of crews and this squadron commander. I knew I was going to fly a lead aircraft in one of the waves and I also knew that the "G"s were going north again. I tried hard not to worry about what was happening later and concentrated on the polite conversation and the laughter that permeated the home of my friends.

I very much admired Ted and John as they were two non-rated officers in a rated officer force, knowing that promotions were scarce for them and yet they worked diligently at their trade and it was a difficult one and I knew it. After a comfortable time had passed and I had digested my meal, I knew that I needed to get on the road, as it could be another long evening and I would need to get organized for the mission. I thanked my hosts for the nice afternoon, the meal and the company, and excused myself and told them that the sorties had to be filled for the 26th of December. I walked out the door to my truck and was aware that I was on an island in the mid-Pacific, far from the combat area, and it was so very quiet as nothing was in motion. The world was in a standown, and Guam was in the center of that world! My stomach started to churn, as the thought of going back to Hanoi wasn't exactly what I had wanted to be thinking about on this day of Christ's birth. Reality stepped in and again I suddenly remembered that tomorrow was my daughter, Mary's first birthday.

Fortunately Guam is where "the day begins" according to the local papers so I had time to make a call home through the command post, a practice frowned on, but one we used as often as possible. I would make a point in calling home in a couple of hours as it was very early in the AM in Sacramento. I got in the truck and sped off to bomber operations (this was sometimes referred to as the Arc Light Center) as I knew the "frag" for tomorrow would be there and I was very curious about how my aircraft would be utilized. I stumbled into bomber operations, out of the muggy heat and into the cool air-conditioned and dark planning area. A few people working on Christmas day looked up as I displayed my badge and asked about the status of tomorrow's flights. The reply was that 8th Air Force headquarters had not yet sent the "frag" down for tomorrow, however I was to start selecting crews as it was going to be very big and it would include the G's, both modified and unmodified going north.

I was very disturbed about the unmodified "G" model being used against SAM sites after our losses on the 18th and 20th. I sought out any planner who could tell me why the unmodified "Gs" were in the mix, however I was told that all the sortie configurations had been made at SAC headquarters and that the "frag" was in concrete for tomorrow. I was more than a bit concerned for the safety of my crews as well as for myself. I could very well be in one of the suspect aircraft. After spilling some venom among this group I decided to go to 8th headquarters and ask some embarrassing questions and if need be, ask to see General Johnson. Fat chance I would get by the outer office!

THE FINGERTIP MISSION

1walked briskly out of the windowless building into a now very cloudy day and one that was threatening rain. As I was about to step into my truck, I heard a voice yelling at me to hold on. I looked back to see one of the intelligence officers, who I had been talking to, beckoning me to come back in the building. Although the "frag" had not really arrived, he knew more than he wanted to divulge as the plans for tomorrow were a result of the Wings coming up with a new plan for engagement based on the enemy's battle performance during the first phase of Linebacker. They had sent the plan forward and it was just a matter of time for it to be returned intact for the immediate mission after standown.

He had decided after he had seen and heard my concern relative to the "G" being used up north, that he needed to clear the air and he would divulge some information to allay my frustration in an attempt to keep me from rocking the boat unnecessarily at 8th headquarters. Once inside he told me that tomorrow's raid would be very big and would indeed include my G aircraft in large numbers, however the unmodified aircraft would not be making a breakaway turn after release, but instead would overfly the target. I was at first stunned, but then assumed that the selected targets would be similar to going to Vinh over the very narrow neck that separated north from south, and I had done that before.

An overfly certainly would not expose the big belly of the B-52 to the enemy radar and would accomplish the desired effect in a mutual ECM environment. I was pretty satisfied with the words I was hearing but wanted more information if I could get it. So I then asked if the targets were essentially the same. He said "yes and no" in an off handed manner and changing the subject said I would have to drop by later for the final count of needed crews for the mission, but to have a large number available. He then turned and walked back into his alcove of secrecy. He definitely had told me all he was going to! He felt my need to know had been fully satisfied, and he was right. Now I really needed to talk to someone, but not of the staff variety, and wondered if I could find Robbie or Herb, and set off to do so.

Knowing full well that Robbie would be one of my lead pilots for tomorrow, I wanted to share the overfly strategy that they were going to utilize on the missions for the 26th. Sworn to not divulge my information and despite the fact that Robbie was the most secure individual I had ever known, I wouldn't tell him a thing. He was going to find out soon enough the details of the new tactics. Slamming open the door to the crew room for Robbie's Barksdale crew, as no one ever seemed to lock their door on this screwy island, there was not only not a Robbie, I found no other member of his crew. I was a bit perplexed, as I was sure he would be around somewhere. I went out on the balcony and walked toward the end of the concrete to access the stairs.

As I rounded the corner I saw the gentle dude from Louisiana running across the grass to the corner of the building. I yelled and he looked up with that puzzled look that wrinkled his brow to the extent that his crew cut stood up straighter. I bounded down the stairs to meet him and pulled up short as I got nearer. He didn't have any running shoes on and for that matter he didn't have any shoes on period. He saw me staring at his feet and smiled as the sweat poured off his shirtless body. "I took up running barefoot on my first tour in Vietnam when I learned that the first thing the NVA would do when they captured a pilot was to take his boots. They knew that we Americans had soft feet and there would be no way we would get very far if we tried to escape".

I wasn't about to ask him if his feet were at a level of toughness that would allow him to run through the jungle habitat, as I was sure he could. I mumbled something about my own plans for survival if I went down up north, but knew that once out of the aircraft, your chances of evasion were slim and none on the ground. If anyone could evade, I could, if anyone could escape, it was Robbie. Everyone had a plan, but only a few tried to increase their odds with the pursuit of a physical regimen that would be needed to get as far away from the scene as quick as possible after exiting your bird and hitting the ground.

Everyone had a personal authenticator (which I have never divulged) that was used to let the SAR (search and rescue) folks know where you were by adding the four numbers to your latitude and longitude coordinates. You also had two questions that you gave them to ask when you were on the ground, to insure that you were who you said you were. My two answers were my mother's maiden name (Phelan) and my brother-in-law's middle name (Duane). Of course you had to be in a position to call the SAR aircraft and have them be able to get to you where you went down first. A clear mind when you hit the ground and a plan was essential before you keyed your radio. Robbie and I were well versed in that need. Looking at Robbie I became a bit thirsty and felt some liquid refreshment was in order. It didn't take too long to get Robbie of a mind to shower and join me for a brew before I had to get a sortie count and review the crew roster for available crews for tomorrow.

I had no sooner started on my first beer than I received a call to report to bomber ops. I left Robbie who had now linked up with one of his buddies from home. As I entered the facility there was a definite buzz among the planners. Herb was already there and was bent over one of the many tables writing something in a notebook he carried around most of the time. I nudged him as I approached the table and as he looked up there was a trace of vulnerability in his face as if he were aware of tomorrow's mission and of the role he would play, as it was his turn as well as mine to go downtown. He was obviously trying to assess the available crews for the sorties that had been programmed in the "frag" order. He said "we have 45 G aircraft scheduled for the mission, and we need to pick the most experienced lead pilots". Well, that wasn't too difficult!

We charted missions flown in all categories. On every flying schedule we listed the number of missions each pilot had flown and the number of times he was the lead pilot on the "Bulletshot" missions. We were also well aware of the flights each crew and staff member had been subjected to during Linebacker? Herb and I set about selecting the lead crews, as the radar navigator was as important as the aircraft commander. Robbie was a lock for one of the leads and one of my Mather crews, Don Bogue, who had 267 total missions and 81 leads, and had performed very well in an earlier lead role, was also a cinch selection. Plus his RN had flown 219 missions and was not one to have a problem with pressure over the target. My acting operations officer, John O'Donnell was another high mission pilot and an obvious lead selection. Then of course there was Herb and I! We amassed the required number of lead pilots, selected appropriate spares and went on to other selections for the raid.

The tactics were another matter, but tonight was not the time to worry about the procedure or the order of battle. That would be briefed in detail at the pre-mission briefing prior to takeoff. It was going to be the biggest raid of the war and it was going to get a lot of people's attention. Herb and I, along with some of the planners, who were interested in who the "bomb aimers" were, completed the crew selection. The lowest sortie count of the selected crews was above fifty missions and most had numbers greater than one hundred. It had to be the most qualified group of crews that ever flew in combat! It also confirmed the suspicions of the crews I had talked to on Christmas Eve.

I left the building with a heavy load on my mind, as I had once again gotten personal and selected a number of my friends to fly this biggest and possibly, the most hazardous mission the B-52's would fly in the Vietnam War. There had been a lot of press about crew members refusing to fly after the first day of Linebacker. It was grossly exaggerated on all counts, at least in Guam. I had a few pilots and others who wanted to spill their guts about the fear they experienced, but all, with no exceptions, just needed to tell someone that they were very concerned about what would happen if they did not come back. I found it very easy to discuss this fear as I too had felt the Wolf rise within me, and told them so.

It was an unfair rap that some liberal journalist picked up on, and blew the story totally out of proportion. It was not hard to find those who would be involved, as after all it was Christmas and people do tend to get together on this holiest of days. The notification of the crews, including spares, taxi-crews and standby, was accomplished and those affected were put into crew rest. Were the crews surprised? Not at all, they were expecting some form of maximum effort and most seemed pleased that they would be a part of the action. I wasn't too sure! It would be another mind game tonight trying to catch some Z's!

After a somewhat restless, but surprisingly sleep fulfilling night, I awoke a bit later than usual. I hadn't left a wakeup call with the orderly, so there was no knock on the door this morning, as he knew I was scheduled for a sortie today. I swung out of bed and walked to the door, flinging it open as the mornings always seemed fresh and clean and smelled of ocean. It was Mary's first birthday! This day on the island of Guam was no different, as it was truly a marvelous day. I nudged my brain to acknowledge that I would experience the same beautiful morning tomorrow. (no negative thoughts). A gentle ocean breeze, cool temperature (only in the mid 70's), clear skies and very quiet. Absolutely no sound! That would change. It was a few minutes after 0600 and I was hungry. I wanted a good meal and so once again decided to go to the club for breakfast.

I've never been one to feel I had to take a morning shower, but I always shave, so accomplishing the latter. I jumped into a clean flight suit, laced up my boots, and grabbed my hat and sun-glasses and started out the door. One of the most experienced of the AC's on the island happened by as I opened the door. It was Major Bob Weaver, a standboard instructor pilot from Robins AFB in Georgia. He was a good friend of Robbie and was the same kind of person, very calm and unassuming and knew every facet of the airplane. He was going to be a wave leader this day and seemed to be preoccupied with some of his own thoughts. I said hello and he looked up and asked, "do you have any idea where the targets are today"?

Not too sure of where anyone was going, I answered "no, but the tactics are definitely changed". He seemed pleased with that response as he had been very critical of the tactics utilized the first three days. I explained as we walked off the second floor landing about the unmodified G overfly of the targets and no breakaway. Bob had flown on day two in the same wave as I had as the Airborne Commander, and had wanted to employ some evasive maneuvers to avoid the SAM firings we had all experienced going to our target. He of course was told to bite his tongue as there would be no evasive maneuvers, period!

I asked if he was going my way and he said that he was not and was going to meet his crew later for breakfast. He just was out to catch some air before they got out of the sack. I stopped at my truck long enough to contemplate waking up someone to go to breakfast and decided they all needed sleep more than food, that is if they were really able to hunker down without the thought of today's mission. I too was having thoughts about today and as I drove my truck to the club I couldn't help but remember the concerns that I had for previous flights I had to make.

My first solo flight in the T-6 was a complete surprise as my instructor Clyde M. Pinkerton, Pinky to most, and I had flown to the auxiliary field near Dexter, from Malden AB in Missouri. Believe it or not, this was a grass field, not paved! After a couple of touch and goes on the grass strip, Pinky told me to full stop, which I did. As I taxied past the mobile tower, he told me to let him out. As I pulled up he crawled out of the back seat, fastened the seat belt to the shoulder harness, patted me on the "green eagle" hat we wore and told me to make three full stop landings and to pick him up after the last one.

I'm not sure if I was just naïve or what, but I had not given a thought to going solo, after all it was a "dual" ride. I was more than nervous. I was going to fly the "terrible Texan T-6" alone? My knees were in total disarray and my mouth, dry as a bone as I taxied away from Pinky and headed to the ill-defined runway for my first takeoff. I gunned the engine and almost forgot the torque generated by this big engine. I quickly pushed in my left leg on the rudder pedal to keep from going into the mobile tower and started down the grass runway, quickly leaping into the air and pulling up my gear I gained the necessary altitude to turn to my crosswind heading. At 800 ft above the terrain I turned downwind and had the auxiliary runway clearly in sight.

As I passed the approach end of the runway I dropped my gear, hesitated for a moment, cut back on the throttle and turned base, milked down my flaps, and started my descent back to the runway below. It was a good approach, however the landing was a tad hard and I bounced into the air. The T-6G was a fun airplane to fly, however at that moment I wanted to be anywhere but in this airplane. After I finally put it back on the grass runway, I really expected to see the red light flashed at me, signaling the end of my solo attempt. It didn't happen so I taxied past mobile, waiting for Pinky to jump out waving his arms to stop me from killing myself. No such luck!

So again I took the runway, pushed the throttles up, remembering to stiff leg the rudder pedal this time and bounced once again into the wild blue. I repeated the first pattern and made a very nice tail dragger landing. Now, proud of my effort, I confidently pushed the aircraft back to the runway and now actually saw my instructor watching my effort. Once again I launched into the very busy sky, as I wasn't alone in my bid to solo. Again I flew a very disciplined pattern and made a wonderful approach and a beautiful landing.

I proudly taxied back to pick up Pinky for the flight home, stopped my Tango-6 and waited for him to climb aboard. He looked at me and finally sauntered over to the wing root and wanted to know why I wasn't making another takeoff. I yelled above the engine noise that I had already made my three landings. He said he only saw two and told me to get back out there and make another. Had he missed the first lousy landing or was it one of my two good ones? Maybe he saw them all, but didn't want to talk about or count the first one. I managed to defy the odds and completed another successful approach and landing, taxied back to pick up Pinky and headed back to Malden. He never mentioned my landings, four in all, with me after I made the additional approach and landing. He crawled into the seat and we silently flew back to Malden, the only comments being something about my first check ride at sixteen hours.

Another sure way to have a restless night before a mission was to have to fly an annual "check" ride. It was really an ego thing to most, however if you happened to be a standboard pilot, which was the hand picked few who evaluated the rest of the wing, then there was lot of prestige and pride to lose. A failure in that capacity meant you had to be replaced in your position and most of us are not proud of this form of very public failure. I always worried about my yearly stanboard rides and I was especially nervous when as a member of standboard and a CCTS (Combat Crew Training Squadron) instructor, I had to fly CEVG (Combat Evaluation Group) flights on what seemed like a much too often basis.

One such evaluation particularly stands out and it occurred at Pease in B-47s. I was the new guy in the seven crew standboard section and the no notice team arrived at our doorstep with the express purpose of flying with wing crews and specifically the check section of the select pilots who evaluated the 509th crews. The schedule was set by the CEVG evaluation team to fly with all the crews over a two day period. I was set to fly on the first day, as was our chief of standboard, George Knott and two other crews. The weather forecast prior to takeoff was for strong winds in the area upon our return some six hours after takeoff.

All my activity as an Instructor was from the back seat of the tandem seating B-47, so that was my crew position for all instructional areas. The remainder of the mission, bombing, navigation, low level etc I would be evaluated while flying in the front seat as any other aircraft commander would. The takeoff was normal despite some turbulence at the lower level, which dissipated by level off at altitude. I changed seats at this point and the evaluator got up front as we prepared for the rendezvous and refueling in the back seat or co-pilot position. Refueling from the back seat in the B-47 was easier than in the front, as you had decent visibility. (This was totally opposed to back seat in the TB-58, where you had to push your head far to the right side of the cockpit and I had to actually stand up, all five feet, six inches, to see the tanker).

The refueling receptacle, which was set to the right side of the nose of the 47 was in plain view and you merely lined up on the tanker inboard engine nacelle. Everything was normal for the rendezvous and contact. I had no difficulty moving into position and making my contact. I managed the prescribed off-load without an inadvertent disconnnect. I then had to demonstrate the "limit demonstration". This involved moving to the various ends of the envelope. I moved smoothly to the limits of the refueling envelope, (full forward, aft, lower, upper and left and right azimuth) and seemed to satisfy the evaluator, who really was a nice guy, with my flying skill.

After a coordinated disconnect from the tanker we headed to our cruising altitude and leveled off. Changing seats again, we did a high altitude navigation leg and then entered the "Orange Tree" low level route that was down in Kentucky. It was a very pretty route over mountainous (or at least hilly terrain) and the weather was kind to us as it was very clear and the air was smooth. Therefore we could fly the VFR (visual flight rules) altitudes and I could assist the Navigator with check points off my map to maintain the route corridors. The bomb run went very well despite some minor radar problems and the scores read back were typical of Jus Rose's capability. He was a "cracker jack" bomb "aimer" and everyone knew it (he was also the wing clown jester and kept everyone loose). He had once come over the interphone on a particularly long takeoff roll on a very hot and dark night and said "I don't care what science says, this hummer won't fly!

It was an uneventful flight and exit from the low level and now we had the long dead head, return flight back to Pease. I had ahead of me the required penetration, GCA, ILS, visual pattern, approach and full stop landing. All of these were standard requirements on any check ride. The weather gods had abandoned me as I entered the holding pattern for my penetration to Pease and received the local report. The winds were gusting to <u>sixty</u> knots varying 20-40 degrees across the runway. The evaluator wanted to attempt to make the approach to Pease and was hoping for the wind to be right down the runway on one of our approaches thus allowing us to make a full stop landing. I didn't protest, although under ordinary circumstances I would have opted to divert to another, more friendly airdrome.

I received clearance for the approach and started the penetration. At approximately 10,000 feet we started to hit turbulence. The lower we went the more severe the turbulence. I leveled out at twenty two hundred feet and was picked up by GCA. I told them I wanted a low approach to runway 34. The turbulence was now so severe that I couldn't read my airspeed indicator. It was rotating somewhere between approach speed and forty knots high. The book called for a variance from approach speed of not greater than five knots for a highly qualified ride.

It was extremely difficult to hold heading and even a semblance of altitude as we were bouncing all over the sky. Never the less the evaluator had me fly a second and then a third pattern under these conditions. My flight suit was wringing wet, my helmet was leaking into my mask and I could even feel my toes swimming in my boots. It was very apparent that we were not going to get the airplane down at Pease. After the third approach the evaluator called the command post and asked for permission to divert to Plattsburg AFB, another B-47 base in upstate New York and only a short distance in air miles from home base.

Getting an approval to divert and a clearance from air traffic control to climb on course, we set our heading to our diversion base and only then did the evaluator allow me to put the bird on auto-pilot, which was a tremendous relief. Throughout the approaches at Pease he had been very supportive and did not give me the impression that there was any problem, so I felt generally at ease, but knew I would still have to make a visual approach and full stop landing at Plattsburg to complete the check ride. Once again we made contact with an approach control and upon being cleared, entered the queue of airplanes at this historical military base. I made a very good visual pattern, as I had flown in there on a number of other diversions and had picked up some visual ground check points to fly my downwind and make my turn to base with. My turn to final was right down the runway and my back seat landing was as good as I could make. The evaluator took control of the aircraft as we rolled down the runway and muttered something that sounded like "good ride", but I couldn't be sure as my helmet had the "gurgles".

We parked, exited the aircraft, debriefed maintenance, and got some wheels to the BOQ. After a shower Jus, Keith Glenn, my copilot and I went to the club, where lo and behold it looked like Pease west, as all the crews and their evaluators were sitting in a group having a beer. I spied George Knott sitting next to my evaluator. He gave me a thumbs up which was very good news. We all had stories to tell as everyone had made at least an attempt to land at Pease, and all were in awe of the turbulence we had encountered. No longer did I need to worry about having to make the move back to the squadron in an ignominious wing type failure, that is if I could safely and according to the "book" get my bird back to Pease when the weather improved. As it turned out the evaluator rode back to Pease the next day in the non-crew position below and hardly uttered a word on the return.

I finished breakfast without any interruptions, but did find out that Colonel Rew did indeed have a lot to say about The Christmas eve bash at the club at the 0500 standup briefing. Luckily I had crew rest to use as an alibi for missing that meeting. I left the club and started for bomber operations to check the targets and routes. The standby target study navigators were milling around talking about the missions and it was apparent they were excited (of course they didn't have to fly). The package for tonight was indeed a change, as it would utilize all of our aircraft to the extent of their capability and not compromise the G with a turn from the target.

Tonight's mission was going to be very different and the crews constant harping to the mission planners and higher echelon on our previous tactics had paid a huge dividend as we were going to compress our time on targets. This in effect eliminated the cell concept. This would allow our bombers to deny the SAM gunners the opportunity to not only reload between cells, but also would keep the first cell from being a barometer for the track and heading for the following cells. The plan was to use a "fingertip" type flight inbound to the target, thus spreading the formation across the target and allowing for a very effective mutual ECM coverage for the aircraft.

The fingertip style formation was being utilized in an attempt to confuse and saturate their command and control system. The crews were going to love it at the pre takeoff briefing! I suddenly realized I was compromising my crew rest so retreated to the squadron to finish some paper work and then attempt a nap before the pre takeoff briefing. I managed a bit of work, rose and told the clerk to wake me no later than 1000 hours, and left the wide open room for the 20 step walk to my room. The room was cool, removing my boots and flight suit I crawled into my sack and closed my eyes. I woke up with a start and wondered if my troops had gone to war without me, but looking at the clock, I had only been asleep for an hour.

It was 0930 hours and I was refreshed and really wide awake. I decided a shower was in order as after all, who knows when I would take my next one? I stepped out to see my clerk, opening the door. He was early, but he wanted to tell me I had a phone call from a former SAC headquarters friend who worked for me in the Career Development Division, Major Joe Nemeth. He was another of the very bright guys I had the good fortune to be associated with and one who definitely kept me from deviating from the proper path in the myriad thinking that is indigenous to the puzzle palace in Omaha. I wrapped a towel around me and hurried to the office.

Joe was in his usual good humor and was merely wondering if I was taking "good" care of myself. I convinced him I was and begged off with the excuse I had a meeting to go to. He read between the lines on this unsecured line and told me to be safe and would talk to me later. I retreated to my room again as the after shower effect, combined with the now very humid and hot conditions made me wonder why I had bothered to take a shower. Once in the air conditioning I was able to get dry and get into my flight suit and boots again. I now felt ready to meet the bus, which was going to be downstairs and then would take my assigned crew and one other to the theater for the pre takeoff briefing by way of the "inflight" kitchen and the personal equipment section.

The gunner was the responsible party for ordering the meals, and everyone usually ordered two as it was a long flight and even though there wasn't much of an appetite going to the targets, there was a lot of nervous eating. Of course on the return flight everyone was ravenous. The meals were a variety of choices, roast beef and turkey sandwiches, fried chicken and others. Each meal came with two small cartons of milk, a candy bar, juice, crackers and some tidbit to remind us where we were. The meals ran the gamut from OK to extremely good, and on Guam they fell into the last category.

We picked up the lunches and a lot of coffee and pushed on to PE (personal equipment). Once there everyone got out to pick up his chute, and survival vest. I was careful to check my 38 caliber handgun and an extra bag of ammunition, along with the standard stuff we had in the vest, matches, flares, gloves, black skull cap and other odds and ends that were very valuable in a survival situation. I had a survival knife on the pocket on the inner side of my left leg that could cut tangled shroud lines and do a decent job gutting a varmint. My business knife was sewn to my boot and was razor sharp, but thankfully never used. Picking up my helmet I checked the mask and oxygen flow from the nearby hookup.

I then threw it back into the bag and along with this large group exited the building amid the voices from the PE staff, asking us to bring the chute back unused and to have a good flight. I loved those guys! Back in the bus we engaged in a bit of small talk on the way to the briefing. We arrived to find a lot of blue busses and I mean a lot, parked around the building and there were still more to come. They filed in one crew at a time. The radar-navigators had seen their targets, but none were aware of the tactics change. Slowly each crew found the right seats, as each was marked by wave, cell and cell position. I was going to be bronze lead tonight, each cell was a different color and each wave a different number.

There were three ships to a cell and depending on the target, a number of cells made up the wave. We already knew our target as my aircraft, along with fourteen other G's in my wave were hitting the Haiphong transformer station. We would stay out over the south China sea until we had gone north of the harbor city and then turn and come back to the target and strike it from the northeast. We would overfly the target and exit back into the sea. Our time over land was almost less than that of our missions at Vinh.

It was also about the same time frame that was needed as an Instructor in the B-58 to qualify a crew for supersonic flight when we flew our demonstration Mach Two flight for our student crew going through the CCTS. We would accelerate from .91 Mach in the turn at the northern end of Lake Michigan, climb at 1.65 Mach, turn south and level off at above 50,000 ft. and finish the acceleration to Mach two plus. Once established at our programmed Mach we would go through an engine failure demo, then give the student control of the aircraft, pass Chicago and decelerate and descend, all in less than nine minutes. It was a real kick to fly at that speed and all you would have to do to realize your speed was to watch a ground reference point pass by the really moving object you were flying in.

I would remember that tonight on my nine minutes to the target, before we go "feet wet", but I would be more interested in the unfriendly objects occupying the space around me and would not be worrying about the amount of time I would spend over Haiphong. Entering the building we found our seats amid the din of a bunch of crew dogs working off their nerves. Ultimately everyone was in his place, and there was nary a seat unoccupied in this large theater. The taxi, standby and flying crews were in place and now everyone was virtually silent. The staff and support personnel who were privy to sit in on the briefing were mostly standing in the rear and spilled down the side aisles.

If this were a movie they would call it SRO. The normal entrance of the senior staff ensued, clattering down the theater aisle. They sat in the empty front row and the briefing began. Wave and cell makeup, along with air discipline, was discussed. The flight paths to the target were shown and the tactics to be utilized were then announced, evoking chatter that almost drowned out the briefer. There was no doubt that this group of crews were much more pleased with the tactics of this, the day after Christmas and my Mary's birthday than those utilized during the first few days of this grand attempt to win this war. Someone had actually listened to the suggestions of the crews and they were pleased that finally the SAC planners, in their estimation, got it right.

The chaplain closed this session as he had all the briefing with a request to God to bring all of us back safely. There are times when prayer is the last thing on some people's mind, however I don't believe that there was anyone in this theater who didn't mutter silently or otherwise a solemn Amen. We exited into the bright sunlight, found our bus and proceeded to aircraft 6503, parked in spot C62, which was about as far as you could go without falling into the ocean. Almost to the east taxiway, but close to the north runway, which we would utilize to get to the takeoff end of the active runway. This was a taxi distance of almost two miles, moving between parked Buffs on both sides, many loaded and going to the same place we were.

Unlike my first Linebacker mission, the aircraft was totally ready for the crew pre-flight procedures and it was fully loaded with its deadly stores. Again a proud, overworked and hot crew chief, presented the 781(aircraft history of discrepancies outstanding) to me for my review. The document was divided into sections, all of which were important to all members of the crew. Maintenance discrepancies are listed in three categories, the red dash, which is usually a very minor item, such as a burned out bulb that can't be reached without causing some down time. Then there was the red diagonal, a more serious write-up, but one that you can fly the aircraft. Finally a red X is a discrepancy that means the aircraft can't be flown until it is cleared with corrective work that eliminates the particular writeup. 6503 had some dashes and a number of diagonals, however no Xs.

One thing stood out about this G model in it's 781, it had not been modified with the latest ECM capability. We would be very careful not to expose our belly to the enemy radar. I briefed the crew on the items that would affect each station and we grabbed our gear and entered the aircraft. It was oppressively hot, sweat dripped from every pore and the point in the checklist where we could connect external power couldn't come fast enough. There were a couple of portable air conditioners pointed through the entry door, but it didn't have much effect upstairs. I opened the side window, hoping for an island breeze, however if one was there, the aircraft was not oriented on the ramp to pick it up.

Start engine time finally arrived and once all eight engines were in the idle position, the cool air started to flow into the cabin. Closing the sliding window, it was almost comfortable by the time we left our parking spot. Checking the brakes and turning right to the 8500 cross over, it was a little more than a 90 degree right turn. The heavy bird which was close to its maximum gross weight of 525,000 pounds, lumbered around the corner, straight ahead for a very short distance and now a left turn to go west to the north runway.

The activity on both sides of the runway was intense. Aircraft were in every state of readiness, some with engines running waiting their turn to taxi with the cell to which they were assigned. Others with maintenance "bread" trucks surrounding them, trying to remedy a just discovered problem, one with a crew hurriedly exiting their aircraft with their gear, heading to a maintenance truck for transport to a spare as their assigned aircraft had a problem that could not be fixed prior to their takeoff time. There were also some aircraft on each side of this overflow parking area that seemed completely engulfed in maintenance activity hanging engines, or repairing a system problem.

The shirtless specialists were transfixed as they turned to watch us taxi by, raising a thumb or throwing a smart salute, pride emanating from every airman on the line. A couple of Ds turned in front of my aircraft, the hard spots on each wing showing a large package of 100 pound bombs and the heated exhaust from their engines, falling and clinging to the ground. Once the two "tall tails" were directly in front of me the massive flaps of the D now blocked my view of the external stores and the huge shark like tail now seemed to be in the form of clasped hands pointing to heaven in a pre-takeoff prayer. Then I saw the gunner in the aircraft directly in front of me. He was moving his turret almost imperceptibly, more than likely trying to find his own personal comfort level. I almost thought he was checking me out, but I'm sure his thoughts were on something other than the G model behind him.

The "taxi tango" of war was once again in motion! Radio transmissions were now filling the air as "Charlie" tower and ground control were simultaneously barking out instructions. Lame aircraft were being shut down and crews were being rushed to spares. It was a minor miracle that there was no confusion. It was orderly to a fault as aircraft after aircraft fell in line in the proper place for the launch. As the first aircraft started to roll, I sensed a feeling of professionalism for everyone who was involved in this massive demonstration of power. I actually had goose bumps as I took the active. It seemed a bit corny, but the "gung ho" spirit of launching an aircraft had overwhelmed me. The lump in my throat was so large I had difficulty announcing "Bronze lead on the roll", however I managed to get it out.

I placed my eight throttles to the wall, fired the water, felt the surge of power and hurtled toward another day in the history of the war in Vietnam. There would be no abort! This day would not be like any other for our adversaries to the north in this, the eighth day of Linebacker. Despite my apprehension, I wanted to fly this mission. It was one thing to visualize the tactics that were to be flown tonight, it would be another to experience them. As we cleared the dark ground cloud the launching aircraft had created, we were in the clear, climbing over the ocean. Our friend, the Russian trawler was somewhere close at hand below. His message would be very clear, "they are coming again-in force".

The exhaust of the engines from the multitude of airplanes climbing westward was a sight to behold. The minimum interval takeoff had placed this large group of big birds in the air seconds apart and the turns by the various leads, designed to get everyone in their appropriate cell positions, became like a large canvas with many painters placing a stroke in the proper place. The high sun slightly to the west only accentuated the scene. One after another cells were making the appropriate join up calls, bronze cell checked in on the assigned discrete frequency. Again, there were some raw and funny comments concerning the launch and join up.

I wondered aloud if Don Bogue pulled his "pirate" flag back in prior to launch. As I had stated Don had a practice of putting a good size "skull and cross bones" flag out the pilot's window on the ground when taxiing, much to the delight of the crew chief of the airplane he was flying on that mission. There was a grunted "roger that" in a voice unmistakably the baritone of Bogue. It was a real thrill watching the aircraft in front of us climbing in trail. The black D was very obvious, silhouetted against the bright sunlight of this fading day. Everyone was scrambling for their spot in this incredible gaggle of airplanes as we reached for our altitude for the enroute portion of this significant event. The Ds would be hitting a tanker for their flight to and from the target, but the Gs would go unrefueled, a tactic that would not only shorten the mission, but would also deplete the fatigue factor. It had been determined that the G could effectively fly this mission without any additional fuel.

The level off at altitude was routine and now the only sound was the buzz of the various electronic equipment in 6503, silence reigned.

With the exception of the call for turns and changes in altitude, there was no radio traffic and there was also very little interphone chatter. Crews were settling into the allowed routine of getting comfortable. Inside our aircraft it was obvious the downstairs pair were alternating as the "station keeper" and the sleeper. The sun was setting pretty much in our face upstairs so I left my helmet on with my sun visor down. The co-pilot tried his sunglasses, but took my lead and went back to his helmet and visor. Finally, the sun was history, as the rapid travel to the west had accelerated its departure.

The reality of the mission was now apparent to all of us, as everyone in all the aircraft were going through the same drill of checking their own personal equipment for the upteenth time, and the aircraft equipment for which they were responsible. The bombing radar and the gunnery radar were most important, not only to hitting the assigned target, but also to sustain our ability to maintain cell integrity. Cell aircraft would inform the lead if they had a problem, and for now there was a merciful silence. We had a tight airplane, no problems with equipment, all eight engines running smoothly, everything humming right along, and yet you could sense the personal tension. The crews were all wondering the same thing. How would these tactics work? Would the Gs that were not modified be able to avoid the scrutiny of a talented gunner on the ground? Would they be as confused as we felt they would be?

Our approach did not require a turn of any high degree of bank after the initial turn from our northwest heading toward the target area, while still out to sea, however after release, we would make a turn to a southeast heading. I intended that to be a minimal bank for the formation. We would still have a short period over enemy territory where our belly would be exposed. We were counting on the massive approach to the target by aircraft from many headings at different altitudes in fingertip formation as an element that would place the gunners on the ground in a state of total disarray. We were hopeful that by the time they gathered their senses we would be back over the water heading home.

The usual wave type bombing that we had exposed the North Vietnamese to on earlier missions had allowed them to accurately set their weapons for our altitude and track, and if they missed the first wave, the second could be patiently expected on the same track and altitude. Now they would have one opportunity and one only as the entire group of Gs was programmed to hit various targets around Haiphong within sparse minutes and at different altitudes. The same applied to the mixed D and G force over Hanoi. This would widen some eyes, hopefully cause some confusion and cause general consternation with their command and control system. We were sure it would work. Silver cell and the other cells in our wave were now splitting off from the second and third waves in our group of Gs.

We were paralleling the coast of Vietnam close enough to make out the shoreline, but quite far enough out to feel a complete sense of safety. There were scattered streaks of light far in the distance as we passed Hue, more than likely some 'hundred millimeter' fire as it was certainly not threatening to us. As we approached Vinh, the activity increased, as someone had awakened the natives in that neighborhood and they were restless. The TAC (Tactical Air Command) guys were busy, along with the carrier based Navy pilots (how can you possibly land on a carrier at night? It must be really fun if you have taken a hit or two!), suppressing the SAM sites and dropping chaff. We understood the F-4s had the chaff assignment tonight, in an attempt to get lower and avoid the high winds that had plagued chaff effectiveness the first three days.

We could now see some fireworks in progress to the north and much farther inland towards Hanoi, but I couldn't discern a SAM firing yet. I'm sure they were waiting for us big guys, which was not a comfortable feeling. We had progressed to a point that I could make out the harbor and the city of Haiphong. Now they had some activity going on and although we couldn't see them, we knew the chaff F-4s and their escorts had penetrated into the lethal protective zone around the city. They were hitting the SAM sites and covering the area with a blanket of chaff to camouflage our approach from the east.

I couldn't make out any large ships in the harbor, but because of our politically sensitive civilian leaders, the ships of all countries had been warned to get out of town as the "buffs were coming". From my viewpoint I would have been happier if they weren't aware that we had an interest in that fair city to my left. Weren't those ships supporting the enemy with supplies that were intended to do harm to our countrymen? It was our impression that we were the expendable ones, not those who traveled in and out of that harbor with a sanction that prohibited our attacking them! It would be a nice show if we could be responsible for blocking their harbor with a hit on one of those large Libyan oil tankers, or better yet, a Russian cargo ship.

At this moment I wasn't worried about our fragile relationship with the Soviet Union, nor did I care one whit what our liberal press would report to the American public, or for that matter to the rest of the world. My rancor was interrupted when the navigator called for the turn that would allow us to approach the mainland from an almost due west heading, and to inform me there would be other sets of Gs directly to our left, to the south of us doing the same thing. We would all hit our targets within mere minutes of the same time, with our wave at a higher altitude and eventually paralleling and in some cases overflying the other waves on our exit. We would enter the Lethal SAM line just about landfall, turn southwesterly, bomb our target, and turn back out to sea, going feet wet within a couple of minutes after our release.

I gave the order for the wave to go echelon right, ascertained that all exterior illumination was indeed extinguished and called for radio silence. The bomb run was in progress with some real intense SAM indications now being seen in the distance toward Hanoi and also radar search modes of the SAM sites around Haiphong were evident to the EW. He gave no indication of anything more than a search mode, no "lock-on" as yet. The Radar was giddy with the bright return of his assigned target. He passed out some derogatory statement about even pilots could find this target as he and the navigator were running the bomb run checklist in a very casual fashion. The PDI hardly moved from 120 TTG to the point where I gave him second station at about 20TTG. A SAM flurry was seen well to our left, but didn't seem to be a threat to anyone. Now there was an obvious salvo of three SAMs to our right and well ahead of us. Almost directly off the nose, the sight of multiple SAM launches were evident, but in the distance. The hundred "mike-mike" was really intense, but below us.

Theodore Roosevelt said: "I think I could face death with dignity—so I shall not go into a war with any undue exhilaration of spirits or in a frame in any way approaching recklessness or levity". I wasn't feeling the least bit reckless, nor do I think there is anything funny about this mission! Press on.

The Ds going into Hanoi were taking a lot of fire as launch after launch of SA-2s and SA-3s were passing through what looked like our altitude and also one below us was exploding, lighting up the sky with a quick flash and a fading fire. There did not seem to be any hits! Fires in the distance were also very visible. 10 TTG, PDI centered, and no real sighting of a threat, no hyper activity from the EW. The call from the bomb aimer of "bombs away" was made. And in that instant I now had control of this beast and it was reacting to the sudden loss of our bomb load. In response to the abrupt nose up movement, I applied a heavy dose of nose down trim as I waited for my time to turn the aircraft. The navigator called down the time and cleared my turn and I started into a left bank back to sea. It was gentle and as I looked down, the area next to the harbor was in flames, not from the buffs, as our stores had a few seconds before their arrival on our programmed target, therefore some fighter jock had found his target not too long before our arrival.

All told there were four waves coming into the target areas near Haiphong, all from the sea, only one, far to the south, would not turn back to sea, but would overfly an area somewhat below Hanoi and exit into Laos. The G wave to the south of us was actually turning into, but under us, to further confuse the gunners below. As I continued to look down I saw a flurry of "hundred millimeter" fire below us and some SAM firings. However none seemed to have an evil motive for us, it was more a declaration of someone who felt he had to launch his missiles, even if he didn't have something in his cross hairs, so to speak. It was a salvo job to save face and hope it hit something in the air. As I rolled out of the turn and was heading southeast, the effects of the G bombs were now apparent. Fires were now raging to my right and left and looking back as far as I could to the left, secondary explosions were lighting the sky. Still there were no SAMs seen in the visible range of the pilots that we could feel had us as a target.

I had no trouble discerning when I was feet wet as the navigator startled the crew, informing us in a rather loud voice of our position over the water. The many fires, punctuated by the visible firing of the Vietnamese anti aircraft guns made the coastline very distinguishable. We were still within the SAM line though, so I was not about to gloat just yet. A few more minutes! It did feel like forever, but finally it was apparent we were in safe waters and out of harms way. There was a collective sigh of relief and as brave chatter filled the interphone, anyone could tell this was a happy and grateful crew.

Time to check the cell and wave composition. Abraham Lincoln once said about those who gave their life for their country "they paid the full measure of devotion". Hopefully, this night, we would not have to use that quote! One by one, bronze cell checked in, followed by the remainder of the cells within this wave. All the calls were similar, name of cell, "out with three", or "feet wet with three". I could recognize the ebullient voice of most of the cell leads who checked in and it was indeed a great feeling to know they were all OK. Everyone was reporting safely over the South China Sea and no damage from hits of any kind. I hoped that the results over Hanoi were the same.

I was to find out later that two Ds were lost, one taking a couple of direct hits and going down close to it's target, and the other hit very badly and making it back to U Tapao, only to lose control and explode on landing. A loss on that crew was an EW, Roy Tabler, who had been on one of my student B-58 crews when I was an instructor at Bunker Hill. He was a quiet, but efficient guy and was a very good EW.

As we got farther away from the coast line and very much out of the range of any meandering MIGs, we started to reform the waves for the return to Anderson. One after another, the cells fell into line, stacked up with 500 foot separation and one mile in trail. Running lights were back on as were the overwing lights for the minute, to facilitate visual join up. It didn't take too much time as the echelon formation had been very tight in order to afford mutual ECM protection for the waves. Now it was a matter of allowing the adrenaline to subside and make the long trek back to home base. For a second I wished we had flown out of UT, as they had such a short return flight from the targets. I then remembered that the crews out of U-Tapao could fly every day, as they did not compromise crew rest with their three to four hour flights. Our total time enroute, including the timing routines we flew, could go as high as fifteen or sixteen hours, thus we flew no more frequent than every other day.

I chuckled to myself as I remembered a flight I got involved with when I was a new second Lieutenant at Roswell New Mexico. I had been dating a young lady whose father was an instructor pilot in the 6th Bomb Wing, the 509th sister unit at Walker AFB before it moved to Pease. He asked me one evening if I would like to go for a ride in the B-36. It was a huge airplane, with six pusher type turbo-prop engines, plus four J-47 jet engines, the same one used on the B-47 that I was then checking out in as a co-pilot. I felt it was a bluff on his part, but I called it and said "sure". He indicated he would clear it with my squadron and let me know when the flight would take place. True to his word, my squadron operations officer, Major Mark Gilles called me up after roll call one bright Monday morning and informed me that I was scheduled to fly with the 6th BW on Wednesday. I was to report to Major Ward for mission planning purposes the next day.

On Tuesday I walked into the briefing and flight planning room and found Major Ward. He told me I couldn't help too much, as I was unfamiliar with the aircraft, but to sit with Lt. Cook, the co-pilot and he would go over his duties. Cookie and I had gone through the "basic" phase of our pilot training together at Laredo. He had always given me the feeling that he felt uncomfortable flying and gave every indication that he was totally frightened by the T-33, our jet trainer. The B-36 was indeed the right airplane for him. I stayed around long enough to get the particulars, when to report and what clothes to bring along and then left. They did tell me it would be a long flight, but not much else! The takeoff was actually going to be early Thursday morning, but the reporting time was late Wednesday night. I really wasn't prepared for any of the pre-takeoff process as there was a real crowd milling around that comprised this one crew.

I didn't see everyone and knew there were more crew members as they told me that the "back end" was picking up my three flight lunches. Three? The pre-flight was long and arduous and I wasn't even involved. Cookie explained the location of the various takeoff positions we would occupy, mine being by one of the gunner bubbles on the left side. A great view! It turned out that Cookie was actually the "third" Pilot and would be in the position exactly opposite me on the right side.

After an obscene period of time we were finally ready to start engines. I observed one after another of the big pusher blades rotate, belch black smoke and spring into life. The taxi was forever and the time on the hammerhead seemed to take more time than the preflight. Finally we took the active and started our roll and surprisingly the takeoff was actually covered in a very short distance down the runway prior to liftoff. Then the fun began! Looking out my bubble, the desert was now very visible as the sun was breaking the horizon. Our climb was at a rate that was embarrassing to this fighter pilot. It was an hour, or so it seemed, to get to our first cruising altitude. There were two radio operators and both were busy making various reports.

I hadn't seen Major Ward since I first reported and now Lt. Cook was preparing a spot to catch some Zs. Flight lunches were being passed out and I was asked if I wanted my hot lunch now or later. I wasn't hungry yet so just took my cold fried chicken lunch and sat back down in the bubble, looking at what was now the blank expanse of Texas below, and opened the juice. It was hours before anyone addressed me again and it was one of the radio operators who told me that Major Ward would like to see me in the cockpit. I felt like asking for directions, but managed to find the "upstairs" pilot location without help, although the path was somewhat busy with the large navigator team milling around their station and an older captain I remembered from yesterday.

There was an empty seat beside the major and he motioned for me to sit down. The captain I had passed on the way forward must have been the real co-pilot. I sat down and fastened the seat belt around my waist. The good major took great pains to show me the intricacies of the cockpit. It was on autopilot and seemed to jerk a bit every time I touched the wheel. He also indicated that the co-pilot was going aft to get some bunk time. I wondered why he didn't bring Cook up, but didn't mention it as I sort of liked being in this fish bowl, looking out from a very lofty perch on what looked like endless desert. It sure beat lying around in the back of the aircraft as I had not brought any reading material. I literally spent hours in the seat, sometimes taking it off AP and flying this huge cigar of an airplane manually. It was a handful!

Darkness fell and I can remember being surprised at the altitude we were at for some simulated bomb runs on Houston. We were at 47,000 ft. I had never been above 35,000 in pilot training or in the initial stages of the B-47 checkout. The co-pilot had returned to the seat for the bomb runs and after they were finished, Major Ward told me to get in his seat as he needed some rest. We flew navigation legs over the Gulf of Mexico, bombed Cuba (simulated of course and before Castro), flew up the East Coast of Florida and climbed to 51,000 ft. The sun had risen and set and we were still in the air. I actually ate my three meals, slept for an hour or two and still didn't get any indication when we would land. Finally, I was told to take a landing position and wandered back to my "bubble".

Cook had gotten a lot of sack time, but never once went forward to "fly" the aircraft and was now strapping in for the descent to Walker AFB. He could have waited, as this very large bird was actually descending in large circles over southern New Mexico. The sun was rising and we were still going in circles, there was no hurry to get this thing on the ground! Mercifully, the gear was finally unlocked. It was closer to being pushed down, as you could actually hear the various degrees of motion as it cranked lower. It too, was in no hurry! Aloud clunk, clunk gave me the indication that the gear was down. Final approach and landing was made in full daylight. After parking I clamored out of the aircraft and then while stretching my weary body outside the airplane I saw eight people exit the rear section of the aircraft, that I had not seen before. They had exited through a rear entry door of the aircraft and upon questioning, I found out they were in the bunk/kitchen area! We had been airborne for almost twenty-five hours.

The B-36 was an incredible beast! It looked like a pregnant cigar with wings that were so wide at the root a crew chief could walk inside, stand up straight and work on systems within the spars. Someone at one time felt it would be the new bomber. I'm sure it was a formidable weapon system, but it wasn't for me. I was becoming very happy with the B-47, despite it's long takeoff role and its reputation of not being a friendly aircraft, especially on takeoff. For a lot of reasons that are too long to enumerate I would not fly the B-36 again and that was despite the fact that Major Ward had been very kind to me and actually logged almost sixteen hours of flying time in my behalf. I know I spent at least that much time in the seat. (I'm not sure the airplane was a factor, but I didn't date his daughter again). I would stick to the six or seven hour B-47 flights, and was satisfied to not be confronted with the "challenge" to fly that big bird again.

The flight back on day eight, like the return on the 18th, was once again peaceful and very quiet. The same sense of relief and accomplishment settled over me. How many more trips would I have to take up north? The odds were going to narrow a bit with each return mission. It was very serene going over the Pacific as the Philippines slipped by, outlined by a myriad of lights on the land and spilling into the surrounding ocean. It was easy to feel giddy on return flights. The sense of relief was very powerful and as always I was in no hurry to get back on the ground. The remainder of the flight was quiet as only an occasional heading change and altitude adjustment was announced from the navigator and passed on to the cell. The flight lunches were finished and conversation picked up in the aircraft as the sun cracked the horizon.

Time for the visor to thwart the sun, and a crew warning to get ready for the descent. We had been in radar contact for some time and when 180 nautical miles of Anderson, we were cleared to start an enroute penetration. This was normal as it would be terrifically time consuming to make a "teardrop" for the massive number of "birds" coming back to roost. The enroute controller passed bronze lead and flight off to approach control. Another "welcome back" boomed into our ears as we made our initial call. It was certain to be another beautiful morning on the island as there were no clouds and unlimited visibility as we started our descent.

Guam people advertise themselves as "Hafadi, where the day begins" and day nine was now really starting in beautiful fashion. The approach and landing were uneventful and once again we exited the runway, taxied to a parallel, opened our bomb doors and were examined for a release of all our twenty-seven bombs. Cleared, we proceeded to our assigned slot and cut the engines, cleaned out our gear and exited the aircraft. "Not a scratch", I was told by a grateful crew chief, "nice job". It's nice to be appreciated, I thought, but even better I was happy that we had brought back the chief's airplane with us in it.

The air was delicious, in fact it was actually cool, probably only around seventy five degrees, and we made sure the bus windows were down to enjoy it on the ride to debriefing. I had finished with the maintenance debriefing when I saw the "Smiling Jack" of the temporary duty pilots, Robbie, walk through the door gesturing to Herb about something. I walked over to find them laughing about the fact that the December 26th mission had gone so well. We had not lost a G, and at that time we were not aware of the D losses. Now joining in, we all agreed that we didn't see any SAMs fired with a deadly purpose from the briefed three sites around Haiphong. All of us had different targets and all of us felt that the enemy gunners near our targets never got it together.

We were joined by other pilots, as they sauntered into the debriefing area and they shared the same opinion. At the intelligence debrief similar statements were coming out about the targets around Hanoi. However, they informed us that two Ds bought it in that vicinity, and crews in their respective wave might have a different thought about the night. The powers to be though were convinced that the enemy was not only confused by the short 22 minutes for all TOT (time on target) for the entire force, but in total disarray in response to the tactics utilized. With that knowledge I grabbed a small bottle of "medicinal" brandy for the walk back to my barracks and began to think about the "frag" for today and how the "G" success would play on the now planned sorties for tomorrow.

It was really quiet in the squadron area. It was, of course very early, and I was the first crew through debriefing, the others were still discussing last night's events when I left. Then, also, tonight's fliers were still in crew rest. I walked into the office, doors wide open as usual and found no one there. I sat down at the desk and opened my short bottle. It was a very settling drink, sipping just a taste at a time until the too few ounces were exhausted. I waved at a couple of crews as they walked past the door and almost fell out of my swivel chair. All at once I was glad I hadn't taken two of those medicinal bottles as I wouldn't have made it the thirty steps to my room. I decided not to look at the list of tonight's day nine fliers, sitting right in front of me. The list was anchored on the desk with one of my paperweights, an empty 20 mm shell casing. Instead I got up and wove an unsteady path to my room and fell into bed. I did remember getting out of my flight suit and boots, but there was no shower.

I woke up with a start, not knowing the time or for a second, the place. I rolled my feet out of the bed and noticed I had slept through the pre-takeoff briefing for tonight. I showered and put on a fresh flight suit and my shower clogs and walked to the office. I felt amazingly rested. It had been the longest sleep I could remember since arriving on the island in September. I gathered the schedule and poured a cup of coffee, while ignoring Al Sweney, my counterpart squadron commander in this squadron office. Herb and Hinch had their office in the real BOQ (bachelor officer quarters) much closer to the club, but a lot farther from bomber operations.

Al was a very strange guy, very knowledgeable of the B-52, a favorite of Colonel Rew, and used often to help on aircraft emergencies due to his expertise, but he had the personality of a closed door. He muttered something about last night and I told him it was a "no brainer". I chose to study the crew alignment and he involved himself in some papers in front of him. I had seven crews flying, a couple of which were from Mather and belonged to Al's squadron on Guam, but I considered them mine. John Mook, from Beale was scheduled, but was still DNIF and was being replaced by Captain York, one of my Barksdale aircraft commanders. It was a very experienced lineup. I wondered aloud where the targets were and Al said all the Gs were going downtown, Hanoi. No milk run to Haiphong! Twenty-one Gs in all, somewhat less than the forty-five of last night, but I felt they were all modified with the latest ECM gear, and that might have been the extent of available aircraft.

A couple of Al's crews walked in, but ignored him and sat on or around my desk. They were curious about their rotation back home as they had reached the magic time to re-deploy. The Air Force would have to give them credit for a full tour if they went over 180 days TDY (temporary duty), and those personnel folks were not about to let that happen. I had a list of crews going home on the next flight out and both crews were listed. They were very pleased as the Guam version of the "freedom bird" was leaving before they could fly another mission. They virtually raced out of the squadron, I assume to get things together for the trip home 24 hours away.

I left the squadron shortly afterwards, curious about the specific targets, and went to where the frag was organized. I found the same mission planners that I had talked to on Christmas, hard at work. It was a short list of targets for the Gs as all twenty-one were going to the Lang Dang railroad yards. A very bad spot, with good gunners. I asked about the tactics and the target selection folks said they were basically the same as last night, but did not provide any details. They were busy trying to select targets for day ten, looking at BDA(bomb damage assessment) and mating that with other intelligence data to ascertain what targets needed more work.

I left feeling awfully hungry and weighed watching the launch or going to the club. I drove to the flight line and pulled through the gate and made my way to a known vantage point and watched the first seven or eight Ds go and decided to get some food. However, I needed to do something first! It was now a typical Guam mid-afternoon, hot and humid. I turned and went back to the room, changed into my running shorts, grabbed my shoes that I always left outside my front door to drain the water (known as sweat to the non-athletes) after runs, and bolted down the stairs. I ran by the mess hall, down the road towards the VOQ (visiting officers quarters), now being used by all the "Charlies" and their maintenance counterparts.

I started running on the triangle field that I often used for my run, as it was handy to the squadron and they would find me there if I was needed. My normal run on Guam was about three to four miles, and once done it felt great to shower and let the endorphins run wild. I cruised back after a few rotations around the triangle and found "Smiling Jack" hanging around my room waiting for me. He wanted to talk to me about last night's mission and started into a litany of the tactics of the mission and how we should have used them all along. Then without hesitation he said that the first two nights probably lulled the powers to be into attempting the disastrous third night raids. I felt that the second night was the key as we fared very well despite the many SAM launches and the near misses that were recorded including my close encounter.

The planners at SAC more than likely became over-confident with the success of day two and the minimal loss figure. Robbie, now joined by a couple of passing crew members seemed to agree with my assessment. Then Robbie threw me a curve and asked me if I would go as the airborne commander in the jump seat with him on the next mission he would fly. The jump seat was not my favorite viewing or comfort position on a flight when you are being shot at. It means in order to exit the burning building your riding in, if necessary, you must go downstairs and roll out of the navigator's hole once he has fired his downward ejection seat.

I guess I must have looked at him in a funny way as he smiled that crooked smile of his, furrowed his always furrowed brow a bit more, and said absolutely nothing. The others standing there looked at me as if they were expecting an answer and suddenly an involuntary voice rose up from within me and said, "sure, why not"! I wondered who said that and realized it was me. Robbie replied "great" and sauntered away, seemingly happy with himself and began to whistle a bit as he looked back and repeated his "great" statement. I was stuck and I knew it. I not only had agreed to go with him on a mission up north but he had witnesses to my agreeing to going. Now, I had flown with Robbie on a number of missions and I was no stranger to the jump seat as that is the normal IP position when evaluating a crew, but this was different.

Others had done this on such missions, namely Colonel Rew and Colonel McCarthy, and returned successfully not once, but twice. However then there was Keith Hagen, who flew with Jim Nagahiro on day three, he didn't make it! We weren't sure of his fate on this day, but we knew that Jim and his radar were POWs and we hadn't heard anything about Keith, which was a very bad indicator. Oh well, as I have been wont to say "fate is the hunter". We'll find out soon enough! Erich Remarque described "chance" as "hovering", and that the existence of chance makes those who are in war, "indifferent". I will continue to call it fate and I'm far from indifferent!

As it turned out day nine was once again very good for the G model aircraft. The 21 Gs out of Anderson all returned and reported very little enemy action against them. The final report indicated no more than six SAMs were expended during the very similar approach to their target, the Lang Dang railroad yards, utilizing the same tactics as our sorties did on day eight. The news wasn't all good however, as one of the Ds out of U Tapao, Cobalt lead, was shot down during its run against the Trung Quan railroad yards. The crew was one of mine from Mather. The aircraft commander, Captain Frank Lewis, was a fiery young pilot, who had a veteran crew. The radar navigator was Major Al Johnson, one of the best in the 441st bomb squadron. I was stunned when I heard the news of their loss and could relate to the turmoil that was going to ensue back home.

Rosemary would be up to her ears in the task of ministering to the wives of the crew members and addressing their needs. I would make every attempt to find out their status through the channels that were available to me. At the present moment I needed a drink and wasn't up to the task of calling home to see if the news of Lewis' crew going down had been received at Mather. I decided to wait and let the official word get there before I got involved. There was absolutely nothing I could do anyway. I aimlessly proceeded to the club and pulling up I saw a group of crew members walking into the club. As luck would have it, one of the crews was that of Ted Goronowski, a very good and experienced, but sometimes a bit too intense, AC from the 441st bomb squadron at Mather.

"Goro" saw me and stopped to wait for me to park my truck. As I approached he sort of held up his hands and asked me if I knew of any survivors out of Cobalt 01, Frank Lewis' aircraft. I said I didn't know except that I had heard from Intel that numerous beepers were heard after the aircraft was hit. Visual accounts from the returning crews indicated a direct hit shortly after the bombs were released. The aircraft, when last seen, was burning wildly and seemed under control, though in a slight descent. I felt that the crew from those accounts were now POWs, and told that to Goro, though I had no verification of that being the case. He nodded and turned to join his crew. I entered the club again to the welcome coolness of the interior, and heard the strains of "Yellow River" and smiled as I remembered the ruckus that the song and other favorites had caused. I would never hear that song again that I wouldn't think of the Anderson O'Club and this time frame and what it meant to these homesick crews.

I walked into the dining area to find a full house and was greeted by a few shouts of "the sheriff has arrived". I waved to the unseen crowd and turned and retreated to the bar. It was quiet in there, a few of the permanent party were hanging around and nodding discretely to me. A couple of crew dogs were sitting around sipping something cool in an attempt to forget either yesterday or tomorrow. It was still December and for many in the states it was time to relax and forget their work. All of the crews knew that unless they had an urgent reason to do so, there were very few people back home who even were aware that there was a war going on. It didn't so much bother us that they didn't know, but it did bother us a great deal, that they didn't care!

The thought of flying a mission in the jump seat crossed my mind as I saw one of my oldest and best friends sitting at the end of the bar, sucking on a beer. Jim Denson was a big, broad shouldered brute of a man. When talking to you he would peer into your eyes and give the impression that he could read the innermost secrets of your soul and then purse his lips and utter statements in such a manner that he confirmed that he had that psychic gift. I sidled up to the stool next to his and said "hi". He nodded and looked at me, but didn't say anything. Finally after a long silent period he asked how I felt about getting drunk tonight, which meant that he was well on the way and was looking for company. The thought seemed pleasant and I said something to the effect that it was a great idea, but I didn't have time. He chuckled his very familiar little laugh and went back to his beer.

This was the normal conversation these days as the other questions centered on the next night's mission and who was flying. Most knew the answers to those topics so it became a bit mundane to even bring anything up. Such was the ways of our war and I would assume, all wars. Jim and I went to dinner and ate without too much conversation. We had been stationed together since our first duty assignment out of pilot training, flown the same airplanes, been in the same wings, knew each other's wives and children, and had the same admiration for each other's skills. Therefore the meal and the night passed with nothing more than grunts and nods. We did discuss briefly the loss of Frank Lewis and his crew last night but it was not an emotional discussion, only a professional opinion on what might have transpired. Both of us agreed that being in the wrong place at the wrong time can be deadly and that based on the witness reports all of the crew should have gotten out of the "burning building". Fate or chance had not been in their corner.

Day ten dawned! Another beauty of a day, and true to form it was hot and humid. Nothing changes except the crews flying tonight are different than those who flew last night. It was obvious from the frag for tonight that we were running out of targets and the BDA we were receiving from the SR-71 photos confirmed that fact. Every photo showed pinpoint bombing accuracy and almost total destruction of the targets. There was no apparent capability by the North Vietnamese to re-supply their defensive stores. Airdromes had no operational runways for heavy aircraft operation or for fighter launches. The harbor at Haiphong was totally blocked with the hulks of ships that ignored the warnings to get out, and mines that were dropped to blockade movement.

If there was a piece of railroad track capable of supporting a locomotive, it had to be in the northern most part of the country. There was not a track system that was intact. We could not see any rolling stock that was not on its side or literally in pieces. There were no fighter aircraft that could be seen except those destroyed on the ground. With all of this evidence and with some degree of concern for a couple of targets and for still existing SAM sites, the command decided to launch a total of only 30 aircraft from Guam and a mere half of them would be Gs. There was to be another 30 aircraft going up north from U-Tapao. Fifteen G aircraft was less than we flew on normal "Bulletshot" days so finding rested crews was really easy. The logistics for that effort were therefore minimal so it gave all of us some time to think ahead to tomorrow.

Yes, there would be some flights going on the next Linebaker raids. In two days this supposed fact would include Robbie, and his squadron commander in the jump seat. However, more news worthy and popular right now was the fact that it was announced there was to be a show coming to the island for everyone to see. As was his scheme for the Christmas season, Bob Hope was coming through on one of his morale boosting war (yes, contrary to popular opinion, there is a war going on) tours on his way back from Vietnam. It would be an around noon show on the twelfth day, so even if I flew I might be able to see him before launch.

That is if I fly on day twelve. I was having second thoughts about my agreement. How could I not fly though as I knew Robbie and his Barksdale crew would go, and I had promised him I would ride in the jump seat? I wonder if I could step in that hole on the triangle field I run in. Could I possibly break a leg? Fat chance of that as I couldn't close my eyes long enough or tight enough to hit my leg in the hole. At any rate Bob Hope would offer good fodder for the next few night's conversations, better by far than our normal fare.

Today's launch went without a ripple and almost no fanfare. All thirty aircraft launched in a very compressed and smooth fashion. Not being anywhere close to a source of the communication traffic, I couldn't discern if there was even a "bag drag" that took place. We had reverted to an almost normal atmosphere, crews were seen sun bathing, going to the gym, running, drinking beer in the afternoon and generally being their home sick selves. I, for one, felt a great sense of relief. A burden of preparing crews and selecting crews to fly was now again a routine matter.

I could get on with a normal pattern of getting things done and right now I better start preparing recommendations for awards and decorations for all the crew members who have already flown missions or it will never get done. This was a chore I didn't relish as everyone felt that they contributed in a special way and despite having to deal with a "hit", their fear factor was every bit as real as that of those, who under an extreme emergency performed in an heroic and now public fashion. Being in the "lethal" SAM area was reason enough to merit an award of some kind. Oh well, that would never fly, but the crews were understanding of the rationale, so I would do what I could and work the system to give them the recognition they deserved.

I worked very late that evening in an attempt to catch up with my squadron duties. I had received another call from George Lockhart's father. It must have been in the early morning hour from where his home was in Virginia. He was certain that we had information that we had not divulged about his son. I had been advised beforehand by Colonel Rew that he might call and that I could tell him everything I knew. This wasn't too much more than I knew in our previous conversations. I was using information that I had received from other eye witness crew reports and the subsequent information we received through other channels which wasn't too uplifting. What I knew was that it was a catastrophic explosion of Randy Cradducks fully loaded aircraft.

Those who saw it did not feel there was a chance of survival, however some say they did hear beepers. This was little solace however, as day three being the disaster it was, they could have come from other aircraft. The "hit" happened at a very critical point inbound to the target when other aircraft crews were experiencing their own personal hell and couldn't be held accountable for what was happening to other aircraft.

There was an unsubstantiated report that the gunners name was released as a POW, which if true could work both ways. It did hold out hope that there were more survivors, as the gunner in the G model B-52 sits in the forward, upper section of the aircraft. On the other hand, why weren't we hearing more names from that crew? Eighth Air Force was receiving names of some of those who went down in the sixth and seventh day. I told most of this to the father, who was a retired Air Force Colonel, without mentioning my own thoughts, and knew he could sort out the facts. He had to know the chances of his son's survival were very remote. After I hung up I felt this sudden loss of perspective. Here I was working on awards and decorations to satisfy the living and I was saddened that I was helpless to do anything for those that were lost.

I decided my heart wasn't in it and walked out into the night oblivious to the rain now coming down in a steady fashion. I walked to bomber ops to ascertain the results of day ten's activity. I sought out my usual sources, a bit wary of the possibility of any negative reports of the mission, however the results were all positive. The crew reports were very factual and straight to the point. All the Buffs released on target and were now over the fence safely. It was a zero loss night! HF(high frequency) traffic indicated very little opposition, no fighters sighted and few SAMs launched and none in a threatening fashion. It appeared that our analysis of the enemy's capacity to wage war was accurate and that it was at a very low ebb.

Hopefully they were not just loading up for tomorrow! Upon the G model crews arrival back at Anderson and while they were in debriefing, those that I talked to said pretty much the same thing. There were very few threats and the SAMs that were fired seemed to be fired with no purpose except to launch them. The pinpoint precision that prevailed the first few days from the gunners on the ground was no longer apparent. Some hundred-millimeter ("mike mike") was seen, but it did not have the carpet effect at the lower altitudes that the crews had seen on early missions. The real analysts shared our thoughts and were guardedly optimistic that the assessment of the BDA damage that we had seen was very accurate and that re-supply of the gun emplacement sites was virtually impossible.

Maybe going back north in the jump seat the day after tomorrow wouldn't be so bad after all. It could be just a walk in the park! Fat chance, but today's mission will give us a little more verification of the real status of the enemy, and if there is a repeat of day ten I will be a lot more relaxed than I have been on the previous two flights I've had up north.

One thing that has come out of this so far "ten day" war using the buffs up north, is that the B-52 drivers have finally been recognized by their fighter counterparts as playing a significant role in the Vietnam encounter. There has always been a tendency by fighter pilots to look down their noses at the bomber guys, not so much for their flying ability, but for the type of aircraft they fly. The role of the "Buff" in the "downtown" raids has turned the heads of the fighter guys and there is a new respect for the big ugly fat fella. It's still a bomber though so the attitude among the fighter jocks will be the same behind the squadron doors. I'm not worried though as I've flown the hottest airplane in the world in the B-58, much hotter than anything we have in country. There are virtually no aircraft that can stay with the 58 in most environments. It had sustained speed, great maneuverability, unparalleled climb capability and it was a single pilot airplane.

However to many it was still a bomber as it had a B in front of its number and it had additional crew members. I've flown the F-102 and the F-106 and various single pilot trainers, and I've talked to my friends who have flown either the F-4 or the F-105 and the B-58 and our opinion is the same, none could hold a candle to the Hustler. I remember one day flying the B-58 we were scheduled to have a fighter intercept mission for an F-106 outfit from some northern base. We were a single aircraft playing the enemy for the fighters to make some passes on us. It was training for the fighters, but it was sheer boredom for my crew, George Holt, the radar and Bob McCormack, the defensive systems officer and myself. We flew straight and level at a flight level around 30,000 ft. Once the intercept was under way, with two 106s in pursuit, we settled in to maintain a constant airspeed.

The ground controller asked us to reduce our speed from normal cruise of .96 mach as the fighters were not gaining on us. Being the good guy that I am, I throttled back to pick up a lower speed. This was not sufficient, so once again I throttled back to the point that my angle of attack was more appropriate for takeoff and climb rather than level flight. Now the B-58, because of its large delta wing, doesn't have stall characteristics similar to other aircraft. It just falls without warning like a leaf leaving a tree. I was managing to keep the aircraft on a step without losing altitude when we spotted the first of the two aircraft making a high angle attack from the seven to eight o'clock position. The second aircraft wasn't too far behind him in timing from about a three o'clock position. They passed in silence after announcing a simulated weapon launch and promptly asked if we would stay around for another pass.

I agreed as I had the fuel and the time and I always want to be nice to other pilots. Again we couldn't pick up speed as their wide-angle turns were killing distance and their ability to close. Finally the two were in a position to make one last set of passes. As the second aircraft came by from four o'clock, he turned parallel to my track, drove in front of me, thanked me for accommodating them and thrust his aircraft into a roll similar to a victory roll familiar to fighter pilots everywhere. Fortunately I had been bringing up my power as they were closing and was now incensed that this guy was (in my opinion) insulting my aircraft. I pushed all four throttles into AB (afterburner), watched my airspeed creep through .97mach, caught the malingering hot dog, insured I was by him and did the best roll of my life.

It did startle him and I'm sure the wake turbulence had some adverse effects on his control surfaces, as he called out "good show" in an awed and trembling voice. I was satisfied I had made my point and now had to pull the throttles back before I had an unscheduled flight above Mach 1. Yes I flew a bomber, but it was hot and could handle anything around. I loved that airplane and wouldn't have traded my time in it for any other bird in the inventory. The "rap" that the bomber guys lived with was that their aircraft wasn't "hot". The show the "buffs" put on was something the fighter guys could only think about as our results over 10 days had placed all aircraft flying combat missions in a position of flying milk runs over the "north". I knew that every fighter guy, who would like to be flying those "milk runs", admired our work. That was truly gratifying!

AN ENEMY DEFEATED AND POLITICS

Day Eleven was dawning and a driving rainstorm that had swept in from the south of the Marianas awakened me. I could have stayed in bed a bit longer, however we were back in a mode of having morning standup plus I couldn't get my phone conversation with Colonel Lockhart last night out of my mind. It kept gnawing at me, as I considered the other downed crew members, some of whom we knew were alive, among them Frank Lewis from Mather, who was seen on TV, but were now POWs and then there were others that we had no information on whatsoever. So I got up and prepared for this bombing day as I have most of the others, except now there was an air of confidence that the enemy was truly finished. My fear and that of others who had witnessed our political meandering at home was that someone would get cold feet and feel we were being too harsh on our foes in the north of Vietnam.

There was no doubt that they had lost their capacity to wage war. If we would just continue to fly minimal sorties against them, there was no way they could recover as they could not defend themselves any longer and there were no means to restock their war machine. However we have talked about the existing western mentality allowing the beaten guy to get back up and then come back at you at a later date and knock you back on your heels. McNamara was a wizard at this practice and subsequently caused the early stages of this war to be almost comical in its tactical evolvement.

I have heard other military authorities who declared publicly that if we had been allowed to bomb the north with the idea that we would destroy their capacity to wage war, it would have taken less than ninety days to end the war, and that was in the early stages. However Mr.

Mac in his great military wisdom ignored the Clauswitz theory and allowed our pilots to fly in and go for meaningless targets in operation "Rolling Thunder", another dismal failure that resulted in filling the "Hanoi Hilton" with downed and frustrated pilots. Tactically it was a disaster and all of us here were hoping against hope that we did not repeat the mistake again and that was despite the fact that none of us enjoyed flying over the north. It would be a long time before we had an adversary in this position again. But that wasn't our call. We would just have to wait and see what road our most astute political leaders would take and we of course would comply, as that was our fate.

It was again going to be a light day for all of us and especially the G model crews as only twelve sorties were fragged. Once again we were going to hit the Lang Dang railroad yards and we also were going after the SAM support and storage areas. I left the half-empty theater in the middle of the briefing as I was asked to talk to one of the wives of a member of my squadron crews that had been shot down earlier. She was at her husband's home base in Blytheville, Arkansas and had asked through channels if she could talk to the squadron commander of the deployed squadron. I had no information that she had not already been furnished, however she asked to talk to me and I was asked to please put in a call back to her. I was getting a little stressed out with my losses and the fact that I was being asked to make such calls, however it was part of the territory.

I called my wife first and she also informed me that the spirits of the wives back home were somewhat improved as they had seen pictures of Frank Lewis as a POW in Hanoi. I asked if there was any information on the other members of the crew and she said that Frank was the only one so far. I told her that things were looking better over here and to tell the wives that we were confident that the flights north were now much more tolerable and safe as the enemy was badly beaten. After that brief conversation, I called to talk to the wife I had been asked to call. She had heard unofficially that her husband was now a POW and seemed overjoyed. I asked who had given her the information, as we were not informed of that news. She said it came from the squadron at Blytheville. I told her it was great news, but to wait for an official announcement. She was so sure though and I didn't want to take away any joy from her news, so said something to the effect that it was indeed great and I would talk to her later.

I walked out on the balcony to see the first aircraft going down the runway, it's water firing and the black smoke from the engines sweeping over the runway. It was followed by the sounds of other aircraft going in the same direction, but the smoke completely obscured the runway, so all I could see was the top of the "D" tails cutting like giant shark fins down the active. It was thrilling to watch and I stood mesmerized at the sight and the sound. The smoke cleared a bit as the first "G" took the runway, it's camouflaged torso throwing water as it turned onto the runway. It straightened out and the water fired and then headed into the dark misty smoke that now permeated the landscape. I looked towards the east and could see the trails of the first three "D" aircraft going into a join up maneuver. I then saw the first "G" rising above the terrain, looking like any other aircraft, except that I knew what he carried in his belly and where he was going to dispose of his "load".

It was a feeling of awe, but also one of concern as that aircraft carried a crew of six, and there was no guarantee that they might not end up in the wrong place at the wrong time. (That thought of "Fate is the hunter" crossed my mind, but I thrust it away. It did, however keep creeping back). As I did often during these days I uttered a prayer for their safety. Turning away, I was caught up in an euphoric moment. What if this was the last day of this type of action? What if the North Vietnamese surrendered? Wow, what a nice thought! We could all go see Bob Hope, and then go home. The thought vaporized as quickly as it appeared though and I knew there was a fat chance of that happening. Anyway it was time to go restock the refrigerator with beer, as the San Miguel was getting low. The crews needed their beer during this "hot" time, and I wasn't referring to the weather.

After the replenishment operation, I returned to the squadron and once again started to work on the awards and decorations. This was a thankless job and though I had enlisted some help earlier, I was now alone trying to write a standard justification for the various flights. All of this resulted in nothing more than a flight into the SAM infested airspace above the city of Hanoi, avoiding any catastrophic activity, releasing the stores on target, being scared witless, and getting back safely. No one in the higher echelon running this war at Pacific Air Force headquarters (PACAF, safely headquartered in Hawaii), would consider it remotely worthy of a medal, yet they were free as could be with giving medals to some other factions in this war.

We would see the bench ridden fighter pilot mentality against bomber activity in the award of decorations to the buff guys. You could bet on it! But I would continue to try to find the correct words as I was convinced that these crews deserved recognition. Some of my crews had flown four missions over Hanoi, and some of the crews at U Tapao had flown seven and eight times. It doesn't sound like much? Try holding a two hundred ton aircraft, laden with a full bomb load, steady on course when you know a SAM is coming up your tailpipe and you have to hold heading through release and then some. You are sitting in the cross hairs of a gunner on the ground that knows you aren't going to maneuver to escape his weapon. I'm convinced that I have to find the right words to insure these guys are recognized.

Robbie walks in and I plop him down in a chair and tell him to get to work. He laughs and complies. We work well into the evening and then decide to get something to eat and maybe even a cool beer or two. The wind is really whipping through the open doors and it's very hot and sticky. My flight suit will need to be washed before I ride in that jump seat tomorrow as my body odor is up to the barely acceptable smell level. We take the stairs down like two possessed men and head for wheels to take us to the club. I'm hungry and very thirsty and ready for anything, especially anyone who has a stupid remark about my going north in the jump seat.

The club is not overly busy and that is a good indication that the crew members have gone back into a semi relaxed mode. Now, crews are going other places to eat and drink. The bar and its coolness were very enticing, however after the obligatory beer and some small talk with a couple of crews, we recognized our crew rest requirements for tomorrow's flight and wandered into the dining room to eat. The dining room was buzzing with rumors of a stand down tomorrow. When queried, I pleaded no contest as I hadn't heard a thing about no flying and in fact was told we were going as scheduled and that the "frag" was being finalized. When we finished eating, I decided I would stop by bomber Ops, just to check.

Everyone there was working, which was a sure sign that we were going, and I even got some not so stupid digs thrown at me about flying in the jump seat for the mission. I was uncomfortable with that, but shrugged it off as a routine, but genuine concern. I didn't fool anyone though as they kept reminding me that I would have to follow the downstairs navigators through their ejection holes if we had to leave the aircraft. I had to remember all of these guys preparing the mission targets were radar navigators. I reminded them that I was fast and might even beat the upstairs pilots out. Now convinced that the flight was going, I casually asked if any information had come back from the 11th day crews and they told me that all reports were in and that there were no losses. Also the information included the fact that there was little or no resistance. Some SAMs were sighted but there was no indication that anyone experienced any problems. Tomorrow's mission was looking more and more like a piece of cake. I decided to retreat to my room, put on my shorts and go down to the laundry room and wash some things. There was no one in the laundry room so finished quickly and got back up stairs to my room. I was suddenly very tired so put my clean flight suit over to the side with my boots and got into bed. I was not experiencing any great feeling of anticipation for the mission and once in bed, fell immediately asleep. The "Wolf" was not bothering me tonight!

BOB HOPE'S VISIT

The morning standup was going to be handled by Major O'Donnell, so I stayed in bed a bit longer, but finally got up, as I couldn't stand lying in bed any longer. My mind was working overtime trying to out think our political oriented leaders. Would they roll back again and allow the NVA an opportunity to regroup or would they sustain pressure on the enemy until they gave up. Henry Kissenger, hopefully was no McNamara!

The monotonous weather was just one factor in wishing I could leave Guam. It just never cooled down and the humidity was outrageous. I should not complain though as I had air conditioning in just about every place that I spent time (the squadron was an exception, but the wind through the front door and out the back was like a warm fan most of the time). I also had to remember that the guys working on my plane were in tents and metal buildings and their only source of coolness was from the hot island breezes. I stepped outside and thought for a minute about walking to the club for breakfast, but changed my mind when I felt the rain beginning to fall. I ran to my truck, got in and decided to go by bomber ops one more time just to make sure I was flying today. You can't say I wasn't persistent!

Nothing there seemed to have changed. Everything I heard indicated it was still a go, but there seemed to be a feeling that maybe something was going on. I didn't pursue it though and hurried to see if I could catch the group that went to standup. They might have more information. I sprinted into the club, avoiding what was now a good downpour. I found them still lounging in the dining area, all sitting by the window watching the rain that would stop before we walked out and eating their favorite fare, eggs benedict. I found a spot at the end of the table, poured some coffee, and casually asked if there was any indication at standup if tonight's sorties were canceled. They looked at me sort of funny and replied almost in unison that everything was going to proceed as planned, however there was some talk, though guarded, that the missions tonight would be held back. We were to be briefed and would target study and go to our airplanes until we were officially told to cancel.

They told me that Colonel Rew had given the first contribution to the OWC Christmas tree fund for the items destroyed on our infamous night before standown. There was an implicit requirement for contributions from the TDY troops and that started with the G squadron commanders. Naturally everyone would kick in for this fine cause. After all the permanent party needed their decorations. The conversation then quickly switched to the Bob Hope show, which was to begin shortly after noon. With any luck they would cancel the sorties early and I could make the show. I ate breakfast and left the group and I was still contemplating their discussion on the scheduled sorties for the day. I wanted to find Robbie and let him know what was going on. I found him still in bed and quickly rousted him. I told him that after the pre takeoff briefing, I would go back to the squadron and get some work done and that he and his crew could finish the prefight and I would come out in time to taxi if there wasn't a cancellation.

I went back to the squadron and tried to put in a call home, but all the lines were busy, so returned to some routine correspondence and then again buried myself in the awards and decorations task. A few pilots came in to discuss their rotation home for their generous twenty eight days R&R and one of them noted that the Bob Hope show was to start shortly. I didn't feel I should leave the squadron just yet so delayed while I weighed whether to go to the show or not. As is my nature, I finally decided that it was too late and that I might as well go directly to the aircraft. I finished some letters to a couple of the families of my missing crew members and was about to leave when Robbie waltzed in.

The mission was officially cancelled, the President had halted what was now the Eleven Day war. Evidently the North Vietnamese saw no sense in what was happening to them and asked to return to the truce negotiations. The results of our continued bombing had reduced them to rubble. The war was virtually won. Our BDA assessments were right on. The North Vietnamese were isolated from the world. There was no conceivable method they could utilize to re-supply their forces in the northern portion of the country or to sustain support for the Viet Cong down south. It should be obvious to everyone that there was no way under the present circumstances that they could continue to wage war if we kept their feet to the fire.

We had paid a terrible price to get to this point. My squadron alone lost three crews and my group from home had lost Frank Lewis' crew. The fear that we had all experienced was all too real and the making of heroes was not far down the road. The crews never backed down. They flew into the worst type of hell and pressed on. The flinching was on the other side, not ours. I was hoping that this would signal the return home for the vast majority of the crews and their aircraft plus all the support personnel that were away from home on this island. After all, with the condition of the North and its capacity to wage war, only a small segment of our B-52 force would be needed to keep their leaders aware that it was over! A three-ship cell of "Ds" a day could ensure their status and ultimately force them to sue for peace. It would be great to see a return to normal. I'm sure home alert would seem a pleasant change. I was not alone in looking forward to some peacetime flying back home. The crews were exuberant! There would be a celebration tonight. My thoughts were on another track. It would be really nice to drink real milk again, eat fruit?

Henry Kissenger was going back to Paris to discuss "Peace". It had to be on our terms, right? The routine returned and we started some "normal" bombing missions down south. They were real milk run flights and seemed non-productive. There were no missions to the North, despite the fact that we could only keep the enemy from regrouping and re-supplying by keeping the routes and harbors shut down. Finally it happened, we were told that congress was cutting off funds for the war. Amazing! We were given a time frame for stopping the bombing. First it was to halt in flights into the storage areas in Cambodia. I flew a "D" in the jump seat on one of the last of those missions and it was to be my last mission over Southeast Asia from Guam. The Gs were only flying sporadic missions and none of them seemed to have a real purpose.

After the first of the year, Colonel Rew notified Herb Jordan and I at one of the morning standups that Herb and I had been promoted to

Colonel. I was obviously very pleased, but somewhat chagrined that we were the only two out of six squadron commanders on Guam that were promoted. I'm sure there were plenty of L/C's (Lieutenant Colonels) fighting the staff war back home who made the new grade. I know these guys here and I know what kind of professionals they are. No Hinch, Dave, Red, what a shame! Herb and I went to the bar that evening and had the cheapest promotion party ever. Not that we didn't buy drinks, because we put the bar bill for everyone on our tab. The liquor was so cheap that despite the fact that we bought for everyone for a few hours, it barely dented our eight-dollar a day "per diem" (for the month that is). It was a great party and we even allowed some of the permanent party pukes to sashay on to our tab. They were good friends despite their status on the island. It became perfect when Red and Dave showed up to partake of the nourishment and seemed genuinely pleased with our promotion. We all drank to the gentle strains of "I Want to go Home". Matter of fact, it played over and over again!

As often is the case we had no idea what would happen now that we were promoted and we both anxiously awaited any notification of our new assignments. I was hoping against hope that I would remain at Mather in some capacity. Both of us were told that we were to be replaced on Guam soon and that we would be rotating home. It was almost at the same time that we were told that our POWs were to be released and would be coming back to the states soon. We had been given a listing of those who were being held and the known KIAs. Steve Rissi headed the last list, but neither list included Bob Thomas, Steve's co-pilot or Allen Johnson, Frank Lewis' radar navigator. There were other glaring omissions on the lists too and we knew that questions were being raised about their whereabouts, however those two stood out as both were black officers.

I have often thought that there was a relationship with their race and they're not being returned, but were never able to find any substantial reasoning for it. Often, later, when this was discussed with the returning crew members, they would swear that those two were alive when everyone left their aircraft, but no one said they were seen on the ground. It could be that both perished in some fashion during bailout or upon their arrival into hostile territory. Whatever, it seemed too coincidental to me. It's more than sheer happenstance though and I'll always believe that they were alive and imprisoned for sometime after the release of the others. There were many rumors to the effect that some of the prisoners were not released. Unfortunately I had no real proof that this was true and despite others who felt as I did, our government never seemed to aggressively pursue this possibility.

I did stay on Guam until March, when I was informed that I was to be the new Director of Operations for the 320th Bomb Wing, my home wing at Mather. I was overjoyed, especially when I heard that Herb was being re-assigned to the Pentagon in a desk job and what's more there was a new policy that if you weren't in a flying billet, you would not get flight pay. He was crushed and my assignment didn't make it any easier on him. We both continued our island duties and flew training flights occasionally and I would remind Herb that he would someday look back on Guam as a wonderful experience and it would prepare him for the rigors of Washington. The crews were now flying what amounted to ordinary training missions. However there was no indication that they were going home. We did not reduce the crew level at all despite the fact that we were not flying missions of war. It seemed as though everyone forgot about us. Morale couldn't have been lower as there was little to keep the crews occupied. Worse, all the "war time rules" for flying went out the window. It was very difficult!

Finally I had a replacement. It was sort of bitter sweet though as I wouldn't be able to greet the POWs when they came through Clark AFB in the Philippines. The commanders who had crews returning were being flown there to greet the guys as they came back. I would leave two weeks too early. I would miss not being there as I felt a close bond with not only my crews, but I had friends who had gone down in the Linebacker raids. Oh well I was going home and was indeed a lucky guy!

Before we left we were informed that the Christmas tree relief fund had surpassed the necessary amount needed to replace everything that was damaged or destroyed. In fact they had enough to ring the swimming pool with trees if necessary. War is truly hell!

B-52D Bombing Mission from Guam 1972

HOMECOMING

I returned from Guam before the aircraft were redeployed as I had hit my 179 day limit in a temporary duty status. My new position as the Director of Operations of the 320th Bomb Wing was truly a great job! However no airplanes within my experience, so I did what any pilot would do, I checked out in the KC-135, our tanker support aircraft. While I had no B-52s I did have some crews who were also on their rotation home. They would be going back if needed, but it was unlikely due to the reduced role in SEA. The peace negotiations had the provision for the return of the Prisoners of War and many came home through Travis AFB, which was close to Sacramento. We went there for their arrival and were proud to be in the large number on hand for their return. The planes did not return until the following fall and with it a real operations position for me. I continued to get time in the KC-135, but now was able to fly the B-52 when I wanted to. It was a wonderful experience and felt I did well running flight operations and keeping crewmembers happy and that was despite the fact that we were now pulling nuclear alert duty. At any rate I was given the position as the vice commander of the wing, which I'm told is a promotion. Life could not be any better as Ken Chapman, my deputy and best friend was given my DO position. His wife and mine were very close and so happiness was once again a matter of daily life.

The B-52 crews still did not return. It was now over seven months since we flew combat missions out of Guam and the aircraft and crews were still there. There did not seem to be a legitimate reason for keeping the aircraft on Guam and all we could see happening was lending credence to the slogan we had used when pressed to find rationale for our presence on the island. "In God we trust and on Guam we rust". The crews were merely flying sorties to keep up their proficiency while there.

Congress had pulled the rug out on combat sorties to anywhere in SEA, so why did we keep the crews there. Who Knew? I had pinned on my "eagles" on the 1st of June amid a fairly vacant Wing, however it was the culmination of less than nineteen years of active duty, and I felt truly blessed. Finally in late September we were notified that our crews and aircraft would return in October. The second week of October the 320th Bomb Wing finally returned to the United States, almost ten months after we ceased our bombing of Southeast Asia. Predictably, the war in Vietnam had begun to heat up as we had not kept the heat on the north.

Our POWs seemed to be all that the administration and the congress really were interested in. Public and media pressure was the reason for that I'm sure. Our leadership had now allowed the North to re-supply and regain momentum, thereby taking the offensive in a war that could have ended so easily. I could never understand the rationale of not ensuring that the enemy's capacity to wage war was not totally stymied. And if we weren't going to fight, why keep an island full of crews and aircraft over there and isolate them from home? I was happy though. I had a great job in a great wing, flying two great aircraft and was located in the best location I could ask for. We were a family again and were leading a normal Air Force life.

Your career is something you think about often, mine had been full. I had experienced war and I had felt the wolf rise in me. I will never forget the eleven days of December. They were a time of turmoil, but also a time of personal growth and maturity. You can only grow so much in a lifetime, but you can continue to mature. There are friends that I will never see again, there are experiences I will never endure again, but the memories of life during those eleven days will be of all of the men who rose to the occasion and did not allow Theodore Roosevelt's "wolf" to conquer them. As he stated "Any man who feel any power of joy in battle know what it is like when the wolf rises in the heart". They were men who deserve to be a memorable part of the history of our great country. They were courageous; they were heroes!

THE PHONE CALL

1 became the Wing Vice Commander on August 12th, 1974 and my best friend, Ken Chapman took my old position as the DO. I was happy to be a part of a great wing and living in a wonderful area. My children were happy in their schools and with life in general and Rosemary had firmly established herself among the wing wives. I happened to be in my office one evening in mid March and the phone rang. It was an ordinary commercial line, not the standard "hot" line from 15th Air Force Headquarters that business was usually conducted on, and not knowing that the Wing Commander was in, I picked up the phone only to hear him talking to the 15th Air Force Director of Personnel, who happened to be mentioning my name. It seemed that I was to be re-assigned. I listened long enough to hear U-Tapao, Thailand, and hung up the phone. I was more than a bit stunned and knew the news would not be too popular with my family. I had been home from Guam just two years and it appeared I was going to leave again. I wasn't pleased! Later, after being officially notified of this permanent change of station I had some real soul-searching to do.

I had over twenty-years of service and could easily have retired, but I truly loved what I was doing and the new assignment was as the Vice Wing Commander of the 307th Strategic Wing. This was one of the most storied of SAC wings and the one which had carried the brunt of the B-52 war to Vietnam. So despite some very difficult decisions about where my family would stay, I was determined to make this as palatable as possible for everyone concerned. Rosemary and I decided to buy a home and stay in Sacramento, so as not to disrupt the children too much. They would continue going to the same schools and would have their friends and Rosemary would have familiar surroundings and facilities, such as the base hospital to use.

I was only given four weeks to get everything in order and leave for, of all places, Guam. I was to be briefed by the 3rd Air Division there and then proceed to Clark AFB in the Philippines for further briefings and to hone some survival techniques. I left California and a very distraught wife and children in mid April. I spent two days on Guam, meeting General Minter, the 3rd Air Division Commander and my future boss while in Thailand. He gave me the distinct impression that he was not pleased with my selection for the Vice-Commander post. I'm not sure why he felt that way and would never find out. (fortunately a short time after my arrival in Thailand he was replaced by General Tom Rew) I was briefed by a myriad of his staff that things weren't going too well in Vietnam and that "UT" could become a very hot area if things didn't improve.

The next day I flew on to Clark, where I was once again briefed on numerous subjects, most of which were centered on the situation in Southeast Asia and the role that the 307th would play under any possible scenario. After a couple of days, going through various briefings and classes, I finally flew on to U-Tapao. I had always felt that I had experienced hot climates. Guam had been bad, and my stop in the Philippines was even worse, but when I stepped off the plane in Thailand, it was surely the hottest weather I had ever experienced. I was met by the Wing Commander, Colonel Caryl Calhoun, a diminutive, energetic guy, who took me to my quarters, a two-bedroom bungalow with a bath tub, supposedly the only one on the base. I met my maid, the smallest women with the widest smile I have ever known. Her name was Lamtien. She immediately counseled me on the "steely boys", telling me to place my valuables where they couldn't find them. I hadn't brought too many things with me of great value and didn't feel I would buy too much while there, but I did listen.

As the time rolled on if I bought anything I would leave it in my office in the headquarters building as there was very little access to it and it was generally busy in the area as our command post was in the same building. Lamtien also advised me to leave everything shut tight to preserve the cool climate in my trailer. Fortunately my new home was air-conditioned, as the temperature/ humidity outside was stifling, both day and night. I was also given my own vehicle. It was also air-conditioned, a real plus. All I had to do was go from my quarters to my car and to my office to keep cool. So armed I set out to find my way to my new office. I only had to head toward the flight line and the sound of the B-52s running down the runway. We only had the "D" model and the whine of their engines was very distinctive.

Though there were no combat sorties, we had twelve aircraft and TDY crews supporting them, flying, guess what, training flights. There were KC-135s and a 99th Strat Wing U-2 contingent under our command and the Thai navy was there as our host. Finding the wing headquarters was fairly easy, as once at the street paralleling the flight line, I could head right or left. I took a left and came upon the building in a matter of seconds. It was clearly marked with a huge sign signifying I was at the right place. I parked my blue vehicle in the spot marked for my position. Walking from my air conditioned car to my air conditioned office, I was greeted by Billie Strecker, the nicest secretary I would ever meet. She was tall, very good-looking and most gracious. I learned later she was also a former Playboy Bunny. She showed me to my office and gave me a schedule of the week's events, with today highlighted.

The commander was out, but should be back shortly. She had called the security people and they arrived and filled out the necessary paperwork for my clearance. This was necessary to obtain access to the various secure areas of the base. It was especially needed due to the type of missions being flown. The U-2 outfit was flying reconnaissance missions twice a day over Vietnam gathering information on the movement of the North Vietnamese army. I was also given a map of the base and a brief outline of the activities and the personnel assigned to the various functions of the wing. Briefings went on well into the evening and at the very end I was given my security badge. All I could think of when they presented it to me was of the many badges at the various bases I had been assigned and of the pain and strain it took to complete everything needed to get the badge. This badge took less than three hours to process and complete! It was the 25th of April and I was firmly entrenched in my new position and I had been gone from home less than two weeks. It would be an interesting, adventurous and fascinating year in Thailand, and as I would find out, it would be chocked full of experiences I would never forget.

That evening I was invited to a Sawadi party, a farewell for some of the staff. It was going to be at the Thai officers club. The Wing Commander was not there and I really didn't know anyone so I sort of introduced myself around. I was really thirsty and looked for a place to buy a drink. Someone asked me what I wanted to drink and I asked for a beer. The following question baffled me as I was then asked whether I wanted a whole bottle or if I wanted to split one. I immediately said I could handle the whole thing. I was presented with a larger than the normal twelve ounce bottle, but not outrageous. It was called Singhai, and as I later found out, it is fermented using formaldehyde. It may be normally used when you have already expired, but as I found out it could certainly hasten you to that state. The next day everyone was aware that I had a headache that emanated as a singular dot in the middle of my forehead, and nothing seemed to phase it. Needless to say, the remainder of my tour in the land of Singhai, I was very careful to split my bottle of beer with anyone who wanted to have a half of a deadly headache that I was most willing to share. This is probably where I discovered a taste for Gin.

The night of my fourth day in Thailand, I was called to a meeting in the command post and was there notified that the situation in Saigon had become very critical. I had been briefed on the possibilities of the fall of Saigon when in the Philippines but had not been too convinced that it would happen this soon. If the city fell, U-Tapao would be the recovery base for most of the aircraft in the area. There would be no U.S. aircrews assisting in the protection of the withdrawl (or maybe we should call it an exit), as we were not allowed to participate in any action in Vietnam. Therefore all the recovering aircraft, though American supplied, would have Vietnamese personnel.

I left the briefing and went back to my quarters. I was still not acclimated to the time change, but was starting to accept the heat, which at 2200 hours was in the 80s. I went to bed, only to be awakened by the command post phone, notifying me that Saigon was under siege and that we were told that we would most likely be receiving aircraft right after day break, which at ten degrees north latitude was about 0615 hours. It was now a few minutes after 0500 hours. I got up, put on my flight suit and headed to the command post. Colonel Calhoun, the 307th Commander was there when I arrived and he asked me to assist in getting the recovered Vietnamese military individuals into some form of debriefing. The powers to be would want as much information as possible from these fleeing crews. It would then be necessary to separate the military from other refugees and provide them with some form of quarters. It would be a monumental task dealing with the civilian refugees and one I fortunately was not going to be involved in, as the base commander was responsible for all the incoming civilians. My duties centered only on the arriving flight personnel.

I left the briefing and set out for the flight line and plunked myself in my air conditioned car on the parallel taxiway about 6000 feet down the runway. I sat on the flight line peering out over the gulf, looking for the first incoming speck in the sky. I couldn't help but thinking that only a little over two years ago we had totally cut off the North Vietnamese from the south and had destroyed their capacity to wage war. We had won the war and now, due to our political melodramas brought on by liberal media pressure, and the Jane Fonda-Joan Baez crowd, we were faced with the reality that this war which was won in December of 1972, was now lost.

All of those airmen who flew so valiantly on those terribly terrifying eleven days and especially those who didn't return had been warriors for naught. I lost good friends and loyal crew members who really did die for no reason. Don Rissi flashed across my consciousness and my own admitted fear of my nights in the air over North Vietnam flooded my memory. I could see once again the exploding SAMs and could feel the tremble they put in the air as they accelerated past my aircraft. And what of the legions who went before our December bombers, those who toiled on the ground and those who spent precious years in Vietnamese prison camps? What must they feel?

Somebody, someplace should take credit for the over fifty thousand war dead and our long list of missing warriors. And someone should face those who returned from the living hell of the "Hanoi Hilton". I knew that no one would ever admit their failure, but it would be obvious to all of those who knew, that this enemy was finished on the eleventh day of our Linebacker raids in December 1972. We were about to see failure and defeat due to a combination of enemy sympathizers, a media that couldn't see the end that was obvious to everyone who had a brain and our gutless politicians, the enemy within, who heard only Jane Fonda and her ilk. They must shoulder the blame. I was sick at the thought and ashamed of my country and those who had placed us in this situation. They had contributed to the greatest country in the world shrinking in stature among the nations to whom we had steadfastly claimed that we would help them in their fight for self-determination. I was not looking forward to facing the escaping warriors from the south that were wending their way to this refuge in Thailand, the last stand for the United States in southeast Asia.

I was getting anxious as I waited for any indication of the first of the evacuating aircraft. We knew that the embassy was in the process of being evacuated, or for all we knew had already been evacuated, that the airport had been overrun and that fighting was going on throughout the city. So far no aircraft had arrived, but we were promised they would come. Saigon was falling and they had nowhere else to go. Our political stalwarts and erstwhile leaders could chalk up another miscalculation! And then suddenly they appeared. The tower had a visual on an F-5 on a final, landing downwind. I looked to the gulf and saw the spec that was to become a plane. It floated toward the end of the runway and touched down. It's roll out was somewhat abbreviated and it slowed and turned off the runway, a "follow me" truck intercepting him and leading him to the parking tarmac. He was now picked up by a crew chief and turned into the designated parking spot. As the engines wound down, we noticed for the first time that the pilot did not have a helmet on, nor did he have on a headset.

The canopy opened and the pilot crawled onto the wing and behind him rose another figure that the pilot must have been sitting on. The two of them were smiling but somewhat wary of the reception they saw in front of them, and what might be in store for them. Another surprise rose from the seat! There had been three individuals in this single place aircraft. After some conversation, we found out that the pilot had taken both his crew chief and his assistant crew chief on their very hurried exit from Saigon. There were no parachute and no personal equipment, but there were three warm bodies. This was to be a day of improvisation and surprise as all of the U Tapao personnel, whether involved in the recovery or not, were to find out.

Our attention was now diverted back to the runway. Our tower people were frantic trying to control the airspace currently full of incoming birds. Aircraft were everywhere. There were planes on final approach going in both directions and there seemed to be very little communication going on with any of them. There were some responses, but there was no clear designation of who was responding. The hand held radios that were being carried by key personnel were screaming with directions being given from various sources for any possible task in assisting in controlling this incoming horde to include the parking of the multitude of aircraft now everywhere. They were on the ramp, the runway, going both ways and in all phases of approach in the air.

I heard my moniker called out over my hand held radio. "Bravo, would you go to the 7000 foot turnoff and supervise the parking of those aircraft with hot guns". "Roger that, I responded and sped off, only to see two F-5s pass each other on the active, going in opposite directions. An A-10 landed just behind the F-5 going north and veered to the right to miss the F-5 going south. As I came to a halt at the designated taxiway, aircraft were coming from all directions on the ground. I spied an MMS (Munitions Maintenance Squadron) "bread truck" and waved him down. I told him to send the "hot gun" aircraft in my direction and he wearily replied "I'm not sure I could tell one from the other"! I agreed with him and decided to head back to the 6000 ft marker.

Larger aircraft were now appearing on the horizon, and from the look of things, there was finally some semblance of conformity to the active runway going north. I could even see some aircraft on a normal downwind, starting their base turn even with "Buddha" mountain, our natural turn point for the north runway. I ground to a halt just in time to see the "follow-me" picking up a set of F-5s that had just turned off the active. I had asked the tower to let the driver of the directional truck know that we wanted to park all the "hot gun" aircraft he could identify on the navy ramp. There were no Navy P-3s on the ramp today and it was completely empty. It also had a high revetment that we could nose the aircraft into. They complied and led them along the parallel to the U.S. navy ramp. As they turned into the parking area I noticed that the guns had been fired and that there were no external stores on either aircraft. They had been busy! As they ground to a halt another MMS vehicle pulled along side of me. I got out of my vehicle and met a "Chief" (Chief Master Sergeant) who informed me they would clear and "safe" the guns. They would also pin any weapon that had not been expended, which didn't seem visually to be a task that needed to be accomplished.

The very normal Thailand day was now upon us. The brief morning respite from the stifling heat had passed. The humidity had hardly decreased, however the heat had now caught up with it. The thin, wispy clouds above offered no relief. The sun bore down on the ramp and the surface temperature had to be above 110 degrees. Standing still, waiting for the pilots to get out of their F-5s, I was dripping from every pore. I knew everyone else on the ramp was suffering the same distress as I. They may have been somewhat more acclimated than I was, but they were still very hot and uncomfortable. I did feel for the MMS guys as they would be working on "hot guns" and any possible unexpended ammo. They had their shirts off and were tanned from the constant exposure. They were the perfect pictures for the heat index. I talked briefly to the team chief, asked if there was any other place we could download if this ramp became saturated and received a negative reply.

I called the command post to inquire if transport was on its way to take these pilots to an "Intellegence" debriefing and received a "roger". I scurried to meet the two pilots walking toward me. The first pilot, clad in a dripping wet flight suit had Lieutenant Colonel leaves on his shoulders and as I got closer I could make out his name tag. It read "Ci" and that was it. It caught my eye as most Vietnamese names are not so brief. I assumed it was a contraction of his real name or a nickname of sorts. I held out my hand to greet him and he said in perfect English. "How are you Colonel, I'm so glad to be here".

I responded in kind as he launched into his final minutes in and his departure from Saigon. He and his three wingmen were taxiing out for takeoff with fully loaded aircraft when the airfield was suddenly overrun by North Vietnamese heavy armor. He and his number two made it past the hammerhead and onto the active and launched. The other two aircraft were cut off by a tank, which prohibited their takeoff. Colonel Ci and his wingman turned back over the airdrome and proceeded to expend their guns and rockets on the oncoming enemy. He saw that the two pilots of number three and four had been pulled out of their aircraft by NVA soldiers and were spread-eagled on the ground. The soldiers were hacking off their hands. Incenced, he and his wingman spent the next twenty minutes firing everything they had at the on-rushing army. When they had exhausted all their weapons they followed the orders they had received prior to takeoff and headed for U-Tapao. I did not have any conversation with the wingman, nor was I able to corroborate his story through any other source. It was obvious to me that he was a disturbed and shaken man and the experience had deeply affected him. I put the two of them in a staff car and they left the ramp. I never saw either of them again. I was angry, not just for him, but for all those going through this unnecessary trauma. The "fat cat" politicians who called themselves leaders had no concept what they had caused. Worse still they didn't care.

I had little time to dwell on this right now as my little piece of the world was getting very cramped and crowded. A C-47 had pulled into the area and its engines were being shut down. Now a C-47 has never been known to carry any guns, so I was wondering why it had been directed to this ramp. There are of course the "Puff" C-47s, which were converted for combat and had numerous guns mounted on its side for close suppression purposes. (They actually gutted the inside and restructured only one side and made it a flying battleship.) This bird, however was not one of them! It was camouflaged, not painted black and did not have openings on its side. I approached the rear door just as the doors opened wide. I was faced with two Vietnamese Marines, tall beyond belief for someone of that ethnicity. They were giants and around their necks were bandoleers of ammunition.

Seeing me they immediately threw off the weaponry that they had on their bodies. Guns, grenades and other deadly objects hit the entry to the aircraft and bounced to the ground. Other military individuals behind them were following suit. Behind the military personnel was a mass of humanity. They were of all ages, some were infants, teenagers, and a large segment of the people were older. All were very frightened and obviously unsure of what would happen to them. We called for a bus, but discovered one would not be sufficient to handle the number of people. All told over ninety people got off that one aircraft, about forty over the normal capacity and there were enough abandoned weapons lying on the floor of the aircraft to outfit a squad of infantry. There wasn't time to think about it though and I directed the weapons personnel to secure the debris while I hurried to a group of A-1Es now meandering into this overstuffed ramp. I asked tower to keep any more C-47s out of the area and asked for someone to get out here and tow the present large resident (the C-47) out of here.

The A1-Es seemed to be coming into the area in droves, each as their propellers stopped rotating, would disgorge a large number of fleeing people. It turned out that some were relatives of the pilot, some were military personnel and some were people who were trying to avoid an unknown and most likely deadly future. I counted ten people getting out of one of the two to three man crew A1-Es, most of them were civilians and they had been crammed into the small cargo compartment. The day continued in that fashion. I had no idea where everyone was going when we placed the masses in busses, and at the moment I didn't care. All I knew was that the aircraft were slowly but surely filling the available ramp space.

As the afternoon wore on the number of arriving aircraft dwindled away. I was about to close down the area when another speck appeared on the horizon. It seemed an eternity in getting close enough to distinguish that it was a twin engine prop driven aircraft, but it wasn't until he touched down that I was able to discern that it was an ancient C-45. I had a couple of hours in the airplane immediately after leaving pilot training to get my monthly flying time for pay purposes. It had been a "base flight" aircraft at Walker A.F.B. in New Mexico and it was taking someone to Nellis AFB near Las Vegas. Another Lieutenant and I were aboard to get time and the (IP) Instructor Pilot was a grizzled LC (Lieutenant Colonel) who probably had been flying the airplane before I was in grammar school. We set off in the afternoon and I was to be in the left seat for the first leg. I received a very quick indoctrination and off we went. It went very well until we were on final for Nellis. The IP was attempting to tell me how to land this beauty and I was just trying to hold heading on the approach. He made the mistake of warning me of the difficulty in getting it on the ground and that it had to be "flown" to touchdown.

I had a lot of training hours in "tail dragging" aircraft, so felt I really didn't need his advice. As I reached the moment of touchdown, cutting my engines to idle, and "rounding" out, I found myself instantly looking into the windows of the base control tower, which were about ten stories high. It was at that moment that I realized that "roundout" was not the thing to do. Flying the aircraft to touchdown meant to keep only the two main gear in contact with the runway until the speed diminished to a point where the tail wheel fell to the runway. I humbly made another approach and landing, this time following instructions. It was a tough airplane to fly and had the disposition of a U-2. You could never relax until you shut down the engines.

My attention was now on the unmarked C-45 which made a perfect landing going in the proper northerly direction and rolled a few hundred feet and left the runway by the first taxiway. It most definitely did not have "hot guns", however it taxied right to my location on the navy ramp. No "follow me" vehicle assisted him, nor, as I later found out, was he directed to my location. But with some purpose in mind, he came to the area and headed directly at the large barriers that separated the concrete ramp from the road and navy buildings, and parked with his nose barely inches from the concrete barrier. The engines were cut and after a short pause, the rear door opened and out stepped a neatly attired Caucasian man, followed by another. They had on dark trousers, white shirts, unbuttoned at the top and had "wheel" hats on. As they exited, they saw me, headed the very short distance toward me, paused for a second and turned back to the door of the aircraft and took off their hats and threw them into the aircraft. Now they turned to me and the first person to exit held out his hand and gave me a set of two keys and said, "It's your aircraft", turned and walked away. There was no transport there for them, nor did they ask for any. They just walked away, never to be seen at the base by anyone again. I knew it was an "Air America" (CIA) crew, who had been told to get lost when Saigon fell and they did just that. (The tail dragging C-45 aircraft was still at U-Tapao when I departed eleven months later, pointed into the same large piece of concrete. It had for company rows of A-10s, now stripped of anything the Thai navy could use).

It was now dusk, Saigon had fallen, over one hundred and twenty aircraft had been recovered, twenty five were F-5s, which the North Vietnamese claimed were their airplanes. How many lives had been lost this day? How many people left behind would be subjected to the terror of paying for their loyalty to the United States? These thoughts were racing through my head. There was little I could do now as I retreated to the command post for a wing staff meeting. A post recovery meeting, but in reality, this day was finally over! We were only rehashing history.

On reflection, over a cool American beer at the O'club that evening, this day was the most unforgettable day of my life, however, unbeknown to me there would be other days that I would recall as this twelve month tour, one of total withdrawal (nee retreat) had only begun. As the last commander of the storied 307th Strategic Wing I would take part in the withdrawal of all the B-52s in Thailand on three very hot days in June. There also would follow the Mayaquez incident where the KC-135s at UT would help sustain the air action against a stubborn Cambodian government. It was also where a Marine commander insisted on invading an island that not only had no value, but also did not hold any members of the Mayaguez crew, and was told these facts well in advance in our attempts to rescue the captured ship. 21 U.S. Marines died needlessly. But that's another story of chaotic bureaucratic and military bungling.

Finally, in less than a year, I would be on the lead tanker taking all the fighters out of Southeast Asia. This effectively ended our role as the "savior" of the free countries of that region. The dominos had begun to fall! There was no value in the presence of the United States and Thailand, in order to satiate the demands of Vietnam, had ordered us to get all of our aircraft out of their country. There would be other widespread ramifications resulting from the fall of South Vietnam. From those who wish failure for the policy of the United States, this was a real sign of weakness. To those who needed our support in Asia, it brought utter despair and to the many others throughout the world, who looked to us as the superpower to fight aggression, doubts in our resolve. And finally to all, there would never be real trust in our word again.

My country proved that it is a hollow giant. Today I had witnessed the tragic outcome of our civilian war. A war that had been won, and barely three years later has been lost, a generation of men damaged, some of my closest friends and men put in my charge, lost their lives to satisfy the misguided minds of an auto management czar and other political hacks. It would be the precedent for mismanaging the waging of war. A political disaster, a national shame, a needless waste!

I often visit the wall. I go directly to the "V". One panel to the left, starting about line 46, the names of the men in my squadron who didn't return from the December, 1972 raids to the north, most are known as KIA (killed in action) and one or two still unaccounted for, are listed. They were brave and they were patriots. The wolf rose within them and they didn't flinch, they deserved better. But here, the names of Don Rissi, Randy Cradduck, Bobby Kirby, Bob Thomas, Alan Johnson, Keith Heggan, Jim McIlvaine, Charlie Poole, Randy Perry, John Stuart, Frank Gould, George Lockhart, Ron Perry, Bennie Fryer, Roy Tabler, and the rest, B-52 crewdogs and friends, will remain as a testament to everyone that this was something they believed in. Unfortunately those who called themselves leaders did not match their resolve and courage. They were mired in a self serving adventure, unable to make command decisions because they were not prepared for the contest which was in front of them. They were the "losers," those on the wall were the real men of our time.

Today it is hard to swallow the protestations of those that could have, but didn't fight. Also those who chose to use their conscience as a tool to hide their cowardliness and fled to Canada or other places and those who observed the war through their opaque glasses and tell the world how unworthy our actions were. To them I would say "they couldn't compare their shallow, meaningless life to those who carried the mail". They will never experience the "feeling of the wolf" rising within. If they had, they too would be considered as heroes and men of honor and possibly the war would have ended differently and the world would indeed be a better place.

Theodore Roosevelt stated it far better than me when he said. "Far better it is to dare mighty things, to win glorious triumphs, even though checkered by failure, than to take rank with those poor spirits who do not enjoy much or suffer much, because they live in the gray twilight which knows neither victory or defeat".

I was the last commander of the 307th SW, although at the time I was acting in that position as Colonel Calhoun was on emergency leave, a status would see him not returning. I therefore was to oversee the departure of the last B-52s in Southeast Asia from U-Tapao. The launching started on June 2nd with the last to leave on June 8th 1975. Our flight schedule cover caption read "Sawadee Buffs". All were going home, with pilot names like Miller, Barngrover, Nelson and Keogle flying the twelve aircraft that departed. This launch was a return to the U.S. bases they came from. It was the end of "Arc Light" and the SAC involvement in the Vietnam War. It was a bitter-sweet moment for me to see the last "Buffs" all "D"s going home. It was the culmination of many sacrifices and untimely losses, but it was also a significant moment in our history and I am proud to have been a part of it.

THE AFTERMATH

My return home would come some months later. The B-52s were gone, but much was still going on in this former war zone. We were flying the U-2 twice daily with signal and communications intelligence intercepts from Vietnam sent down to the downlink station at Ramisson in northern Thailand. We were still supporting all of the fighter groups in Thailand with our fifteen tanker 135s, which gave me many opportunities to get airborne. There was a lot of pressure to remove all of our aircraft as the North Vietnamese were threatening the Thais so it was a bit difficult to face many of the government officials who had access to the base. At one point there was an increase in our 135 contingent due to the increase in our need to support various activities such as the Mayaguez. A reporter asked me one day why the number of 135s had doubled and I told him we had been given the new two tailed tankers and he believed me and it was printed in the Bangkok Herald the next day.

We had many problems with the Thai navy on the base as their commander, Captain Vichit was the ringleader of a bunch of thieves. My Air Division commander was now General Tom Rew, my former wing commander on Guam. He was concerned about the loss of our equipment, especially when our yellow fire truck disappeared out the front gate and then perimeter chain link fence started to vanish into the night. But what really tipped him was after I had put a curfew on our personnel as we had been having an outbreak of enlisted personnel being accosted and beaten by locals and many were being placed in jail due to drug use. Within days of the curfew there was a reported bounty on my head and the price to get rid of me was very lucrative. He wanted to talk to the MAAG commander, General Heini Aderholdt about the situation. He came from his headquarters on Guam to U-Tapao expressly to address the problem. I then flew with General Rew from U-Tapao to Bangkok in our base shuttle aircraft. We were picked up at the military side of the commercial airport by General Aderholt and his driver and drove through the city to the MAAG headquarters which was in the same area as the embassy. The drive through the main part of the city was as usual very busy with traffic. There is little control and few traffic lights in this very populated city and we were just crawling along and General Rew was stating his case about his concern for my health. Finally, General Aderholdt told the driver to stop and then as he motioned the driver to open the dashboard, which he hit with his fist and the bottom dropped down, displaying a virtual arsenal with an array of weapons enough to stand off more than a few "unfriendlies" then he stated he had many contracts out on him, whipped on his running shoes and got out of the vehicle and took off down the street, telling his driver to get us to our destination.

Later Gen Aderholdt came to the base at U-tapao to meet with Admiral Samut, the ranking officer in charge of all Thai military operations in southern Thailand. The meeting would include Captain Vichit and his chief of security, along with other ranking Thai personnel. The meeting was chaired by the admiral and he expressed his concern about the security and thefts at the base. Everything was being conducted in English, however while he was talking Captain Vichit and his security officer were quietly engaging in a Thai dialogue. They were sitting next to General Aderholdt, who suddenly turned and was speaking in Thai to the two officers. It appears they were making comments about the thefts and were incriminating themselves in a boastful manner, thinking they were safe speaking their native language. What they didn't know was that the General had lived in Thailand for many years and in fact had been an agent in the early days working with the government and could speak the language fluently. Admiral Samut, embarrassed, ordered the two officers out of the room. He then told us that from that day forward his own navy police would secure and patrol U-Tapao. I never saw Vichit or his security chief again and the theft and security problems ceased that day.

The 307th Strategic Wing had a storied existence throughout the Vietnam War as B-52s had launched from there throughout its entirety.

The last B-52s departed on that very hot Sunday in a three ship cell mid day. As the current wing commander, Wayne Calhoun was home on leave, I was in charge of the departure. There was a big crowd on the ramp and I told the lead bird's aircraft commander to do a low fly by to close things out. He did so, in fact we were all concerned that he would lose his lower ECM antennas in the process. He rose up, wagged his wings and disappeared into the hot haze of the day. I officially became commander of the 307th on August 12th, 1975 and I went down in history as the last commander of that wing. Due to the drawdown the wing was disbanded in late August. The 135 now being our only aircraft and our role was to support the PACAF aircraft up country, we became the 901st Air Refueling Squadron. Even that didn't last too long as our flight operations in support of SEA ended in December of 1975. Our contingent of U-2s under Colonel Jerry Sinclair were still flying missions and the tankers were still supporting the withdrawal of fighter aircraft from upcountry, providing refueling support for their return to bases in the CONUS (CONTINENTAL US). This role was to be completed by 20 March, 1976 by decree of the Thai government.

I left U-Tapao in late March of 1976 to a new assignment at Barksdale AFB in Louisiana with the memories of never to be forgotten experiences, as I participated in the complete withdrawal of all combat aircraft from southeast Asia, the Mayaquez operation on 15 May, which was one of the biggest examples of poor command and control between Marine command and in-country intelligence agencies to include the 307th SW. I had information and documentation sufficient to hang the marine colonel in charge, but was told to not release it. We had taken an entire battalion of marines from Okinowa into U-T, housed them and then using our helicopters transported them to the invasion of Koh Tang island, which we had learned earlier, contained an entire battalion of the Cambodian army and it was also communicated to the marine command that the Mayaguez crewmembers were no longer on the island. To our dismay and to my personal disgust the colonel stated directly to me with the highly classified message in my hands that he was going to invade Koh Tang. The cost was at least seventy percent of our helicopter aircraft and I would say the needless loss of 21 marines.

"Sawadee" U-Tapao, Last B-52 to leave Southeast Asia,
June 8, 1975

THE LAST HURRAH~BARKSDALE~
KI SAWYER~MARCH

When I left U-Tapao I left as part of the departure of the last military aircraft, the KC-135 from SEA. I also left the remnants of a wonderful group of dedicated officers and enlisted personnel who would close the base and insure most of our equipment would be returned to the US and not fall into the hands of the Thai Navy. I did have one traveling companion as I took with me our wing mascot, Pete the python, our 26 foot docile snake, but that's another story. My new position was to be the 2nd Bomb Wing vice commander in Shreveport Louisiana, but I would return by way of Omaha then Sacramento. I dropped Pete off at the Henry Dorley Zoo in Omaha Nebraska, attended a commander's conference at Offutt AFB and finally went to Sacramento to prepare Rosemary and the five Ms for the next move. It would have to wait for the end of the school year as four of the five were two months away from the end of a pleasant year and I didn't want to uproot them, so I once more would live a solo life, this time in the rural south. The 2nd was a large B-52G and KC-135 wing and I would find many of the crews I had flown with on Guam during the "Bullet Shot" operation. It was a learning experience, flying peace time missions again and conforming to the many rules of that type of flying. My first commander was a colonel named Jerry Wechter. He was a very unhappy person as his days were numbered as the wing commander. He was succeeded by a very personable guy named Jerry Barnes, a true future general, whose star had already been pre-determined. While Jerry was the commander the base was to be visited by President Gerald Ford and I was named as the project officer for his one day and night stay in Schreveport. It was very revealing to associate with the secret service and I was given many opportunities to direct and monitor the security surrounding of a president. It did not hurt that the visit was of particular interest to our 8th Air Force commander, General Dick Hoban. He was very complimentary about my efforts during and after the visit.

Ultimately Jerry Barnes was to be sent to Carnegie Mellon for an MBA and I was to be left with the wing. For a time there was no official notice of my being named as the commander, but ultimately in February of 1978 I was officially named as the 2nd BW CC. It was short lived though as I was notified in late April that I would become the wing commander of the 410th BW, a B-52H/KC-135 "super wing" (meaning it had more aircraft and crews per squadron)in the Upper Peninsula of Michigan, very near Marquette. It had been a troubled outfit, having suffered a major aircraft accident and had other morale problems associated with their daily operations. The H model was a giant step forward in the B-52. It did not require water-injection on takeoff as it had a more powerful set of eight engines. It had greater range and a greater capacity for bomb load. It was to be another step forward in flying for me and I was very excited for the opportunity.

Going to the Upper Peninsula of Michigan was a greater treat than we would imagine as it is a wonderful place and the people were the most giving and patriotic I would find in my career. They just couldn't do enough for us! The 410th was an outstanding unit and rose to the forefront of other wings in the command. It was chosen by SAC Headquarters as the wing to prove that the Air Force had the capability to search and find the Russian fleet as it came out of port in early May. I was honored to fly on that mission as the wing commander. Two B-52H aircraft were to depart from K I Sawyer AFB, to find the Russian fleet. They were to be somewhere in the North Sea, departing from their now open port of Riga and that was the only real detail we were given. It was obviously going to be a long arduous mission with launch from the interior of the US and a flight over the Atlantic to an area north of Ireland. After a refueling over the Atlantic we arrived in the search area to find that we would have to penetrate into a very dense cloud cover. Using our aircraft radar and air to air Tacan to maintain clearance between the two aircraft we penetrated through the clouds and finally broke out about four to five hundred feet above the very angry and cold water. It was a very ragged ceiling and visibility was very limited. We would at some point have to go to 200 feet to remain visual. (Needless to say any ship in the area would be a bit surprised to see a 500,000 pound aircraft almost at the highest level of their boat.) We told the second aircraft to search to the south of the penetration point and we went north. After a number of false alarms, as it was a very busy area for ship transit, we picked up a massive radar return and turned to intercept it. We came upon the entire fleet which consisted of their sole aircraft carrier, the Kiev, and all of its escorts. We told the other aircraft to join the fun and proceeded to take photos as proof of our intercept. We were close enough to see the sailors on the deck and they certainly saw us. Being careful to not break any International rules we flew close enough to get incredible pictures of the fleet. The Russians were concerned enough to turn on their uplink search radar, which we all recognized due to our experiences in Vietnam. They finally decided we weren't a threat and it backed off. After around an hour in the murky weather and low enough to have salt stains on our aircraft we bid adieu and climbed back to altitude and proceeded home. After almost twenty hours in the air we were diverted to Wurtsmith AFB as KI was closed due to weather. We were met by a courier who was to fly our photography to the Pentagon for disbursement to our congressional leaders as proof of our capability. Through sources we found out the pictures were distributed to congressional leaders the very next day.

KI was a dream assignment that ended too soon. A complete snafu by the 8th AF Bomb-Navigation Directorate ended up misidentifying offsets for targets on the no-notice Operational Readiness Inspection (ORI) and the result was that the 410th BW and six others in 8th Air Force failed the inspection. It was a dramatic error and it resulted in all of the wing commanders, myself included, being placed in a position of losing a chance for promotion. It was ironic that the head of the inspection team was the wing commander I had replaced a year earlier. Prior to that event I was to have assumed command of the largest B-52 command training wing at Castle AFB in California. That assignment was cancelled and I was now chosen for a new position as the 15th Air Force Director of Operations. It would constitute another move this time to Riverside California. It was a return to my roots. Although I would still have a flying position, time in the air would be tough to come by. My responsibility was all the western half of the Strategic Air

Command, to include Alaska and Hawaii. All operational flying and missile wings would fall under my purview.

It was a dramatic two years in the position as I was instrumental in the incorporation of the AF National Guard and AF Reserve units being placed operationally into the SAC mission environment. It also provided me with intimate knowledge of the use of our many assets in Alaska and of the strategic role of our Missile wings and their use in the overall command mission. It was also an eye opener into the role of reconnaissance as I was able to involve myself in the 9th Strategic Wing which had the SR-71 and the U-2 in their inventory. I was involved in many highly classified operations as a result and felt very fortunate to see history unfold. A highlight was a mission in the U-2 where I flew to above 75,000 feet. I could see the curvature of the earth and felt I had done everything I could do as an Air Force officer. I had flown two and a half times the speed of sound and had been "limited" to an altitude of fifty five thousand feet up to that time and now I had ventured into the range of an astronaut. Oh happy days! I opted to retire and left the Air Force the first of July, 1980. It was a great life!

**Last Command 410ᵗʰ BW
KI Sawer AFB Flight Line
KC-135A and B-52H**

U-2 Flight Activity